DATE DUE

GAYLORD   PRINTED IN U.S.A.

VARIETIES OF CAPITALISM IN SPAIN

PREVIOUS PUBLICATIONS

Do Isolamento a Integaçào. Lisbon: Instituto de Ciencias Sociais da Universidade de Lisboa. 2004.

Royo, Sebastián and Paul C. Manuel, eds. *Spain and Portugal in the European Union: The First 15 Years*. London: Frank Cass, 2003.

'*A New Century of Corporatism?*' *Corporatism in Southern Europe: Spain and Portugal in Comparative Perspective*. Westport, CT: Greenwood Publishing/Praeger, 2002.

From Social Democracy to Neoliberalism: The Consequences of Party Hegemony in Spain 1982–1996. NY: St. Martin's Press, 2000.

Varieties of Capitalism in Spain

Remaking the Spanish Economy for the New Century

Sebastián Royo

First published in 2008 by
PALGRAVE MACMILLAN™
175 Fifth Avenue, New York, N.Y. 10010 and
Houndmills, Basingstoke, Hampshire, England RG21 6XS
Companies and representatives throughout the world.

PALGRAVE MACMILLAN is the global academic imprint of the Palgrave Macmillan division of St. Martin's Press, LLC and of Palgrave Macmillan Ltd. Macmillan® is a registered trademark in the United States, United Kingdom and other countries. Palgrave is a registered trademark in the European Union and other countries.

ISBN-13: 978–1–4039–6412–0
ISBN-10: 1–4039–6412–2

Library of Congress Cataloging-in-Publication Data

Royo, Sebastián, 1966–
    Varieties of capitalism in Spain : remaking the Spanish economy for the new century / by Sebastián Royo.
        p. cm.
    Includes bibliographical references and index.
    ISBN 1–4039–6412–2
    1. Capitalism—Spain. 2. Spain—Economic policy. 3. Spain—Foreign economic relations. I. Title.

HC383.R69 2008
330.946—dc22   2007045893

A catalogue record for this book is available from the British Library.

Design by Newgen Imaging Systems (P) Ltd., Chennai, India.

First edition: May 2008

10 9 8 7 6 5 4 3 2 1

Printed in the United States of America.

To my twin brother Pepe—you are my light, my role model, and inspiration. You always lead the way.

Contents

List of Tables and Figures

Tables

Figures

Preface and Acknowledgments

This book has taken me altogether too long to write it. I started thinking about the application of the Varieties of Capitalism framework to Spain over seven years ago, when I listened to Peter Hall and David Soskice discussing their path-breaking and seminal work at the *Minda de Gunzburg Center for European Studies* at Harvard University (later published in 2001). As they described the institutional differences among the political economies of the developed world, I considered where the Spanish economy would fit within the proposed framework, and pondered how the pressures for convergence generated by globalization and technological change would affect it. While Hall and Soskice have convincingly showed that there is more than one path to economic success in the global economy, their emphasis on the "institutional complementarities" that link labor relations, corporate finance, national education, and corporate governance systems, seemed to suggest that it is very difficult for countries that lack "appropriate" institutions to develop coordination.

The following pages are the product of my struggles with that conclusion and with the challenges posed by globalization. I am far more optimistic about the prospects of institutional change in non-coordinated market economies than other people. In Spain, globalization and economic integration have promoted rather than undermined the development of coordination mechanisms among the economic actors. Furthermore, the analysis of the Spanish case has further convinced me that in the global economy we flourish by diversifying, not by converging toward an Anglo-Saxon model.

The foundations of this book were built while I was a student at Boston University when I started working on corporatism in Southern Europe. My original plan was to publish a book that would also cover Portugal and some Latin American countries. Yet, unexpected professional detours prevented me from finalizing that project and from finishing it earlier. My work as program officer at Laspau-Harvard University gave me the chance to travel throughout the Americas and to learn a great deal about the institutional framework and economic structures of the Latin American countries, where I also had the opportunity to interview scholars, policy makers, and business leaders. As I was moving forward with the project, the dean of the College of Arts and Sciences at Suffolk University, Kenneth Greenberg, asked me to become director of the campus that Suffolk University has in Madrid. This started a fascinating journey that has allowed me to become more deeply involved with my native country and to explore in far more depth the issues that I wanted to examine in this book. As a result I decided to focus exclusively on the Spanish case for this book, and to leave the wider analysis of Latin American countries for a future research project.

Over the years my thinking about the political economy issues has been influenced by many people. I would like to acknowledge the insight of the following people: Joaquín Almunia, Michael Baum, Nancy Bermeo, Katrina Burgess, Cesar Camisón, William Chislett, Carlos Closa, Xavier Coller, Francisco Conde, Alvaro Cuervo, Omar Encarnación, Miguel Angel Fernández Ordoñez, Bonnie Field, Robert Fishman, Mauro Guillén, Paul Heywood, Peter Hall, Kerstin Hamann, Diego Hidalgo, Richard Locke, Paul C. Manuel, Andrew Martin, Cathy Jo Martin, Felix Martin, Fernando Moreno, Carlos Mulas, Victoria Murillo, Rafael Myro, Emilio Ontiveros, Andrés Ortega, Sofía Pérez, Charles Powell, Marino Regini, George Ross, Joaquín Roy, David Rueda, Mark Rush, Vivien Schmidt, Philippe Schmitter, Ben Ross Schneider, Miguel Sebastián, Kathleen Thelen, Pablo Toral, Mariano Torcal, David Cameron, Ana Evans, Pepper Culpepper and José Ignacio Torreblanca.

Drafts of chapters of this book have been presented at academic conferences, including meetings of the American Political Science Association, the International Studies Association, the Conference of Europeanists, and the Latin American Studies Association. I want to thank all the people that participated in those panels for their valuable insight and comments. Professor Joaquín Roy has also invited me to present this work at conferences that he has organized at the University of Miami. I am very grateful to him.

My research was greatly facilitated by the active collaboration of the people that I interviewed for this project. The list of people who assisted with my field research in Spain includes former cabinet members, business leaders, entrepreneurs, union leaders, scholars, national and regional administration officials. They were all extremely generous with their time and interest. I am indebted to them. In particular I would like to acknowledge the help from Rafael Myro, Emilio Ontiveros, and Jesús Alberdi and the leaders of ADEGI, in helping me schedule interviews and facilitating contacts. Sandra Zerbo has provided editorial and research assistance for the book.

This book would not have been possible without the help and inspiration of a number of people. I owe a great debt of gratitude to the many institutions and people who have supported my research over the years. In particular I would like to thank my colleagues and students in the Government Department at Suffolk University for providing a cordial and supportive environment, as well as my colleagues and students at the Suffolk University Madrid campus. Working with them has been an extraordinary experience. This project would not have been possible without their motivation and assistance.

The *Minda de Gunzburg Center for European Studies* at Harvard University, in which I am an affiliate and co-chair of the Iberian Studies Group, has also provided an exceptionally supportive institution for my research. I want to thank Peter Hall for his constant guidance and inspiration. My greatest academic debt is to him. I also want to thank David Blackbourn, Patricia Craig, Charles Maier, and Andrew Martin.

During the past year I have had the fortune to work as associate dean of the College of Arts and Sciences at Suffolk University for Dean Kenneth Greenberg. Ken is not only my boss, but an extraordinary person as well. He has been a mentor and an inspiration, and I have learned a lot from him. Ken has been incredibly supportive throughout my career at Suffolk, and I am forever indebted to him for all the opportunities that he has given me. I feel enormously privileged to work for him and to count him as a dear friend. I would also like to thank Lauri Umansky for her guidance and help since I joined the Dean's Office. I am very fortunate to work with an amazing group of people at Suffolk University.

On a more personal note I would like to thank all the members of my family. My parents have always been incredibly loving and supportive. They are my role models and the sources of the best in me. My brothers Borja, José Antonio, and Rocío as well as their families have always been champions of my work. My daughters Abigail, Andrea, and Monica have been a joy and a constant source of happiness. They have taught me the most important lessons in life. Abby was born when I was finishing the manuscript and has brought with her sleepless nights that have made it easier to finish the book. Last but not least, I want to thank my wife Cristina. We have shared 15 extraordinary years. She is an exceptional wife, mother, and professional. Cristina is the best thing that ever happened to me. Nothing that I have achieved, including this book, would have been possible without her love, patience, dedication to her family, incredible hard work, and support.

As this book goes to press my twin brother, Pepe, has been diagnosed with liver cancer and he is starting a fight that he will surely win. Pepe is one of the few true leaders that I have ever known. He is not only the smartest, kindest, and most generous person that I have had the privilege to meet, but more importantly he has been the most influential person in my life. We have shared everything and he has always led the way. I would not be who I am without him, and I would have never accomplished anything without his love, leadership, inspiration, and constant support. I dedicate this book to him.

SEBASTIÁN ROYO
Boston, Massachusetts
September 2007

Introduction

Reconceptualizing "Varieties of Capitalism" for Spain

Introduction

This book is situated within the political economy literature's growing attention to the impact of institutions on economic policy and performance. It focuses on domestic responses to, and policy consequences of, economic integration, as well as the threat posed by the globalization of markets and the intensification of international competition. This research project seeks to account for the responses of Spain and Spanish firms to the pressures exerted by these processes.

This book is positioned within the Varieties of Capitalism (VoC) debate about liberal market economies and coordinated market economies. The VoC literature explains differences and similarities in economic policies and economic performance (Hall and Soskice 2001). It focuses on the institutional frameworks of market economies and identifies complementarities between institutional arrangements. The VoC approach looks at the role that institutions play and how they condition policy, and it seeks to address questions such as what features distinguish one type of policy from another? How are the main VoC constructed? It takes as a starting point the neoclassical view, which uses as a reference the economic success of the Anglo-Saxon countries during the past decade, and contends that competitive market relations are the best way to assure strong economic performance. Yet it disputes this conclusion and argues that there is more than one route to economic success.

This literature has examined whether a liberal direction can be identified or whether countries are more or less locked into already developed paths because of the complementary character of their institutional framework. It has also analyzed the forces and mechanisms that make institutional change possible (see Crouch 2005). There is much discussion in this literature on questions such as the following: national economies are changing, what are the implications of the changes on the VoC approach? How does this framework understand institutional change? Can we expect national economies to converge? How do institutions change? This book wants to contribute to these discussions by taking recent changes in the Spanish political economy as a point of departure. It seeks to explore and explain why, when, and how institutions develop and change and it examines the relationship between institutions and the interests of economic actors and their experiences. In addition, it seeks to investigate the need for countries to develop and sustain coordination while adjusting for economic change. The book also seeks to build on recent efforts to bring together the VoC approach with other approaches that focus on the dynamics of firm behavior and to study how firms develop new capacities and learn new ways of doing things (Morgan, Whitey, and Moen 2005).

Against Convergence

The proponents of globalization contend that countries are now converging in one model of capitalism—the Anglo-Saxon one. In the opinion of some scholars, the combined impetuses of globalization and the process of economic integration have imposed exigencies of increasing competitiveness on national economies and firms, which have compelled countries to deregulate their labor markets, welfare systems, and industrial relations (Crouch and Streeck 1997). According to this view, these pressures for change have undermined coordinating capacity, hence pressuring governments to implement uniform policies based on deregulation and further liberalization. This type of explanation perpetuates the extended myth that there is only one economic model to operate in a global economy based on a set of institutions that promotes market efficiencies and entrepreneurship. While states' steering capacities are being constrained by developments beyond their national boundaries, this does not mean a loss of state control or convergence in a neoliberal direction (see Royo 2000).

   This book seeks to challenge the argument according to which the Anglo-Saxon countries (and in particular the United States, and to lesser extend the United Kingdom) have institutions and policies that other countries must follow to achieve economic success in a global world (See Table I.1 for basic socioeconomic data of a number of Western countries.) In recent years there have been constant references to the economic decline of Europe, and scholars have pointed out to the fact that in the last 20 years the continent has lost ground vis-à-vis the United States. They highlight economic data suggesting that the European economies have stalled. For instance, in the first 30 years after the war Europe reduced its per capita GDP distance from the United States by half (from 42 percent to 80 percent), yet since then it has gone down to 70 percent of the U.S. level (Alesina and Giavazzi 2006, pp. 4–5). Other data seem to confirm this trend. While productivity growth in the United States increased from an annual rate of 1.5 percent between 1973 and 1975, 2.5 percent between 1995 and 2000, and 3.5 percent between 2001 and 2005, in Europe productivity growth has been slow: only 0.9 percent after 1998 (although the latest data seem to indicate that Europe is catching

Table 1.1 Basic socioeconomic data of a number of Western countries: Employment rates (15 to 64 years), standardized unemployment, income inequality, and poverty rates (defined as income lower than 50 percent of median)

	Employment rate				Standardized unemployment rate					Gini coefficient	Percentile ratio 90/10	Poverty rate
	1990	2003	2004	2005	1990	2003	2004	2005	2006			
Australia	68.40	70.00	70.30	71.60	6.70	5.90	5.40	5.10	4.80	0.32	4.25	13.01
Austria	—	68.70	67.80	68.60	—	4.30	4.80	5.20	4.70	0.26	3.15	7.74
Belgium	54.40	59.30	60.50	61.00	6.60	8.20	8.40	8.40	8.20	0.28	3.28	7.88
Canada	70.30	72.20	72.50	72.50	8.10	7.60	7.20	6.80	6.30	0.32	4.19	12.37
Denmark	75.40	75.10	76.00	75.50	7.20	5.40	5.50	4.80	3.90	0.23	2.75	5.39
Finland	74.10	67.40	67.20	68.00	3.20	9.10	8.80	8.30	7.70	0.25	2.90	5.38
France	59.90	62.50	62.40	62.30	8.50	9.50	9.60	9.70	9.50	0.28	3.45	7.31
Germany	64.10	64.60	65.00	65.50	4.80	9.00	9.50	9.40	8.30	0.28	3.37	8.36
Ireland	52.10	65.00	65.50	67.10	13.40	4.70	4.50	4.30	4.40	0.31	4.48	16.15
Italy	52.60	56.20	57.40	57.50	8.90	8.40	8.00	7.70	6.80	0.33	4.47	12.76
Netherlands	61.80	71.80	71.20	71.10	5.90	3.70	4.60	4.70	3.90	0.23	2.78	4.91
Norway	73.00	75.80	75.60	75.20	5.80	4.50	4.40	4.60	3.50	0.25	2.80	6.40
Spain	51.80	60.70	62.00	64.30	13.00	11.10	10.60	9.20	8.50	0.34	4.69	14.16
Sweden	83.10	74.30	73.50	73.90	1.70	5.60	6.30	7.30	7.00	0.25	2.96	6.53
Switzerland	—	77.90	77.40	77.20	—	4.20	4.40	4.50	4.00	0.27	3.38	7.56
UK	72.50	72.60	72.70	72.60	6.90	4.90	4.70	4.80	5.30	0.34	4.57	12.46
USA	72.20	71.20	71.20	71.50	5.60	6.00	5.50	5.10	4.60	0.37	5.46	17.05

Sources: OECD: http://stats.oecd.org/WBOS/Default.aspx? QueryName=251&QueryType=View

OECD Factbook 2007: http://masetto.sourceoecd.org/vl=4023467/cl=27/nw=1/rpsv/factbook/

Luxembourg Income Study (LIS) Key Figures as of 13 August 2007: http://www.lisproject.org/keyfigures.htm.

up: in 2006 productivity grew in the EU by 1.5 percent, whereas in the United States it increased only by 0.9 percent).[1] Furthermore, the number of patents granted per working person between 1990 and 2003 has been 3.6 in the United States, but less than 1 in the United Kingdom, France, and Germany; continental output per hour is still about 90 percent of U.S. levels, and only 75 percent of those in working age in France and Italy were in employment, against 87 percent in the United States. This has led observers to call for further liberalization and market-led change in Europe that will put in place the right incentives to take risks, and work (Alesina and Giavazzi 2006, pp. 168–172).[2]

The Nobel laureate Edmund Phelps, highlighted in his Nobel lecture, the failure of European economies to deliver neither dynamism nor high employment, and attributed the recent economic underperformance of these economies to "the continent's corporatist economic system (or systems), a system constructed of big unions, big employer confederations and big banks, all mediated by a big public sector—a system that has been built up starting in the 1920s on the belief that it would be better than capitalism." While he supports a system that combines high dynamism with social inclusion, he advocates market-led change.[3]

Yet, this book will defend that in the global economy we survive by becoming more diverse and by focusing on what we do best, not by copying the United States. While it is true that Anglo-Saxon countries have experienced strong economic performance in the last decade, there are many other indicators that point to significant weaknesses in their economic performance and social well-being. According to UN reports on child welfare and child poverty, the United States and the United Kingdom are the two worst industrial countries in which to grow up: child poverty doubled in the United Kingdom between 1979 and 1998, and in the United States a baby from a family in the bottom 5 percent of U.S. income distribution will have a life span 25 percent shorter than a baby from the top 5 percent. On the contrary other countries, such as Sweden, Norway, and the Netherlands, countries traditionally associated with Social democratic governments and corporatist models of capitalism; score higher than the United States in almost every indicator of well-being: inequality, poverty, and economic insecurity are all lower.[4]

Along the same lines, Pontusson (2005) provides a comparative overview of the two systems (what he calls the "liberal capitalism" of the United States and Britain, and the "social market capitalism" of northern Europe) and examines the presumed trade-off between equality and economic growth. He makes the case that it is not clear that liberal economies generate more wealth. While he acknowledges that Americans do make more per capita than anyone else ($36,000 a year in 2002) some of the European countries closely follow it (Norway is right behind at $35,000), plus the difference with the other continental European nations (ranging from $26,000 to $29,000) is not large enough to claim unambiguously the superiority of the U.S. system. He points out that inequality is higher in liberal capitalist countries: their poverty rate of 15 percent (11.5 percent in the United States) is more than three times higher than in the social market countries. Finally, he notes that while unemployment is higher in Europe the divergences are not so large either: the social market economies have a 5.2 percent unemployment rate between 2000 and 2003, while the liberal capitalist economies had a 5.6 percent.[5] The key difference among these countries is the importance that they attach to social cohesion. Pontusson shows that social market economies can produce growth and employment without the inequities of the liberal capitalist countries. According to him, Europeans seek to share the benefits of economic growth and mitigate the adjustment costs; hence their policies are geared toward improving both social and individual welfare. The institutional setting of these countries makes these policies and these choices possible.

Models of Capitalism

Indeed, there are several viable models to succeed in the global economy. In the last few years there has been a growing body of literature outlining different models of capitalism. In addition to the ones just outlined, Amable (2003) identifies five different models: the market-based Anglo-Saxon model; Asian capitalism; the Continental European model; the social democratic economies; and the Mediterranean model, and examines the institutional transformations that have taken place in Continental Europe to argue that Continental European economies will not converge with the Anglo-Saxon model.

Baumol, Litan, and Schramm (2007) also advance four different archetypes of capitalism: state-guided, oligarchic, big-firm, and entrepreneurial. They show that developing countries tend to be state-guided or oligarchic, whereas developed economies tend to be characterized by big-firm capitalism (Continental Europe, Korea, and Japan) or a mix of big-firm and entrepreneurial capitalism (the United States) (pp. 60–92). From this typology they make the argument that for countries to reach (and maintain) the living standards of the rich countries they will need to adopt some combination of big-firm and entrepreneurial capitalism, and they outline the four ingredients necessary for building and maintaining the mixed form of capitalism: easy to start a business, rewards for productive entrepreneurial activity, disincentives for unproductive activity, and keeping the winners on their toes (pp. 95–121). In other words, they make the case that countries have to move toward the U.S. model of entrepreneurial capitalism.

Other scholars have developed other typologies. According to Andre Sapir, there are at least four political economy models in Europe: The "Nordic model" (Denmark, Finland, Sweden, and the Netherlands) characterized by highest public spending on welfare and social protection, relatively unregulated labor markets, and active labor market policies; the "Anglo-Saxon model," which provides generous social assistance; weak union and unregulated labor markets (Ireland and the United Kingdom); the "Rhineland model," (Austria, Belgium, France, Germany, and Luxemburg), which relies on stronger protection than in the Scandinavian countries, relatively powerful unions, as well as social protection for the unemployed; and finally the "Mediterranean Model," characterized by support for early retirement, regulated labor markets that protect employment, as well as provision of pensions (Greece, Italy, Portugal, and Spain).

Sapir examines the impact of these models on the levels of employment and poverty and concludes that the Nordic and Anglo-Saxon models have better employment performance, while the Rhineland and Nordic models have a better record in eliminating relative poverty. According to his analysis the Mediterranean model (which includes Spain) performs poorly on both objectives. Hence the conclusion is that countries such as Spain should become either more Nordic or more Anglo-Saxon.[6] The problem is that it is not easy to move in the Nordic direction because these countries have specific institutional features (e.g., highly educated population, solidaristic culture, high levels of taxation and public spending, as well as some of the most developed welfare states in the world) that are not easy to replicate. Therefore, he seems to suggest that the most likely option for these countries would be to move toward the Anglo-Saxon model.

Yet, this book will show that a movement toward an Anglo-Saxon model is not preordained. It supports the conclusion by other authors, such as Eichengreen (2007), who have claimed that there may be more than one combination of institutions capable of producing the same level of efficiency. Competition will generate growing pressures for European countries to "deliver their preferred mix of public and private good more efficiently," but there are European countries, such as the Scandinavian ones, who have been very successful at finding the right equilibrium to maintain their social protections while enhancing the efficiencies of their production system. Moreover, as we have seen, European have different preferences; therefore, their institutions should also differ.

VoC in Spain

This book shows limitations of the institutional models—Liberal Market Economy (LME) and Coordinated Market Economy (CME)—that Hall and Soskice have developed and argues that it is possible to develop coordination capacities in countries that lack a strong coordination tradition. Using the tools provided by the VoC literature it seeks to explain how mechanisms of coordination develop and work in Spain, an economy that does not fit nicely into either model.

It challenges the interpretation according to which increasing exposure to trade, foreign direct investment, and liquid capital mobility have prompted a pervasive race to the neoliberal bottom among countries. As we have seen, the proponents of this thesis contend that European countries are now converging on an Anglo-American model of capitalism. In this regard, some have claimed that Spain is moving toward this Anglo-Saxon model because in open economies corporatist models are no longer sustainable, and have argued that despite strong state intervention, the lack of articulation of the Spanish institutional model precludes the evolution toward a CME because the country is now too complex to move toward institutionalized coordination.[7]

Contrary to this prediction, this book shows that in Spain globalization and European Monetary Union (EMU) have promoted rather that undermined coordination among economic actors. Unable to escape from economic interdependence the Spanish economic actors have developed coordinating capacities at the macro and micro levels to address and resolve tensions between economic interdependence and political sovereignty.

In this book I show that institutional change is a political matter and, therefore, it is possible to develop coordination capacities in countries that lack the strong tradition of CMEs. For instance, in the realm of industrial relations the trajectory of chance in Spain parallels development in the CMEs more closely than those in the LMEs. A central argument is that successful coordination depends not only on the organization of the social actors but also on their interests and strategies. This book looks at the evolving interests of capital and the structural and political constraints within which economic actors define and defend their interests. It seeks to shed further light on political approaches to competitive pressures that tend to promote the interaction of the state and economic actors in new innovative ways that create further coordination capacities.

The study of the Spanish case will confirm that the link between changes in the international economic environment and the process of domestic policy making also depends on domestic political and economic factors. They provide their own set of incentives for domestic actors to entertain certain political strategies. The main argument will be that actors' preferences and policy outcomes are constrained by the quality and configuration of institutional frameworks, political deals, and the economic structure.

Furthermore, Spain conforms, to a large extent, to the so-called state capitalism model or State Influenced Market Economies (SMEs) (Schmidt 2006), in which the state is still a major institutional actor and leads business-labor relations. I argue that Spain better conforms to an intermediate model of a State-Influenced Mixed Market Economy (SMME).[8] This book argues in favor of the need to complement the VoC focus on the "micro-tier" of firm-centered relations with a "macro-tier" analysis of state action (see Molina and Rhodes 2005; Schmidt 2006). Yet, while this book follows a two-tiered approach and looks at state intervention and the fragmentation of interest associations (Molina and Rhodes 2005, pp. 7–8), it will dispute the notion that this fragmentation has hindered "the consolidation of a stable framework integrating the social partners into the policy-making system" (Molina and Rodhes 2005, p. 8). Structural fragmentation has led to the development of different logics of coordination and interaction among economic actors; yet in Spain this shortcoming has been mitigated by factors such as the strong articulation of the business sector around an umbrella organization, the *Confederacion Española de Organizaciones Emresariales* (CEOE), by the strategic unity of action between the two leading confederations (Comisiones

Obreras, CCOO; and Unión General de Trabajadores, UGT), and in particular by the role of the state.[9] In short, I claim that the Spanish state, with its distinctive interests and relative power, has been a central factor in the development and consolidation of coordination in the country. It has played a crucial role in affecting coalition building,[10] while providing the resources to sustain particular and distinctive varieties of coordination within the country.

Furthermore it will show that despite the absence of strong ties between the micro- and macro levels at the national level, the strong ties between the micro/meso and macro levels at the regional level have made it possible to develop strong and complex coordination mechanisms at the micro level. Like in Italy, in Spain the economic actors have been able to share information, form alliances, build trust, and hence negotiate the process of industrial adjustment (Locke 1995, p. 175).

In sum, this book challenges the institutional determinism that sometimes has been associated with the conclusions of the VoC literature.[11] It maps the politics of institutional change in Spain, and it argues that countries have choices beyond the bleak prospects for welfare provisions of a liberal-market path, and that institutional change is possible.

Finally, an additional objective of the book is to reflect on how far Spain has come over the last two decades, in order to better understand where it is headed at the dawn of the twenty-first century. Hence it examines the impact of globalization, liberalization, and European integration on Spain from an economic and institutional standpoint. Spain has been remarkably successful at responding to the new "trilemma": balancing the budget, while achieving high levels of equality and employment growth. The roots of this success have to be explained and this book provides a detailed analysis of the development of the Spanish economy over the last two decades. Drawing on empirical research the book offers an up-to-date assessment of institutional change and economic policies in Spain.

Spain

The focus of this book is on Spain, which has become one of Europe's hitherto most successful economies. While other European countries have been stuck in the mud, Spain has performed much better at reforming its welfare systems and labor markets, as well as at improving flexibility and lowering unemployment. Indeed, over the last decade and a half the Spanish economy has been finally able to break with the historical pattern of boom and bust, and the country's economic performance has been nothing but short of remarkable. Propped by low interest rates and immigration, Spain is (in 2007) in its fourteenth year of uninterrupted growth and it is benefiting from the longest cycle of continuing expansion of the Spanish economy in modern history (only Ireland in the Eurozone has a better record), which has contributed to the narrowing of per capita Gross Domestic Product (GDP) with the European Union (EU) (and according to the government, in 2009 or 2010 Spain will overcome Italy and Germany in GDP per capita).[12]

Unemployment has fallen from 20 percent in the mid-1990s to 7.95 percent in the first half of 2007 (the lowest level since 1978), and Spain has become the second country in the EU (after Germany with a much larger economy), which creates the most jobs (an average of 600,000 per year over the last decade).[13] In 2006, the last year with official data, the Spanish economy grew a spectacular 3.9 percent. Economic growth has contributed to per capita income growth, which has almost reached the European average (97.7 percent), and employment.

The performance of the labor market has also been spectacular: in the last 10 years, 33 percent of all the total employment created in the EU-15 has been created in Spain. In 2006 the active population increased by 3.5 percent, the highest in the EU (led by new immigrants and the incorporation of women to the labor market, which has increased from 59 percent in 1995 to 72 percent in 2006); and 772,000 new jobs have been created. The public deficit has been eliminated (the country has had a *superavit* for two years running, which reached 1.8 percent of GDP, or 18,000 million euros, in 2006), and the public debt has been reduced to 39.8 percent of GDP, the lowest in the last two decades.[14] The construction boom has also been remarkable: more than 400,000 new homes have been built in and around Madrid in the past five years.

The economic success has extended to Spanish companies that have expanded beyond their traditional frontiers (Guillén 2005; Toral 2001). In 2006 they spent a total of 140 billion euros ($184bn) on domestic and overseas acquisitions, putting the country third behind the United Kingdom and France.[15] Of this, 80bn euros were to buy companies abroad (compared with the 65bn euros spent by German companies).[16] In 2006 Spanish FDI abroad increased 113 percent, reaching 71,487 billion euros (or the equivalent of 7.3 percent of GDP, compared with 3.7 percent in 2005).[17] In 2006 *Iberdrola*, an electricity supplier, purchased *Scottish Power* for $22.5bn to create Europe's third largest utility; *Banco Santander*, Spain's largest bank, purchased Britain's *Abbey National Bank* for $24bn, *Ferrovial*, a family construction group, concluded a takeover of the *British BAA* (which operates the three main airports of the United Kingdom) for 10bn pounds; and *Telefonica* bought *O2*, the U.K. mobile phone company.[18] Indeed, 2006 was banner year for Spanish firms: 72 percent of them increased their production and 75.1 percent their profits, 55.4 percent hired new employees, and 77.6 percent increased their investments.[19]

The country's transformation has been not only economic but also social. Spaniards have become more optimistic and self-confident (i.e., a recent Harris poll shows that Spaniards are more confident of their economic future than their European and American counterparts, and a poll by the *Center for Sociological Analysis* shows that 80 percent are satisfied or very satisfied with their economic situation).[20] Spain is "different" again and according to a recent poll it has become the most popular country to work for Europeans.[21] Since 2000, some 5 million immigrants (645,000 in 2004 and 500,000 in 2006) have settled in Spain (8.7 percent of the population compared with

3.7 percent in the EU15), making the country the biggest recipient of immigrants in the EU (they represent 10 percent of the contributors to the Social Security system). This is a radical departure for a country that used to be a net exporter of people, and more so because it has been able to absorb these immigrants without falling prey (at least so far) to the social tensions that have plagued other European countries (although there have been isolated incidents of racial violence) (Calativa 2005).[22] Several factors have contributed to this development.[23] First, economic growth, with its accompanying job creation, has provided job for the newcomers while pushing down overall unemployment. Second, cultural factors: about one-third of the immigrants come from Latin America, and they share the same language and part of the culture, which facilitates their integration. Third, demographic: an ageing population and low birthrates. Finally, the national temperament characterized by a generally tolerant attitude, marked by the memory of a history of emigration, which make Spaniards more sympathetic to immigrants (according to a recent poll no fewer than 42 percent state that migration has had a positive effect on the economy). The proportion of children from mixed marriages increased from 1.8 percent in 1995 to 11.5 percent in 2005.[24]

These immigrants have contributed significantly to the economic success of the country because they have boosted the aggregate performance of the economy: They have raised the supply of labor, increased demand as they spent money, moderated wages, and put downward pressure on inflation, boosted output, allowed the labor market to avoid labor shortages, contributed to consumption, and increased more flexibility in the economy with their mobility and willingness to take on low-paid jobs in sectors such as construction, and agriculture, in which Spaniards are no longer interested.[25]

As a matter of fact most of the 772,000 new jobs created in Spain in 2006 went to immigrants (about 60 percent).[26] Their motivation to work hard also opens the way for productivity improvements (which in 2006 experienced the largest increase since 1997, with a 0.8 percent). It is estimated that the contribution of immigrants to GDP in the last four years has been of 0.8 percentage points.[27] Immigration has represented more than 50 percent of employment growth, and 78.6 percent of the demographic growth (as a result Spain has led the demographic growth of the European countries between 1995 and 2005 with a demographic advance of 10.7 percent compared with the EU15 average of 4.8 percent).[28] They have also contributed to the huge increase in employment, which has been one of the key reasons for the impressive economic expansion. Indeed, between 1988 and 2006, employment contributed 3 percentage points to the 3.5 percent annual rise in Spain's potential GDP (see table I.2).[29]

As we will see throughout the book, however, economic success is marred by some glaring deficiencies, because it is largely a "miracle" based on bricks and mortar. The foundations of economic growth are fragile because the country has low productivity growth (productivity has contributed only 0.5 percentage points to potential GDP between 1998 and 2006) and deteriorating external competitiveness.[30] Spain has not addressed its fundamental

Table I.2   Economic summary Spain (2006–08)

	2006	2007*	2008*
Total GDP (€bn)	976	1,045	1,113
Total GDP ($bn)	1,226	1,359	1,454
Real GDP growth (annual % change)	3.9	3.6	3.4
GDP per head ($)	27,767	30,289	31,918
Inflation (annual % change in CPI)	3.6	2.6	2.7
Industrial production (annual % change)	3.0	3.0	2.5
Unemployment rate (% of labor force)	8.5	7.8	7.7
Money supply, M2 (annual % change)	23.8	5.9	4.5
Government expenditure (% of GDP)	38.2	37.9	38.1
Government budget balance (% of GDP)	1.8	1.3	1.1
Current account balance ($bn)	−108	−127	−142
Merchandise exports ($bn)	216	245	260
Merchandise imports ($bn)	317	349	353
Trade balance ($bn)	−101	−104	−93

Note: * Forecast.
Source: Economist Intelligence Unit. From *Financial Times: Special Report*, June 21, 2007, p. 6.

challenge, its declining productivity, which has only grown an average of
0.3 percent in the last 10 years (0.7 percent in 2006), one whole point below
the EU average, placing Spain at the bottom of the EU and only ahead of
Italy and Greece (the productivity of a Spanish worker is the equivalent of
75 percent of a U.S. one). The most productive activities (energy, industry,
and financial services) only contribute 11 percent of GDP growth.[31]

Moreover, growth is largely based in low-intensity economic sectors, such
as services and construction, which are not exposed to international competition. In 2006 most of the new jobs were created in low-productivity sectors
such as construction (33 percent), services associated with housing such as
sales and rentals (15 percent), or tourism and domestic service (30 percent).
These sectors represent 75 percent of all the new jobs created in Spain in
2006 (new manufacturing jobs, in contrast, only represented 5 percent). The
labor temporary rate reached 33.3 percent in 2006, and inflation is a recur-
rent problem (it closed 2006 with a 2.7 percent increase, but the average for
the year was 3.6 percent), thus the inflation differential with the EU (almost
1 point) has not decreased, which reduces the competitiveness of Spanish
products abroad (and consequently Spanish companies are losing market
share abroad).[32]

Moreover, family indebtedness reached a record 115 percent of disposable
income in 2006, and the construction and housing sectors accounted for
18.5 percent of GDP (twice the Eurozone average). House prices have risen
by 150 percent since 1998, and the average price of a square meter of
residential property went up from 700 euros in 1997 to 2,000 at the end of
2006, even though the housing stock has doubled. Many wonder whether
this bubble is sustainable.[33]

Between 40 and 60 percent of the benefits of the largest Spanish companies come from abroad. Yet, in the last few years this figure has decreased by
approximately 10 percentage points, and there has been a decline in direct
foreign investment of all types in the country: it has fallen from a peak of
38.3 billion euros in 2000 to 16.6 billion euros in 2005.[34] The current
account deficit reached 8.9 percent of GDP in 2006, which makes Spain the
country with the largest deficit in absolute terms (86,026 million euros),
only behind the United States; imports are 25 percent higher than exports
and Spanish companies are losing market share in the world. And the
prospects are not very bright. According to the European Commission (EC),
exports will grow by 6 percent in the next two years but imports will grow by
8.5 percent (and 9 percent in 2008). The trade deficit is expected to reach
9.5 percent in 2008.[35]

While there is overall consensus that the country needs to improve its
education system and invest in research and development to lift productivity, as well as modernize the public sector, and to make the labor market
more stable (i.e., reduce the temporary rate) and flexible, there are disputes
about whether the country is heading for a hard landing. Spain spends only
half of the Organization of European Co-operation and Development
(OECD) average on education; it lags most of Europe on investment
in Research and Development (R&D); and it is ranked twenty-ninth
by the UNCTAD as an attractive location for research and development.
Finally, other observers note that Spain is failing to do more to integrate
its immigrant population, and social divisions are beginning to emerge (see
Calavita 2005).[36]

These successes (as well as these shortcomings) make Spain an ideal case
to explore how countries can respond to the challenges of globalization, and
the role played by institutions and economic actors.

The Myth of Globalization

The analysis of this book is framed within the ongoing debate about the
impact of globalization on national economies and on the policy autonomy
of governments. Globalization, defined as "the growing economic interdependence of countries worldwide through the increasing volume and variety
of cross-border transactions in world and services and of international capital flows, and also through the more rapid and widespread diffusion of
technologies,"[37] is considered the great economic event of our era because it
involves the expansion of capitalism on a global scale and it is transforming
the twentieth-century managerial capitalism into a new global financial one.
Some scholars have noted that "much of the institutional scenery of two
decades ago—distinct national business elites, stable managerial control over
companies and long-term relationships with financial institutions—is disap-
pearing into economic history."[38] As a result, large part of the world behaves
like a single economy, which means "an increase in the geographic range of
locally consequential social interactions" (Tilly 1995).

While globalization is widely considered as the defining process of our time, this phenomenon is still highly contested and misunderstood. It has been the result of three processes: Technology development, and in particular enhanced communications and lower technology costs; second organizational innovations from Transnational Corporations (TNCs), which have been powerful engines of global economic integration; and finally, economic and trade liberalization. In the last few decades it has been promoted actively by TNCs, states, international organizations (such as the World Bank or the International Monetary Fund), and civil society.

It accelerated after World War II: The ratios of exports to output have risen from 12 to 17 percent since 1970; and there has been a deepening on the integration of financial markets: $2 trillion per day; as well as a dramatic surge of technology transfers all facilitated by governments bound by multilateral agreements. However, it is not a new phenomenon, nor it is only a Western one (Sen 2002). On the contrary, it could be argued that there has been an even higher degree of integration in previous decades. For instance, between 1870 and 1914, the United Kingdom's capital outflow in 1914 was 9 percent of GDP, twice as big a share of GDP as outflows from Germany and Japan in the 1990s; gold was the world currency; and there as even greater labor mobility at that time than nowadays. The key difference now is the explosion and impact of free trade and capital mobility. The financial sector is now unbound.

Indeed, as noted by Wolf,[39] finance has exploded: the ratio of global financial assets to annual world output has increased from 109 percent in 1989 to 316 percent in 2005, and in that year the core of the global stock of core financial assets reached $140,000 billion. Furthermore, finance "has become far more transnational oriented" because financial markets are increasingly performing the intermediation role that banks traditionally did, and new players (such as the hedge funds and equity funds) and products ("derivatives") are transforming the opportunities for managing risk and providing additional sources of funding. In addition, this new form of financial capitalism is more global than ever: for instance, international financial assets and liabilities from residents of high-income countries have increased from 50 percent of GDP in 1970 to 100 percent in the mid-1980s, and 330 percent in 2004; and the value of mergers and acquisitions jumped from $850 billion (in 9,251 deals) in 1995, to $3,861 (in 33,141 deals) in 2005. Finally, the share of developing country products in the manufactured imports of high-income countries has doubled since the early 1990s.[40]

Hence, some authors claim that globalization is "not a choice [but] a reality," which has to be accepted because it is here to stay and even question whether it means the end to geography (Friedman 2000). It has brought about the "flattening of the world" (Friedman 2006). According to many it is the cause of outcomes in many spheres from production processes to public policies; as well as changes in areas such as culture, the environment, transnational cooperation, or migration patterns.

However, globalization is becoming highly controversial, as unease about the effects of globalization has been building during the past decade, and more and more people view it as an overwhelming negative force. Recent polls provide evidence that the citizens of rich countries feel that globalization is more a curse than a blessing.[41] The opponents of globalization claim that it is responsible for industrial desertification, higher unemployment, reduced social protection, increasing poverty, and inequality; it has a negative impact on small farmers, and lower wages that result from higher imports from developing countries. Furthermore, they contend that outsourcing also puts downward pressure on wages, that technological changes and global supply chains displace jobs, and that they foster labor fragmentation and weaken unions, while leading investment toward developed countries. This is so because employers are using the exit threat to move their operations offshore to take advantage of cheaper labor, as a bargaining chip in their negotiations with unions, thus resulting in a shift in power and income from labor to capital. In short, globalization weakens the bargaining position of unions. As a result, salaries have been shrinking as a proportion on national income in OECD member states. Furthermore the integration of countries such as China and India in the global economy with their cheap and abundant labor, and the outgrowth of outsourcing of manufacturing and services are also putting downward pressure on wages. Consequently in the U.S. real hourly wages have been virtually flat (while productivity has increased by 70 percent).

Recent data show that the trend toward increased inequality is continuing and even accelerating. Indeed, according to the Congressional Budget Office data, in the United States since 1979 the pretax income of the top 1 percent of the population has increased by $664 billion or $600,000 per family, a 43 percent increase. In contrast, for a median family the pretax income has only increased 14 percent from 1979 to 2004.[42] Other reports show that from 1966 to 2001, the median pretax inflation-adjusted wage and salary income grew just 11 percent—versus 58 percent for incomes in the ninetieth percentile and 121 percent for those in the ninety-ninth percentile (Scheve and Slaughter 2007).

At the same time, it is argued that globalization fosters job insecurity for workers because it makes companies more vulnerable to external shocks, such as exchange rate fluctuations (OECD 2007). Finally, some scholars contend that globalization causes extensive harm to the environment and people (i.e., patents), and that TNCs violate labor laws, pay low wages, damage the environment, and abuse workers (see Milanovic 2003; Shiva 2000; Dollar and Kray 2002; Wade 2003; D'Mello 2000; Millen and Holtz 2000; Stiglitz 2002, 2002a).

The supporters of globalization, however, challenge these arguments and claim that, on the contrary, it promotes economic growth, thus reducing poverty and fostering equality; that developed countries benefit extensively because as a result of globalization new jobs are created in other sectors and there are more exports to developing countries. They further argue that it promotes investment, productivity, and development; generates economic efficiencies that result from specialization, economies of scale, and lower costs of production, thus allowing countries to improve their competitive position, and brings benefits for consumers (Wolf 2004; Friedman 2000, 2006; Bhagwati 2004).

These scholars contend that the transformation of capitalism is a good thing because

> active financial investors swiftly identify and attack pockets of inefficiency, [thus improving] the efficiency of capital everywhere; they impose the disciplines of the market on incumbent management; they finance new activities and put old activities into the hands of those who can exploit them better; they create a better global ability to cope with risk; they put their capital where it will work best anywhere in the world; and in the process, they give quite ordinary people the ability to manage their finances more successfully.[43]

To support their claims the advocates of globalization dispute the notion that investment is flooding toward developing countries, among other reasons because most trade (94.5 percent) takes still place among industrialized countries; imports from developing to industrialized countries are only between 3 and 8 percent of the latter's production, while imports from developing countries increased only from 1.1 percent of all imports in 1967–68 to 5.4 percent in 1987–89 (only 1.2 percent of OCDE countries' GDP). They recognize the impact of offshoring—moving production abroad, but they point out that offshored inputs have been moving more slowly than total trade, and its rise has been driven by skilled (not unskilled) inputs.[44] They also highlight that unemployment and lower wages affect both qualified and non-qualified workers as well as manufacturing, service, and construction workers (which are largely shielded from external competition and should not suffer as much the effect of outsourcing) and that the percentage of TNCs production outside of their countries of origin is only 6 percent of their total production and 0.2 percent in services.

Indeed, the latest OECD report shows that trade appears to make only a modest contribution to increases in inequality and suggest that such increases may have more to do with technological changes (see OECD 2007). Finally, they claim that there are other factors that help account for wages' stagnation such as technological changes, or the fact that most new jobs are being created in the service sector with lower productivity (e.g., in the United States there was a reduction in the number of workers in the manufacturing sector from 28 percent to 16 percent between 1964 and 2000).

They also dispute the claim that globalization has resulted in lower investment in developed countries, highlighting the fact that capital stock invested in developing countries is only 3.1 percent of all fixed capital; that most investment still takes place in developed countries; and that investment to developed countries decreased from 30.6 percent in 1967 to 23.4 percent in 1991, while the external debt resulted in higher flows to developed countries. Indeed, while North America accounted for 40 percent of global private equity in 2005 (down from 68 percent in 2000), Europe increased its share of investment from 17 percent to 38 percent.[45]

The empirical evidence shows that the impact of globalization is uneven. Globalization has resulted in cheaper imports and this has benefited the entire economy. While it is true that most of U.S. TNCs' sales (70 percent), fixed capital (78 percent), employment (73 percent), and value added is still based in their home country and also that other factors such as infrastructure, productivity, and skills play a critical role in economic outcomes; it is also true that globalization has shifted the balance of power between workers and employers in favor of the latter. Furthermore, while citizens throughout the world express legitimate concerns about the impact of globalization over the falling share of wages in national income and increasing wage inequality, the evidence has shown that such concerns are often overestimated. Indeed the argument that globalization is the culprit for the stagnation in real hourly wages in the last 25 years, despite a huge increase in output, has been contested. Globalization, technological change, and labor market policies all have had an impact in labor income share. For instance, a new study has examined the wage-productivity gap and has shown that the 70 percent increase in productivity of the last 25 years is largely accounted for by rising nonwage benefits such as health insurance (60 percent), by using the correct deflator to adjust wages, by the shift of the workforce toward higher-skilled employment, which increases output and average wages (but not for those who are unskilled and work hourly), and by labor's smaller share of national income. According to this analysis real hourly wages have not been as flat since the early 1980s, as they have risen by roughly 1.5 percent a year. Furthermore, it shows that without globalization economies would have grown more slowly, and hence most wages would have increased at a slower pace as well.[46]

Moreover, according to a recent OECD report, wages in the OECD countries have been increasing in real terms in spite of offshoring, but the gap between the richest and poorest workers has widened in 18 of the 20 OECD countries (see table I.3). In 16 of the member states the earnings of the best-paid 10 percent grew faster than those of the lowest paid 10 percent between 1994 and 2005. Interestingly, for the purpose of this book, only in Spain (plus Ireland and Japan) the wages of the highest-paid did not outpace those of the lowest-paid. In 1995 in Spain the top 10 percent income earners made 4.2 percent more than the bottom 10 percent; in 2005, this proportion had decreased to 3.5 percent.

In Spain, despite the large numbers of jobs created (with a record employed population of 20 million workers), income from labor has reduced its weight in the total national income from 62 percent in 1992 to 54.4 percent in 2005 (in the EU this decline was more moderate: from 61.6 percent to 57.6 percent). This is owed to the poor quality of new jobs (typically not very productive, with little remuneration), which have pulled down the average salary around 4 percent between 1995 and 2005 (it is now about 20,000 euros).[47] Yet unemployment in the OECD countries was still set to fall (from 33.6 million in 2006 to 32 million in 2007) (see OECD 2007) (see figure I.1).[48]

Table I.3 Employment and salaries in OECD countries

In euros*	Average annual salary 2005	Average annual salary 2005 with price parity	Employment rate 2006 (%)	Unemployment rate 2006 (%)	Per capita GDP 2006 (UE-27=100)
Austria	28.909	26.396	70.2	4.8	129
Belgium	31.972	28.547	60.4	8.4	123
Denmark	39.672	26.751	76.9	4.0	127
Finland	28.199	21.581	68.9	7.8	117
France	28.305	24.197	62.3	9.8	113
Germany	27.880	25.172	67.2	10.4	113
Greece	18.404	19.719	61.0	8.9	89
Holland	32.308	28.846	72.4	44.4	131
Ireland	38.819	29.428	68.1	4.4	144
Italy	22.781	20.340	58.4	6.9	104
Portugal	13.538	14.701	67.9	8.1	75
Spain	19.754	20.093	65.7	8.6	102
United Kingdom	32.996	29.728	72.5	5.4	118
United States	33.428	33.428	72	4.7	—

Note: * Original data in USD. Exchange Rate applied, 1.363 USD per euro.
Source: European Commission, OECD and *Eurostat*. From: *El País*, Sunday, July 8, 2007, p. 73.

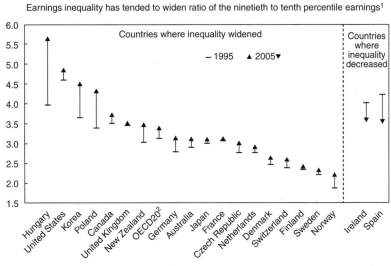

Earnings inequality has tended to widen ratio of the ninetieth to tenth percentile earnings[1]

Figure I.1 Earning inequality

Notes: The figure shows that in all countries except Ireland and Spain, the earnings of the 10 percent best-paid workers increased more than the earnings of the 10 percent least-paid workers, over the 1995–2005 period (i.e., earnings inequality widened).

1. Full-year, full-time workers. The data shown are consistent over time, but not entirely comparable across countries owing to differences in pay reporting periods and coverage of workers.

2. Unweighted average of countries shown in the figure.

Source: OECD database on Earnings Distribution. From OECD *2007 Annual Employment Outlook*.

In the end, the key is to understand the impact of globalization on labor markets, institutions, and domestic structures. This is precisely one of the objectives of this book.

At the same time this books seeks to challenge the arguments from some of the proponents of globalization who contend that countries are now converging in one model of capitalism—the Anglo-Saxon one (see Crouch and Streeck 1997). This argument is partially rooted in the belief that globalization reduces governments' autonomy to develop their own domestic policies. According to this view, globalization has resulted in the dismantling of borders and has transferred power to business, individuals, and transnational communities.

Yet this view oversimplifies the consequences of globalization and minimizes the power of governments. Authors such as Garrett (1998) have strongly contested this argument and have shown that domestic partisan politics, institutions, and other forms of social organization still have an important impact on economic policy and performance. Indeed, governments are not "prisoners" of markets. The role of governments was questioned long before the globalization process intensified in the 1980s. It was the crisis of the 1970s that led politicians to question previous policies and led to deregulation, liberalization, and economic integration, which in turn accelerated the globalization process. However, these decisions were implemented by democratically elected governments and supported by voters. It was this process of deregulation, liberalization, technological diffusion, and economic integration that really weakened governments' powers.[50]

Indeed, the decisions to eliminate barriers between commercial and investment banking (such as the Glass-Steagall Act in the United States or the famous "Regulation Q," which forbade the payment of interest on demand deposit) or dismantle foreign exchange controls were all domestic decisions taken by national governments, and they contributed to the dramatic growth of financial intermediation that led to changes in the global economy and influenced the balance of power among economic actors. This process was hastened by the development of new technologies in computing and communications, and the revolution in financial economics, which contributed to the emergence of new financial instruments.[51]

Yet, the empirical evidence shows that governments are not "prisoners" of markets. Indeed, governments' intervention in the economy has not decreased: for instance, public spending as proportion of GDP—which determines the level of intervention of governments in the economy—has increased systematically (30 percent in 1960 and 45 percent in 2005) (see figure I.2). If governments are prisoners of markets, how is this possible?

While it is true that corporate taxes have declined, how is it possible to explain that governments have been able to maintain income taxes (see figure I.3)?

Indeed, governments are still able to determine social policies. While they have a cost, they are also beneficial because they help cushion the negative impact of globalization and technological change. In fact the evidence shows

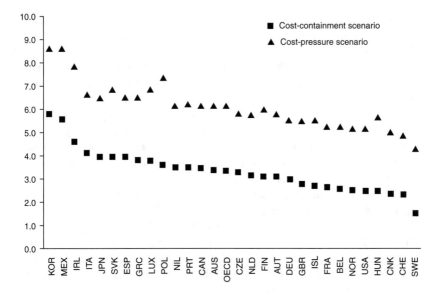

Figure I.2 Total increase in health and long-term care spending by country, 2005–2050
Source: OECD calculations.

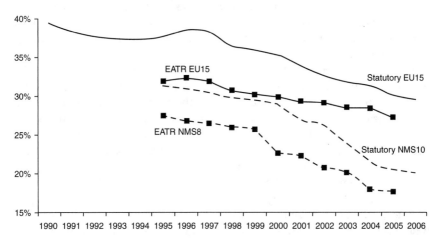

Figure I.3 Corporate tax rates in EU25 1990–2006
Source: Devereux, Griffith, Hal and Klemm (2005), Eurostat, KPMG for statutory rates; Overesch (2005) for EATR (Effective average tax rates).

that governments can implement policies that promote employment and increase the incomes of the low-paid (see OECD 2007a). Finally, while it is true that there are limits in monetary politics and levels of public debt, high levels of debt have been possible with stable monetary policies (i.e., in Italy or Belgium with levels of debt higher that 100 percent of their GDP).

On the contrary, in this book I make the case that success in the global economy demands national government actions, and that it does not need to be based necessarily in convergence, but on diversification and differences. In fact, I argue that in the global economy we survive by becoming more diverse and focusing on what we do best, not by copying other countries or economic models. The question should be not so much about the costs and benefits of globalization (there are both), but how to distribute the benefits. In fact globalization can help generate the resources to develop social policies. It is the inequity in the balance of institutional arrangements that results in unequal benefits. Some scholars are advocating for a "New Deal for Globalization" based on a reform of the tax system to share the benefits more widely, in order to make globalization more tolerable for citizens who have experienced little real income growth (Scheve and Slaughter 2007).

I argue that we should not build a wall against the world beyond. Success will be based on the elimination of tariff and nontariff barriers by rich countries, the establishment of appropriate policies and institutions, the development of adequate adjustment assistance and efficient financial systems, regulated migration, and strong governance. According to a recent OECD report, globalization is "compatible with employment rates, provided the right policies are in place" (OECD 2007).[52] Governments should respond to citizens' concerns about the negative effects of globalization (it creates losers) and address the growing gap between the successful and the unsuccessful. The solutions are well known: better education, flexible economies, improved infrastructure, and safety nets. They may ignore these solutions at their own peril.

Government leaders should remember that capital markets are also mediated by public institutions and political decisions. Politics are not only desirable but also inevitable in dealing with the political and economic effects of globalization. Citizens, who feel threatened by a phenomenon that is perceived as a profit-making and inhuman machine, want governments to shield them from the insecurities of the age, and powerful coalitions are forming to curb the increasing power of global capitalist interests and elites. Yet, it is important to remember that many of the current challenges are transnational (i.e., climate change, energy security, terrorism, migration, demographic changes, global pandemic, increasing competition, or proliferation of weapons of mass destruction) and they cannot be addressed effectively alone by national governments.

In sum, governments are not "prisoners" of markets. They nearly have as much (or as little) control over their economies as they had in the past. This has been a convenient argument to deflect political pressures and justify unpopular policies. Governments should be responsible of their own choices and policies. They should act to configure markets. As some scholars have pointed out,

> Globalization's soft underbelly is the imbalance between the national scope of governments and the global nature of markets. A healthy economic system

necessitates a delicate compromise between these two. Go too much in one direction and you have protectionism and autarky. Go too much in the other and you have an unstable world economy with little social and political support from those it is supposed to help.[53]

In the end, markets and democracy are both necessary to fulfil the ideals of liberty, solidarity, and equality that are intrinsic to Western values. The main challenge is one of global governance because economic globalization is moving faster than political and institutional one (Stiglitz 2006).

Objectives of the Book

This book pursues several objectives. First, the aim is to review the political economy literature on institutions and to explain the ways in which they affect the behavior of economic agents. At a time in which there are significant competitive pressures across countries to deregulate and increase competitiveness it is important to analyze the impact that different institutional settings have on business activities and strategies. It is also necessary to explore the prospects of building coordination capacity in countries that lack a propitious institutional framework. Thus, this project (which includes the analysis of instances of cooperation at the micro level) will help to answer key questions such as the following: What kind of institutions favor enhanced competitiveness and promote entrepreneurship and innovation? How can firms exploit to their advantage the institutional setting in which they are operating? How much institutional change is possible? And, can the knowledge and experience accumulated during institutional reforms in industrialized countries be used in other countries?

At the same time, this book seeks to explain the ways in which institutions affect the behavior of economic agents in Spain. For instance, it seeks to understand how factors such as the extent of the informal economy, vulnerability to takeovers, sensibility of capital investors to profitability, capacity for long-term contracts with employees, and the degree to which networks provide an informal coordination capacity all contribute to affect firms' preferences.

Moreover, since companies are the locus for wealth creation, it becomes crucial to understand how local contexts and institutional settings could enhance their competitiveness and foster markets for ideas, capital, and people (Hamel and Prahalad 1996). It seeks to address key questions such as: What kind of institutions favor enhanced competitiveness and promote entrepreneurship and innovation? How can firms exploit to their advantage the institutional setting in which they are operating? How can multinational firms enhance their competitive position by modifying local institutional configurations? How much change is possible? And, can the knowledge and experience accumulated during institutional reforms in Spain be used in other countries?

In addition, access to capital has traditionally been an important challenge for Spanish entrepreneurs and firms (Pérez 1997). While the larger companies have been able to raise money in international markets by issuing depository receipts, small- and medium enterprises have had significant difficulties raising capital. Indeed, Spain—helped by the integration of the country into the EU—has benefited in the last two decades from strong inflows of capital from European and world companies investing in the country. Yet, small firms still face significant constraints accessing capital. This development has a lot to do with the way that international and domestic capital markets have developed. How can Spanish financial institutions address this problem? What kind of institutional framework should they promote?

Moreover, at a time when Spanish firms are investing heavily all over the world (and in particular in Latin American countries) it will be important to examine the impact that different institutional settings have on Spanish business activities and strategies. Thus, this analysis should help to answer key questions such as the following: How can firms modify the institutional configuration in which they operate to enhance their competitive position?

The political economy literature has mostly focused on the study of industrialized countries but Spain does not easily fit into the categories developed for advanced economies. As we will see, the institutional framework of the country is substantially different and its impact over microeconomic actors' behavior has to be explained, particularly at a time in which the level of economic integration in this country has intensified as a result of economic liberalization and foreign investment. Therefore, it is necessary to study how economic, political, and social conditions determine the level of institutional development in Spain and vice versa, as well as analyze how the country's institutional setting impacts the behavior and performance of economic actors.

Finally, this research project seeks to shed light on how institutional frameworks influence preferences and policy outcomes. Such comprehensive analyses will help develop an empirical framework that describes the linkages among institutional factors and facilitates policy making for increasing competitiveness. It will also illustrate the ways in which nations respond to the pressures of international interdependence and technological change.

Overall, this book aims to

1) examine the impact of globalization and economic integration on Spain;
2) analyze the influence of the institutional frameworks on public policy making, and the impact of institutions on the behavior of microeconomic actors to show that there may be several models of capitalism that allow firms and countries to flourish and compete successfully in international markets;
3) examine how the configuration of institutional frameworks contributes toward explaining disparities in economic actors' preferences and performance; and
4) explore the obstacles that will crop up when reforms aim to transform institutional settings.

Finally, the analysis of institutional factors will provide in future projects the instruments and data necessary to develop a comprehensive and systemic framework of analysis of institutional sources of competitiveness that can be applied to other countries.

Methodology

In order to examine the development of coordination mechanisms in Spain, this book has chosen an historic and institutional approach that considers the objectives of policy makers and social actors, as well as the way that they interpret existing economic and political conditions. This approach allows the researcher to examine the ways institutions structure the relations among actors and shape their interests and goals, thus constraining political struggles and influencing outcomes (Steinmo, Thelen, and Longstreth 1992, p. 2).

Most of the research material for this project has been gathered in Spain. In order to pursue this analysis, the author conducted an extensive review of the secondary literature and has interviewed scholars, social actors, and policy makers. The author has met with employers and representatives from the main business confederations in Spain, and has conducted interviews with the leaders of the employers' association and the major trade unions, as well as leaders and representatives of the main political parties. In addition, the author has interviewed former and current high-ranking officials from state agencies: ministries of labor, economics, the central banks, and the institutions in charge of fostering social bargaining (the *Consejo Económico y Social*). Finally, the author has conferred with leading scholars and specialists in politics, industrial relations, and economics in Spain and the United States. Overall, the author has interviewed over 40 people.[54] In addition, secondary sources of data come from the libraries and records of selected government departments and the social actors.

Theoretical Framework

Basic factor endowments such as labor, land, or capital influence economic and business strategies and condition managerial decisions. The role of these factors has been extensively analyzed by the literature (Porter 1990; Kotler et al. 1997; Fairbanks, Lindsay, and Porter 1997). Institutional factors also hinder or facilitate the strategies of governments and companies. Nevertheless, lately the political economy literature has attempted to explain cross-national patterns of economic policy and performance (Hall 1999; Iversen 1999), and institutional theories have focused mainly on the analysis of organizational change (Powell and DiMaggio 1991). In this manner, institutional economists have attempted to explain the ways in which institutions and institutional change affect the performance of national economies (North 1990; Alston, Eggertsson, and North 1996).

Building on the new economics of organization, a group of scholars has developed a new theory of *comparative institutional advantage*, which offers new explanations for the response of firms and nations to the challenges of globalization and economic integration (Hall and Soskice 2001).[55] The roots of this approach are in the 1960s (Shonfield 1994; Zysman 1984; Johnson 1982). At that time, the central dilemma for Europe and Japan was the modernization and recovery of their economies, but also how to develop institutions that would allow them to compete with the United States. The governments of these countries decided that the development of institutions that gave government a large measure of control over their economies would support a faster process of recovery and modernization. They were convinced that institutions would affect outcomes because they influence power (i.e., they offer sanctions and/or rewards), and also because they promote socialization. The result of this approach was the dramatic recovery of Western Europe and Japan, and the surge of their economies (particularly those of Japan and France).

In the 1970s the neocorporatist approach (Calmfors and Driffill 1988; Przeworski and Wallerstein 1988; Cameron 1984; and Goldthorpe 1984) emphasized the value of centralized and coordinated wage bargaining as a central instrument to promote wage moderation to control inflation and reduce unemployment. This institutional model helped to address collective-action problems and acted as a matrix of sanctions and incentives. The Scandinavian countries emerged as the main paradigms of the success of this model.

In the 1990s the central problem for government and economic actors, as we have examined earlier, has been how to respond to new competitive pressures and the free flow of goods and capital associated with globalization. The VoC approach argues that the institutional frameworks within which firms operate conditions what they can do. It makes the following two core contentions: First, firms are the central actors of the economy (moving away from the neocorporatist's focus on labor unions) because they are the agents of adjustment; and second, it has a relational view of firms: Their success depends on a core of set competences that they develop, which in turn depend on the quality of the relationship with other actors. Therefore, according to this approach, success is contingent on coordination, and hence coordination is the central challenge.

Hall and Soskice propose two types of coordination: *Market Coordination* characterized by arm's-length relations and formal contracts, intense competition and clear market signals, which encourage investment in general assets that can be used for different purposes; and *Strategic Coordination*, based on the collaboration among economic actors with substantial knowledge of each other, which encourages investment on specific assets. Each one of these models of coordination requires specific institutions. *Market Coordination* demands institutional support for the effective enforcement of contracts and regulation to encourage competitions, transparency, and factor mobility whereas *Strategic Coordination* requires institutional support to provide regulatory regimes that places limit on competition and contract laws that allow for incomplete contracts.

This approach provides a comprehensive summary of the institutional, economic, and organizational differences between countries categorized as liberal market economies (LMEs) and coordinated market economies (CMEs). It argues that both models have institutional advantages for growth. LMEs are organized around market-based linkages. These countries are competitive on the basis of their flexibility. CMEs, on the contrary, base their competitiveness on high levels of coordination, which fosters compromise among economic actors.

As Hall and Soskice (2001) have emphasized, the field of political economy has been separated from the theoretical work developed in business schools and, although institutional reform has been a focus for policy makers since the mid-1990s, the study of political structures and practices is still an uncharted territory in many areas. For instance, institutional economists frequently ignore the fact that companies operate and structure their relationships within an institutional framework of incentives and constraints. In fact, a major shortcoming of this literature has been the failure to explain how institutions affect the behavior of economic agents.

These theoretical deficiencies are particularly evident when firms try to adapt to a rapidly changing economic environment characterized by low inflation, increasing integration of economies, keen competition, and rapid trade liberalization. Indeed, there is a lack of understanding of how institutional settings hinder or facilitate firm-level adjustment to international competition and why they may determine the success—or failure—of their strategies (Hall and Soskice 2001). At the aggregate level, performance of national economies is also determined by institutional arrangements (Milgron and Roberts 1992).

From a company standpoint, the most important institutions that influence firms' micro behavior and performance are (Soskice 1999) as follows:

1. *Industrial relations institutions:* that is, wage determination, collective bargaining, and in-company industrial relations.
2. *Education and training systems:* that is, vocational training, industry training linkages, research programs, universities-companies linkages.
3. *System of company financing:* that is, shareholder systems, banking-industry linkages, public financing.
4. *Corporate governance and rules governing intercompany relationships:* that is, technology transfer, standard setting, competitive policy, corporate accountability and the role of boards, the relationship between corporations and financial markets.

Indeed, different institutional frameworks influence companies' strategies because they allow for cooperative or uncooperative behavior between them (Hall and Soskice 1999). For instance, financial systems permit short- or long-term financing of companies; industrial relations system may allow for cooperative industrial relations within firms and coordinated wage bargaining across companies (or deregulated labor markets that facilitate unilateral control by managers). In addition, the educational and training system may foster training for young people or incremental skill acquisition, in which firms may be closely involved. Lastly, the intercompany system may enable technology and standard setting cooperation among companies (or strong competition).

As a matter of fact, institutions set the "rules of the game." They determine the capacity of coordination among businesses and consequently, their competitive advantage in world markets. Also, in an interdependent global economy, institutional structures provide support for particular types of inter- or intra-firm relations, and, therefore, the reduction of uncertainty levels while rendering commitments more credible (Hall and Soskice 1999). Since institutions are responsible for establishing standards and setting rules, and also for monitoring, rewarding, and/or sanctioning behavior (depending on the case), firms should be able to address coordination failures in order to correct the potential adverse effects of cooperation (Soskice 1999).

Hall and Soskice (2001) propose that economies are organized around two sets of institutional choices: one institutional set is about workers, training, and labor markets; the other one is about finance, corporate governance, and interfirm linkages. According to their argument, the ways in which firms make choices around these two institutional sets generate specific and distinct institutional arrangements. These arrangements, however, come in packages and are tightly linked. Therefore, according to this literature there are two types of ideal institutional models: the LMEs and the CMEs. The LMEs, like the United States and the United Kingdom, are organized around a decentralized model based on general skills and market-based linkages, deregulated labor markets, strong competition policy, education and training systems focused on general skills, and a financial setting with relatively fluid capital markets and public information. On the contrary, the CMEs of Northern and Central Europe are characterized by a large number of nonmarket-based cooperative institutional mechanisms, such as long-term finance ties through which firms secure capital in ways that do not depend solely on their short-term performance (such as networks of cross share holdings in other companies and financial institutions), and regulated labor markets in which wages are set through coordinated collective bargaining. According to them, differences across countries in the quality and configuration of these institutional frameworks contribute toward explaining disparities in firms' behavior and performance. It is, therefore, essential to construct a theory of "comparative *institutional* advantage" (Soskice 1999; see also Porter 1990).

The VoC approach is built around the concept of "institutional complementarities." According to this concept institutions are complementary to one another when the presence of one raises the returns available from the other. In LMEs (or CMEs) institutions supporting effective market (strategic) coordination in one sphere of the political economy are usually complementary to institutions in other spheres. In other words, the VoC literature claims that the institutional structure of the national economy matters because it becomes advantageous for firms to move in a certain direction and not in another. It shows that economic growth has been impacted by the interaction between coordination of labor relations and corporate governance: growth improves where there is congruence between labor relations and corporate governance, and performance is better at the two ends (i.e., the more or less coordinated). Hence it is not adequate to make changes in one sphere without taking into account the impact on the other. For instance, liberalizing the labor market may not lead to improved economic performance because it also hinges on the character of coordination with corporate governance.

For instance, in CMEs, a system of corporate governance that limits hostile takeovers provides firms with capital tied to reputation rather than profitability, thus making it more feasible for a firm to make decisions taking into consideration the long-term effects, and a labor relations framework that restricts layoffs offers long-term tenure to workers and gives workers a voice in wage negotiations and working conditions, making it easier for firms to operate production regimes that demand high levels of specific skills, employee autonomy and commitment, cooperative work teams, continuous process innovation, and high levels of quality control.

One of the key conclusions of the VoC literature is that that there is more than one path for economic success and that nations do not have to converge to a single Anglo-American model. They reject the notion of global convergence and explore the foundations of cross-national diversity.

The focus of this literature, however, has been on the so-called *liberal* and *coordinated* industrialized economies of Western Europe, North America, and Asia (see table I.4). This research proposal builds on these findings and

Table I.4 Corporatism and coordination scores for Western Europe and the United States (mid-1990s)

Countries	Average corporatism score* (Scale 1 to 5)	Coordination Index**
Austria	5.000	1.0
Belgium	2.840	0.74
Denmark	3.545	0.70
Finland	3.295	0.72
France	1.674	0.69
Germany	3.543	0.95
Ireland	2.000	0.29
Italy	1.477	0.87
Netherlands	4.000	0.66
Norway	4.864	0.76
Portugal	1.500	0.72
Spain	1.250	0.57
Sweden	4.674	0.69
Switzerland	3.375	0.51
UK	1.652	0.07
USA	1.150	0.00

Notes:
* Of the corporatism ranking of 13 different inquires by different authors. Siaroff (1999).
** According to Hall and Gingerich (2001, p. 46).
Source: Becker (2006).

tests these hypotheses in a country, Spain, which cannot be easily classified as either a *liberal* or *coordinated* economy. While this literature is ideal to define categories for empirical work it is not clear how countries that do not fit easily into either category should be classified. As we will see, in the case of Spain the presence of an effective and active decentralized state and the relative weakness of labor change the dynamics or coordination. Indeed, the institutional framework that exists in Spain defies easy classifications. Does this warrant a new category?

According to the VoC literature, Spain (like France or Portugal) is characterized by strong strategic coordination in financial markets, but not so in the field of labor relations. In these countries there have been historically high levels of state intervention, and the coordination of labor relations has been led by the state (i.e., the minimum wage or the ability to translate a wage increase in a firm to the entire sector). Hence some VoC scholars argue that as states become more reluctant to coordinate labor relations in these countries, they will become less coordinated. Yet, this book shows, developments in Spain point in the opposite direction.

Indeed, it challenges the conclusion advanced by other scholars (Hancké 2001, 2002; Culpepper et al. 2006), according to which

> the retreat of the state left the trade unions of Spain [and France] in a weak position, and firms have taken advantage of the opportunity to move wage bargaining toward the firm level, reduce job security, and render work relations more competitive. Large firms have rebuilt some forms of strategic coordination, notably with suppliers, but the markets for corporate governance in these political economies have become substantially more competitive than they once were. (Hall and Thelen 2005, p. 36)

Furthermore, the VoC literature stresses that institutional arrangements come in packages that cannot be easily unbound, in which arrangements in one domain are dependent on arrangements in another. It does not specify which institutional arrangements can shift independently of others. Reforms in one area would demand reforms in other areas. Hence, institutional change is problematic and for countries that do not have coordinated institutional arrangements it is very difficult to develop them. Therefore, the most likely route for economic success for such countries would be to move the LME model. Contrary to this prediction, however, the Spanish institutional model is not converging toward an Anglo-American model. In other words, the VoC, with its essentially static analysis, cannot easily account for developments in Spain.

Research Question and Hypotheses

In Spain, liberalization, technological changes, capital markets integration, and postindustrialization have influenced the balance of power among the social actors as well as their strategies and preferences. These developments have unleashed new processes that have resulted in different policy outcomes and patterns of regulation. Despite the trend toward market liberalization, deregulation, and fiscal consolidation, the Spanish economy continues to differ in the mix of economic and social policies chosen. Variances derive, at least in part, from differences in domestic and political arrangements. Following the *varieties of capitalism* framework, a key contention will be that in a globalized economy policy outcomes are largely influenced by the preferences of employers, which in turn are determined by their organizational capacity. However, since governments are the ones that make public policy, *how can we explain differences in policy patterns? How can we explain the behavior and strategies of the economic actors?*

The main hypothesis is that actors' preferences and policy outcomes are constrained by the differences in the quality and configuration of their institutional frameworks, political deals, and the existing economic structure. While firms operate within existing institutional constraints, these institutions are constructed as political solutions to political problems, and they are the result of political deals. Hence, institutions evolve as a result of shifting political and economic circumstances, as firms can force changes in the political constraints.

First, different institutional frameworks influence policy outcomes because they set the "rules of the game" and allow for cooperative or uncooperative behavior among firms and social actors For instance, as we have seen, financial systems permit short- or long-term financing of companies; and industrial relations system may allow for cooperative industrial relations within firms and coordinated wage bargaining across companies (Hall and Soskice 2001).

In addition, governments face different political and constitutional constraints. Indeed, the structural capacity of governments determines their ability to change, initiate, or continue policies (Wood 2001). These constraints influence the ability of economic actors (such as firms) to pursue different policy preferences. The Spanish state, with its distinctive interests and relative power, has been a central factor in the development and consolidation of coordination in the country, and it has played a crucial role in affecting coalition building, while providing the resources to sustain particular and distinctive varieties of coordination within the country.

Moreover, policy patterns have been influenced by the position of Spain in the international division of labor. The predominance of labor-intensive low value-added based firms over high-skilled based ones has influenced the choices of governments and firms and determined their policy preferences. This is so because in Spain, with a predominance of low value-added firms, firms base their competitiveness mainly on low costs, high versatility, and the ability to adjust rapidly to changing market conditions. Hence, there is a greater need for generalized labor market flexibility, and a lesser one for the development of a highly educated and cooperative labor force (Regini 2000). Spanish firms derive their institutional competitive advantage from the capacity of their institutional context to efficiently provide firms with weak collective goods, high versatility, and rapid adjustment to changing markets. This competitive advantage is predicated on "weak institutional regulation and effective but unstable voluntaristic regulation" (Regini 2000).

The transformation of the Spanish economy in the last 20 years has modified the economic and political constraints and has altered the balance of political and economic power. Its integration in the global economy is not only changing the policies required to sustain growth but also has transformed the division of labor, the structure of employment, the skills required, and the location of production. These changes have affected the interest of different groups, and have led to the formulation not only of new interests but also of new coalitions and groups. They have forced economic actors to seek new political deals, and have led them to resolve the challenges presented by their integration into the global economy by developing new institutional arrangements. It is hence essential to account for the shifting interests and new politics of creating groups. Like some authors have claimed, in this context, "the politics of political economy become more central."[56]

Finally, the analysis of the Spanish case confirms the thesis that coordination is a political process and that strategic actors with their own interests design institutions (Thelen 2004). Institutional change is a political matter because institutions are generated by conflict, they are the result of politics of distribution, and hence they are politically and ideologically construed and depend on power relations (Becker 2006, p. 9). Institutions are important for firms and workers because they influence interests and impact coalitions, and in a context of structural changes we have to examine the political settlements that motivate the social actors. In other words, this book contends that institutional change is driven by politics. It agrees with Thelen (2001, p. 73) that the focus on the "political dynamics" helps to underline that coordination is not just a "thing that some countries have and others lack." Indeed, the Spanish experience shows that coordination is possible in countries that "lack" the appropriate institutional setting, and that it can be sustained over a period of time. This book explores whether the dichotomous typology developed by the VoC literature of CMEs and LMEs is in fact sufficient to account for the complexities of the political economic realities and to account for processes of change (Kenyon and Robertson 2004).

The Relevance of the Spanish Case

The rationale for selecting Spain was based on the following factors: first, Spain differs along a range of dependent and independent variables from the LMEs and the CMEs, which allows for the evaluation of competing arguments. Second, coordination has flourished in Spain, yet there are significant differences in the degree of coordination within the country over time. The examination of Spain's experiences provides numerous comparisons across periods of interactions between business, unions, and the government. Finally, the historical analysis of the development of coordination over the last two decades also provides fertile ground for the examination of causal factors over time.

In addition, the analysis of the Spanish case offers insights that are relevant to the field of comparative political economy. There are four main reasons why Spain provides an ideal setting to study the impact of institutions on economic policy and performance. First, much of the political economy literature has examined differences among the political economies of the so-called organized and liberal economies of Northern Europe, Asia, and North America. This project highlights one of the main shortcomings of these analyses, namely, their failure to account for developments in countries that do not fit easily into these defined institutional categories.

The main conclusion of these scholars is that there are two main economic/institutional models for firms and countries to respond to the challenges of globalization: the organized model of the Northern European countries, or the liberal one of the Anglo-American ones. Given the difficulties of transforming institutional settings to build coordinating capacities, for countries lacking the institutional capacities of the organized market economies—such as Spain—the only alternative would be to follow the Anglo-Saxon model. As we will see in this book, this has not been the case in Spain. On the contrary, the Spanish governments, firms, and the social actors have attempted to develop new solutions and change outcomes based on new institutional settings that do not always conform to the liberal model.

The second reason that Spain is an ideal venue for examining the relationship between institutional arrangements and competitiveness is that it offers some of the few instances in which institutional reforms to build coordination capacity emerged in a context markedly different from that of the small European states of Northern and Central Europe where social democratic parties had ruled for years. As we have seen, Spain cannot be classified as liberal market economies (i.e., like Britain, Australia, or the United States), nor as organized market economies (i.e., like Germany, Japan, Sweden, Austria, or the Netherlands). On the contrary, Spain displays what some authors have referred to as a distinctive style of capitalism (Rhodes 1998). Hence, it offers an opportunity to research the impact of a different institutional setting on economic performance and the behavior of firms.

Finally, the analysis of the Spanish experiences shows that arguments about the demise of national autonomy in the global economy are overdrawn. Increasing foreign direct investment, exposure to trade, and liquid capital mobility did not prevent the emergence and consolidation of new institutions that facilitate coordination capacities. Spain joined the EU 20 years ago. In Spain, governments faced strong political incentives to cushion, through institutional reform, the dislocations generated by the integration of the Spanish economy in the global economy. In this country the combined impetuses of globalization and monetary integration promoted in some instances, rather than hindered, cooperation and the development of institutional mechanisms that promote cooperation and the provision of collective goods.

What Is Unique about This Book?
(Contributions to the Field)

Following are the main features of this book:

1. The analysis of the Spanish case. The book integrates the Spanish experiences, which to date have been studied almost solely from the standpoint of the literature on political transitions to democracy, into the literature on comparative political economy.
2. It examines the consequences of globalization, liberalization, and economic integration from a multi-institutional standpoint.
3. It analyses the effects of globalization and liberalization in a new democracy. The Spanish experience with liberalization offers one of the few instances in which integration into the world economy (and Europe in particular) took place in an economic, political, and institutional context markedly different from that of the other developed countries. Therefore, an additional objective of this book is to explore the impact of liberalization and economic integration on democratic consolidation.
4. The book also examines the impact that institutions have on the competitive advantage of nations that do not conform to the CMEs-LMEs framework developed by the *varieties of capitalism* literature. It seeks to study the impact of institutions on the behavior of microeconomic actors to show that there may be several models of capitalism that allow firms and countries to flourish and compete successfully in international markets.
5. The Spanish case also challenges the VoC assertion that growth improves where there is congruence between labor relations and corporate governance, and performance is better at the two ends (i.e., the more or less coordinated). In the last decade, economic growth in Spain has outperformed that of every other EU country with the only exception of Ireland, and this despite the "apparent" lack of congruence between financial markets and labor relations.
6. At the same time, following the VoC framework this book brings the firm back into a central position of our understanding of the political economy of Spain. A final goal is to use the empirical analysis to develop a model of comparative institutional advantage useful to enhance firms' competitiveness, and to explore the obstacles that will crop up when reforms aim to transform institutional settings.
7. The Spanish experience with institutional development and change also illustrates the economic, social, institutional, and cultural challenges of this undertaking and provides useful lessons for other countries.
8. This book also illustrates how liberalization, technological changes, capital markets integration, and postindustrialization have influenced the balance of power among the social actors as well as their strategies and preferences. These developments have unleashed new processes that have resulted in different policy outcomes and patterns of regulation.

Plan for the Rest of the Book

The first two chapters of the book look at the transformation of Spain and the Spanish economy over the last three decades. In the second half of the 1970s Spain experienced a model transition to democracy that led to the establishment of new democratic institutions and paved the way for the successful incorporation of the country to the EU, a long-stated goal that was not feasible as long as the country had an authoritarian regime. Spain joined the EU in 1986 and the processes of democratic consolidation and European integration were closely intertwined. At the same time, European integration was the final catalyst to convert the Spanish economy into a modern European capitalist economy. Over the following two decades the economic structures of the country were profoundly reshaped. Spain was a founding member of the EMU and during the last decade the performance of the Spanish economy has been remarkable. Yet EMU and European integration have not been quite enough to push for the economic reforms necessary to address some of the shortcomings of the Spanish model, notably its very low productivity growth and the loss of competitiveness. Chapters 1 and 2 inform the rest of the book and help place in perspective the subsequent discussion about the strategic choices of the economic actors.

Chapter 3 outlines the theoretical framework and places the discussion about the Spanish economic model in the context of the VoC literature. This chapter examines some of the shortcomings of this approach and describes the development of social coordination in the country. The focus on social bargaining is based on the conviction that it represents an important form of institutionalization of coordination in the realm of industrial relations at the macro level.

A central puzzle of this book is to explain why unions and employers have pushed for further coordination and have supported distinctive process of social bargaining. Chapters 4 and 5 examine the strategic choices of unions and employers. It looks at the endogenous and exogenous factors that led them to reconsider their strategic choices and to support the institutionalization of further coordination in order to address socioeconomic challenges and to respond to competitive pressures.

Finally, while national institutional arrangements and legal frameworks shape economic behavior, I argue that even within these constraints there is a range of possibilities open to economic actors. Hence the book underscores the need to look at complementarities at the micro level and tries to shed further light on the strategic choices pursued by the social actors within the existing institutional setting. Chapter 6 examines strategies of coordination in one Spanish region, the Basque Country, and examines the way "sociopolitical networks" influence the strategic options open to these actors. By looking at subnational differences, we find out that we get coordination where we least expect it. The book concludes with a reflection on the Spanish model, its perspectives, and the challenges facing the Spanish economy.

Chapter 1

European Integration and the Modernization of Spain

Introduction

Today it is not possible to understand the Spanish economy without examining the impact of the process of European integration.[1] The European Union (EU) is the source of norms and regulations that influence the behavior of economic actors, as well as the source of funds that have influenced public investment and the economic development of Spanish regions. It is also a large market with more than 400 million consumers that offers strategic opportunities, and competitive challenges, to Spanish firms. Europe has been the goal and the reference, and it is a crucial factor in understanding the behavior and choices of the social actors, which is the focus of this book. Hence, it is only fit that we open the book with an analysis of the impact of European integration.

After decades of relative isolation under authoritarian regimes, the success of processes of democratic transition in Spain in the second half of the 1970s paved the way for full membership in the European Community (EC). For Spain and their EC[2] partners this momentous and long-awaited development had profound consequences and set in motion complex processes of adjustment.

There was no dispute that Spain belonged to Europe. This was not just a geographical fact. Spain shared its traditions, culture, religion, and intellectual values with the rest of Europe. Moreover, it had historically contributed to the Christian occidental conceptions of mankind and society dominant in Europe. Without Spain the European identity would only be a reflection of an incomplete body. Spain belonged to Europe. Its entry into the EC was a reaffirmation of that fact, and it would enable it to recover their own cultural identity, which was lost since the Treaty of Utrecht, if not before.

At the same time, the Iberian enlargement strengthened Europe's strategic position in the Mediterranean and Latin America, and led to the further development of a European system of cohesion and solidarity. Spain (and Portugal) offered a new geopolitical dimension to the Union, strengthening

it southward, and ensuring closer ties with other regions that have been
peripheral to the EC. This process was fostered with the Spanish accession to
NATO on June 1982, after a long controversy within the country.[3]

In order to understand the preferences of the economic actors it is essential to explain the transformation that Spain has undertaken as a result of the
combined processed of democratization and European integration. Hence,
the purpose of this chapter is to examine the impact of European integration
in Spain as an opportunity to reflect on what has happened to the country
since 1986. It will identify the basic changes in the Spanish economy and
society that occurred as a result of this process.

Entry to the EC has brought many benefits to Spain. In 21 years Spain has
successfully turned around the unfavorable conditions of the accession
treaties. EU membership has improved the country's access to the European
common policies and the EU budget. At the same time Spain's trade with
the Community has expanded dramatically over the past two decades, and
foreign investment has flooded in. One of the main consequences of these
developments has been a reduction in the economic differentials that separated the country from the European average. Since 1986, Spain's average
per capita income has grown from 56 percent of the EU average to about
98 percent. The culmination of this process was the participation of the
country as original founder of European Monetary Union (EMU) in 1999.

From the standpoint of European policy, EC membership mattered to
Spain because the EC's decisions affected the country directly. Indeed, some
of the decisions adopted by the EC had an even greater impact over its economy than some decisions of its national administrations. In this regard, entry
into the EC has allowed Spain to have influence on decisions taken at the
European level, which affected the country, and over which before accession
they had little influence, and in any case, no voting power. Since the accession
Spain has played an important role in the process of European integration
and has become again a key actor in the European arena. At the same time, it
has contributed decisively to the development of an institutional design of
the EU that has been largely beneficial to its interests. Finally, Spain has
participated successfully in the development and implementation of the
Single Market and the EMU (see Royo 2006).

The process of integration into Europe has also influenced cultural developments. As part of its democratic transition and European integration,
Spain has attempted to come to terms with its own identity, while addressing
issues such as culture, nationality, citizenship, ethnicity, and politics. At the
dawn of the new millennium it would not be an exaggeration to say that
Spaniards have become "mainstream Europeans," and that many of the cultural differences that separated the country from its European counterparts
have dwindled as a consequence of the integration process.

EU integration, however, has also brought significant costs in terms of
economic adjustment, loss of sovereignty, and cultural homogenization. In
addition, accession has also brought more integration but also fears (exacerbated by issues such as size, culture, and nationalism).

This chapter proceeds in two steps. I analyze first the political and economic consequences of the EU integration for Spain. The chapter closes with some lessons from the Spanish experience.

Consequences of EU Integration

Political and Sociological Consequences

Nearly 40 years of authoritarianism, which kept Spain in the margins of the process of European integration, increased further the desire to become part of the EC. Indeed, in the second half of the past century, the EC epitomized in the eyes of Spanish citizens the values of liberty, democracy, and progress absent in the country. In the words of a famous Spanish philosopher, Ortega y Gasset, "Spain is the problem and Europe the solution"[4]. In addition, Spanish entrepreneurs knew that their only future lay in Europe. Belonging to the European club was a mission not to be questioned. After years of relative isolationism, Spain finally joined the European integration process with the expectation that it would help consolidate its newly established democratic institutions, modernize its outdated economic structures and finally, normalize relations with their European neighbors.

Over the last 21 years Spain has undergone a profound transformation. The democratic regime installed in the 1970s has lasted far longer and attained a greater degree of stability than earlier democratic episodes. EC membership finally ended the political isolation of both Iberian countries. As one illustrious Spanish intellectual stated:

> For the last two centuries Spain has practically been neutralized in the international field. Having our country had ceased to be an active element in the process of world history, we Spaniards have lost, not just the necessary mental habits, but also the very notion of sharing our destiny in the march of the Universal History (Sánchez Albornoz 1977, p. 281).

Indeed, EC membership paved the way for the complete incorporation of the country into the major international structures of Europe and the West, as well as the normalization of Spain's relations with their European partners. Spain has become, again, an important player in Europe. At the domestic level, Spain undertook deep processes of institutional, social, and cultural reforms. Hence, from a political standpoint EU integration has been an unmitigated success, as Spain has consolidated its democratic regime and institutions. The two processes—European integration and democratization—are thoroughly intertwined.

The EC (and international pressures in general) were unquestionably important in this development.[5] When the EC was founded, it pledged to protect the principles of peace and liberty. Whatever other difficulties or problems may arise, this was the fundamental objective of the Community. Given this commitment, the still young democracy of Spain needed to be given a positive answer regarding its integration. Otherwise, it would risk the weakening of this new democracy, which Europe had committed to defend.

This objective was clearly stated by European leaders, "The accession of Spain to the Community emanates from a political purpose, aiming at the stability, the consolidation and the defence of the democratic system in Europe" (Rippon 1980, p. 107). The European Commission itself recognized the fact that the integration to the EC was essentially a political choice. The opening of the negotiations was an explicit recognition that major changes had taken place in Spain, which needed to be protected and consolidated within the European context. In other words, the political, economic, and social stability of Spain were perceived as stability factors for the Community itself (González 1980, p. 47).

In Spain, integration was viewed by the political and economic elites as the best way to consolidate the fragile structures of Spanish democracy, and, therefore, Europeanization and democratization were considered complementary processes. Formal accession negotiations to enlarge the EC began with Spain in February 1979. Accession was viewed as a means to consolidate political and economic reforms in the country. After almost forty years of authoritarianism and very little democratic experience, democracy was still uncertain. In Spain, the failed *coup d'état* led from Colonel Tejero on February of 1981 was a rude awakening to the reality of the fragility of the new democratic regime and provided warnings about the potential pitfalls of a transition gone adrift. Spain still had to go a long way to strengthen its democratic institutions. On the other hand, the Spanish king's firm stance in favor of democracy, as well as the rejection by the overwhelming majority of the population of Tejero's attempt, offered good perspectives for the new-born democracy. In this context, with its application for membership Spain sought to strengthen its young democratic process. Indeed, it is generally acknowledged that the main underlying reason for the integration of Spain in the EC was mostly political, and political forces were particularly dominant in shaping the direction of events in the enlargement as well as in determining the terms of accession. In many cases not only the general public but also political parties had not fully grasped the full economic consequences of the integration (Vaitsos 1982, p. 243).

Some scholars have theorized on the influences that European integration has had on the democratization process, focusing on its symbolic impact (i.e., "the identification of EU with liberal democracy and political freedom"), the pressures induced by the democratization prerequisite for membership; the effect of membership prospects on domestic policies and policy direction; and finally, the involvement of political and economic elites in European institutions during negotiations as well as their participation in European transnational networks (Pridham 2002, pp. 185–186).

In the Spanish case the EC played a significant role in the success of this process. In addition to the EC's demonstrative and symbolic influence due to the EC association with democracy and freedoms, the EC had important indirect levers, particularly during the negotiations for accession, to influence the direction of events and the decisions of policy makers and economic actors (i.e., economic incentives). During the early phases of the democratization processes, the most important lever was, obviously, the democratic precondition for EC entry. Brussels defined explicitly the institutional conditions that would satisfy this requirement and European leaders made them very clear to the Iberian leaders. According to Pridham these conditions included "the inauguration of free elections; the predominance of parties supportive of liberal democracy; the existence of a constitution; and evidence of a reasonably stable government led, if possible, by a political figure known and approved in European circles" (Pridham 1991, pp. 234–235). European leaders stated that accession negotiations would not proceed and the application from Spain would not be considered as long as the country did not demonstrate significant progress in these areas.

Moreover, the repetitive refusals to consider the Spanish application for membership during the Franco years strengthened the position of opposition groups and economic actors supporting democracy. They used EC membership as an additional inducement to support democratization and convince the Spanish people of the potential benefits of membership. In addition, the democratization process received explicit support from the EC. Following the failed *coup d'etat* of 1981 the European Parliament (and many European leaders) passed a resolution condemning it and expressing support for the young Spanish democracy. The message was loud and clear: the success of the coup would have resulted in the immediate cancellation of the accession negotiations. The decision to proceed with negotiations was, therefore, the ultimate lever in the hands of the EC to push for democratization. These developments obviously had an impact on Spanish economic and political actors during the transition and contributed to the consolidation of the new democratic regimes. Finally, the Spanish leaders used the fragile and unstable situation of their country as leverage to push forward the accession process and to obtain financial and institutional support from the European governments, which they used to strengthen their domestic position as well as to legitimize the system and the new democratic institutions.

EC membership has also contributed to the consolidation of the new democratic regime (Pridham 2002, pp. 195–205). Pridham argues that membership has had the following impact: First, it helped link "enhanced national self-image with possible feelings for democracy." In addition, financial contributions from the EC budget as well as the economic benefits of membership (i.e., foreign direct investment [FDI]), contributed to improve economic conditions and mitigated some of the negative effects of liberalization and modernization of the outdated economic structures of the country. In turn, improved economic conditions and better prospects for social and political stability influenced public opinion and helped to legitimize the new system and to strengthen support for democracy. Membership also forced Spain to align its institutions to the *acquis communautaire*, which reinforced democratic practices and induced democratic governments to push for administrative reforms and decentralization. Finally, membership also promoted elite socialization and the development of transnational networks, which, for instance, proved vital for the strengthening of interest groups and political parties (such as the Spanish Socialist party, which received substantive support from its European counterparts). The development of economic interests and networks at the European level also strengthened the support of economic actors for democracy.

The EC, however, lacked the direct intervention instruments (such as armed intervention) that could have had a systemic effect on the Iberian democratization processes. Hence, it is essential to look at interactions between the international environment and domestic politics. The actors involved in the transition had the powers to influence events and, hence, they were the ones that ultimately determined the final outcomes. Domestic dynamics are thus critical. The process of European integration interacted with a wide variety of domestic social, political, and economic factors that shaped the new democracies. In Spain, a radical and unparalleled process of devolution to the autonomous regions has led to a decentralized state that has culminated with the development of the State of Autonomies.[6] In Spain the transition was consensus-oriented. These developments illustrate the limitations of research attempts that have sought to causally link the Spanish democratic transition to internationally rooted and domestically supported pressures for European integration. In the end, as it has been correctly stated by Fishman (2001, p. 8), "the political motivations guiding their assessment of Europe during the crucial years leading up to EC membership were strongly shaped by the Iberian's held attitudes toward democracy and regime transition, attitudes formed within the context of the distinctive political experience of each case."

From a sociological standpoint EU membership has also resulted in attitudinal changes that have influenced the political culture. From the beginning there was strong support from public opinion and elites for the integration into Europe as a means to consolidate the new democratic regimes. Spaniards viewed democratization and European integration as part of the same process. Hence, successive governments associated European integration with the modernization of the country and this helped shift public opinion's attitudes toward the government and democracy. In addition, other scholars have noted that by allowing for the active involvements in European institutions, European integration contributed to change the "isolationist-fatalist attitude" of the political classes (Magone 2002, p. 225). Public opinion surveys from *Eurobarometer* and Madrid's *Centro de Investigaciones Sociológicas* (CIS) have shown a sustained increase in positive ratings effects for the functioning of democracy. Support for the relationship between Spain and the EU has been widespread in the country since 1986 despite fluctuations. This almost unanimous consensus in favor of integration into Europe may be explained as a consequence of Spain's need to overcome its historical isolation from the rest of Europe since the nineteenth century until the end of the authoritarian regimes in 1970s. This development contributed to the legitimating of the new democratic system (and thus the consolidation of democracy).

However, the greatest consensus elicited toward the EU is largely instrumental because the levels of diffuse affective support for the EU are relatively low (although high in comparative perspective). The polling data collected by the Madrid's *Center of Sociological Investigations* and *Eurobarometer* show that Spaniards feel linked by geographical and affective feelings to Europe and the Europeans. However, they do not identify closely with a so-called common European culture. The reason for this is that despite a shared history and traditions, there is an absence of a premodern common past and a European heritage that would have allowed for the emergence of a unified European identity. Therefore, the image of a "European community" among Spanish people is very weak.

Indeed, they perceive the EU as an economic community, not so much as a community of Europeans. The *Eurobarometer* and CIS polling data show that the perceptions of citizens about the personal and collective benefits derived from EU membership are one of the key factors that help explain their attitudes toward the process of European integration (see table 1.1). Consequently, it is not surprising that polling data show that Spaniards have a utilitarian and instrumentalist concept of the EU—that is, they evaluate the consequences of membership over issues such as living costs, infrastructures, job opportunities, wages, and so on. It appears that Spanish citizens develop an implicit cost/benefit analysis and based on this evaluation adopt a position in favor or against European integration. Hence, approval of Europe seems to coincide with the economic cycles: low during economic recessions, and high during periods of economic growth. Finally, when comparing the attitudes of Spanish citizens vis-à-vis other European citizens the former support the EU more, but also stress further the need to build a social Europe (CIS 1999, pp. 131–132; Magone 2002, pp. 223–233).

Above all, it is important to stress that in terms of political behavior, EU membership has not transformed activism and political participation in Spain. Levels of support for democracy as a legitimate political regime, preferable to any other alternative, have usually remained high (around 80 percent of the responses in surveys), and Spaniards declare themselves satisfied with the functioning of democracy. Yet, political cynicism continues to be a major component of political attitudes and the political behavior of Spanish citizens. Spain still has the lowest levels of participation of Western Europe and membership in political and civic associations remains very low. At the same time, citizens do not have a feeling of political influence and express strong sense of ambivalence toward political parties and the political class, which is

Table 1.1 Support for EU, EMU, CFSP, and enlargement

	EU membership is good	Trust the European Commission	Support EMU	Support CFP	Support CSP	Support new members
Spain	63	62	68	68	76	58

Source: *Eurobarometer*, October–November 2000.

translated into a rather low interest in politics (Pérez-Díaz 2002, pp. 280–284; Magone 2002, p. 232; Fishman 2004).

Economic and Social Consequences

Economic conditions in Spain in the second half of the 1970s and first half of the 1980s were not buoyant. The world crisis caused by the second oil shock in the late 1970s and the lack of adequate response from the collapsing authoritarian regime intensified the structural problems of the economy. By the time of accession Spain was the EC's fifth-largest economy.[7]

The economic crisis of the late 1970s and the first half of the 1980s had devastating consequences in the country and made any additional adjustments caused by the accession to the EC a daunting prospect. The high unemployment levels, which reached 22 percent on 1986, suggested that any additional adjustment cost would have painful consequences (Hine 1989, p. 7). In addition, the country was unprepared for accession—that is, Spanish custom duties remained on the average five times higher than the EC's and EC products faced a major disadvantage in the Spanish market because the country had a compensatory tax system and restrictive administrative practices that penalized harder imported products.[8] Slow license delivery was common, and constructors that sold vehicles in the county did not have import quotas to introduce cars into Spain from abroad. Finally, when Spain called to the door of the EC for accession in 1977, protectionist institutions—which were incompatible with EC rules—were still fully operative. For instance, the Spanish government controlled through the National Institute of Industry (INI) a considerable size of the economy, and subsidized public enterprises such as the auto-making companies (SEAT, ENASA), as well as the metallurgic, chemical, ship construction, and electronic sectors. This situation provided a considerable advantage for Spanish manufacturers, which were highly protected from foreign competition.

In this context, EC integration became a catalyst for the final conversion of Spain into a modern Western-type economy. Indeed, one of the key consequences of the country's entry into Europe has been that membership has facilitated the modernization of the Spanish economy (see Tovias 2002). This is not to say, however, that membership was the only reason for this development. The economic liberalization, trade integration, and modernization of the Spanish economy started in the 1950s and 1960s and the country became increasingly prosperous over the two decades prior to EU accession (Estefania 2007, pp. 53–116).

Yet, the economic impact of the EC started long before accession (see Eichengreen 2007, pp. 204–216). The Preferential Trade Agreement (PTA) signed between the EC and Spain in 1970 resulted in the further opening of European markets to the country, which paved the way for a model of development and industrialization that could also be based on exports. Also, the perspective of EU membership acted as an essential motivational factor that influenced the actions of policy makers and businesses. Henceforth, Spain took unilateral measures in preparation for accession including increasing economic flexibility, industrial restructuring, the adoption of the VAT, and intensifying trade liberalization. Through the European Investment Bank Spain also received European aid starting in 1981 to mitigate some of the expected adjustment costs (e.g., on fisheries).

In addition, the actual accession of the country after 1986 forced the political and economic actors to adopt economic policies and business strategies consistent with membership and the *acquis communautaire* (which included the custom union, the VAT, the Common Agriculture and Fisheries Polices, and the external trade agreements, and later the Single Market, the ERM, and the EMU).

EU membership also facilitated the micro- and macroeconomic reforms that successive governments undertook throughout the 1980s and 1990s. In a context of strong support among Spanish citizens for integration, membership became a facilitating mechanism that allowed the Socialist government in the 1980s to prioritize economic rather than social modernization and hence, to pursue difficult economic and social policies (i.e., to reform their labor and financial markets), with short-term painful effects. Moreover, as we will see in chapter 2, the decision to comply with the EMU Maastricht Treaty criteria led to the implementation of macro- and microeconomic policies that resulted in fiscal consolidation, central bank independence, and wage moderation.

Nevertheless, the process of EC integration also brought significant costs in terms of economic adjustment and loss of sovereignty. Under the terms of the accession agreement signed in 1985 Spain had to undertake significant steps to align its legislation on industrial, agriculture, economic, and financial polices to that of the EC. The accession agreement also established significant transition periods to cushion the negative effects of integration. This meant that it had to phase out tariffs and prices, and approve tax changes (including the establishment of a VAT) that the rest of the Community had already put in place. This process also involved, in a second phase, the removal of technical barriers to trade. These requirements brought significant adjustment costs to both economies.

Since 1986 the Spanish economy has undergone profound economic changes. EU membership has led to policy and institutional reforms in the following economic areas: monetary and exchange rate policies (first independent coordination, followed by accession to the ERM, and finally EMU membership); reform of the tax system (i.e., the introduction of the VAT, and reduction of import duties); and a fiscal consolidation process. These changes have led to deep processes of structural reforms aimed at macroeconomic stability and the strengthening of competitiveness of the productive sector. On the supply side, these reforms sought the development of well-functioning capital markets, the promotion of efficiency in public services, and the enhancement of flexibility in the labor market. As a result markets and prices for a number of goods and services have been deregulated and liberalized; the labor market has been the subject of deregulatory reforms; a privatization program was started in the early 1980s to roll back the presence of the government in the economy and to increase the overall efficiency of the system; and competition policy was adapted to EU regulations. In sum, from an economic standpoint the combined impetuses of European integration and economic modernization have resulted in the outcomes that are listed in figure 1.1.

This is not to argue, however, that these outcomes are all the result of the process of European integration. As I indicated before, the modernization of the Spanish economy started decades earlier with the implementation of the stabilization plan in 1959 (Estefanía 2007, pp. 53–116). Furthermore, while the success of the Spanish economy in the last two decades has been largely attributed to the liberalization of the economy and European integration, the process was also marked by intense interventionism, the targeted protection of certain economic sectors (such as banking and telecommunications), and a privatization model characterized by explicit attempts to keep out international players (Etchemendy 2004).

In terms of *static effects*, EC accession has resulted on trade creation in the manufacturing sector. Indeed, it has had dramatic effects in trade patterns.[9] As a matter of fact, in the early 1980s the Spanish economy was the least open to industrial trade with any of the EC members. Hence, the participation in a custom union such as the EC has resulted in the dismantling of trade barriers for the other members of the union. Trade liberalization also exposed the highly protected and noncompetitive sectors of the economy to foreign competition.[10]

• The end of economic isolation	• Increasing competition
• Institutional reforms	• Industrial restructuring
• Tax harmonization	• Capital flow liberalization
• Openness of the Spanish economy	• Deregulation
• Nominal convergence	• Lower inflation
• Capital infrastructure effort	• Fiscal consolidation
• Financial liberalization	• Cohesion policies
• Central Bank independence	• Lower nominal interest rates
• Privatization	• Internationalization
• FDI	• Higher efficiency
• Labor market reform	• Deregulation
• Reduction in government subsidies	• Economic growth

Figure 1.1 The Spanish economic transformation
Source: Royo (2002).

Some EC products already had preferential access to the Spanish market as a result of the 1970 Preferential Trade Agreements (PTA). Trade creation was reasonably expected given the high level of protection before accession to the EC as well as the similarity of the structure of industry in Spain and the EC.[11] Accession did not have negative consequences on non-EC suppliers because Spain's tariffs on non-EC imports were aligned to the common external tariff, which in general was much lower than Spanish tariffs on non-EC imports prior to accession. Furthermore, as a result of the 1970 PTA, Spain had already benefited from a substantial cut in the external Common Customs Tariff; therefore, Spanish exports to the EC did not have discriminatory effects on other non-EC suppliers. Finally, the opening of the Spanish market has led to an increase of intra-industry trade, and hence less acute labor adjustments problems.

At the same time, however, for Spanish manufacturers, accession to the Community also resulted in more competition. Since Spanish nominal tariffs averaged 10–20 percent before EC entry, and generally speaking manufacturing EC products were cheaper and more competitive, membership resulted in an increase of imports from the EC and, therefore, in a worsening in the current account balance (and the closure of many industrial enterprises in Spain). The intensity of the adjustment, however, was mitigated by the behavior of exchange rates and by the dramatic increase in the levels of investment in the country. Spain has been an attractive production base since it offered access to a large market of 40 million people, and a well-educated and cheap—compared with the EC standard—labor base. In the end, the transitional periods adopted in the treaty to alleviate these adjustment problems and the financial support received from the EC played an important role minimizing the costs for the sectors involved.

As I mentioned earlier, Spain had also benefited from the PTA with the EC on manufacturing products. However, this agreement left the country outside of the Common Agricultural Policy (CAP). While the composition of GDP had changed significantly throughout the 1960s, in the 1970s agriculture was still a critical sector for the Spanish economy with more than 10 million people—17 percent of the population—earning their livelihood from it. Spanish agriculture accounted for 9 percent of GDP and its agricultural output was 16.5 percent of the Community total.

The Spanish government, however, was much more effective in achieving reasonable compromises in the manufacturing sector during the accession negotiations than it was in the agricultural sector. Arguably, this might have happened because in the industrial sector the governments had to satisfy their workers (an important electoral constituency) as well as the unions that were well organized and had influence in the Socialist party. Spanish farmers were not so well organized and hence were not as effective in pressuring for a better agreement. It is also true that some EC members, particularly France, held more intransigent positions on agriculture during the negotiations.

The integration of Spain in the EC offered opportunities for both trade creation and trade diversion in agriculture. Since Spain had been kept out of the CAP before accession, EC membership gave better access conditions to Spanish agricultural exports to the Community. This was particularly true given the good quality of these products and their lower price—compared with those of the EC. At the same time, the increase of Spanish agricultural exports to the Community displaced imports from other countries. The main source of adjustment problems was trade creation because greater import penetration led to a contraction in domestic production. For Spain one of the main challenges of accession was the result of the regional diversity of its agriculture because it has not been easy for farmers affected by the CAP to switch to other products given the differences in the environment, weather, and fertility conditions (Hine 1989, pp. 16–18). From an agricultural standpoint the fears of trade diversion materialized to some extent after accession (in favor of other EU members such as Italy or France), which contributed to increasing migration from rural areas to the cities.

At the time of accession, it was considered that a critical factor to determine the final outcome of integration would depend upon the pattern of investment, which would bring about important *dynamics effects*. Spain had a number of attractions as a production base including good infrastructure, and educated and cheap labor force, and access to markets with a growing potential. In addition, EC entry would add the incentive of further access to the EC countries for non-EC Iberian investors—i.e., Japan or the United States. As expected, one of the key outcomes of integration has been a dramatic increase in foreign direct investment, from less than 2 percent to more than 6 percent of GDP over the last decade. This development has been the result of the following processes: economic integration, larger potential growth, lower exchange rate risk, lower economic uncertainty, and institutional reforms. EU membership has also resulted in more tourism (which has become one of the main sources of income for Spain) (Pack 2006).

Another significant dynamic effect has been the strengthening of Spanish firms' competitive position. As a result of enlargement Iberian producers gained access into the European market, which provided additional incentives for investment and allowed for the development of economies of scale, resulting in increasing competitiveness. By the 1980s Spain was already facing increasing competition for its main exports—clothing, textiles, leather—from countries in the Far East and Latin America, which produced all these goods at cheaper costs by exploiting their low labor wages. As a result of this development, the latter countries were attracting foreign investment in sectors where traditionally Spain had been favored. This situation convinced the Spanish leaders that their country had to shift toward more capital-intensive industries requiring greater skills in the labor force but relying on standard technology—e.g., chemicals, vehicles, steel and metal manufacturers. In this regard, Spain's entry to the EC facilitated this shift. It gained access to the EC market, thus attracting investment that would help build these new industries. Finally, Spain also benefited from the EU financial assistance programs—i.e., the European Regional Development Fund, the Social Fund, the Agriculture Guidance and Guarantee Fund, and the new

Table 1.2 Compliance of the EMU convergence criteria (1996–2006)

		Spain			
		1996	1997	2004	2006
Inflation	%	3.6	1.9	3.3	3.5
General government deficit	% GDP	4.6	2.6	−0.3	−1.8
General government gross, debt	% GDP	70.1	68.8	62.6	39.8
Long-term interest rates	%	8.7	6.4	3.64	3.82

Source: Commission and EMU Reports. ECB.

created Integrated Mediterranean Program for agriculture, and later on from the Cohesion Funds.

EU integration has also allowed the Spanish economy to become integrated internationally and to modernize, thus securing convergence in nominal terms with Europe. One of the major gains of financial liberalization, the significant decline in real interest rates, has permitted Spain to meet the Maastricht convergence criteria. Indeed, on January 1, 1999 Spain became a founding member of the EMU. At the end, Spain, which as late as 1997 was considered an outside candidate for joining the Eurozone, fulfilled the inflation, interest rates, debt, exchange rate, and public deficit requirements established by the Maastricht Treaty. This development confirmed the nominal convergence of the country with the rest of the EU (see table 1.2).

The EU contributed significantly to this development. Article 2 of the Treaty of Rome established that the common market would "promote throughout the Community a harmonious development of economic activities" and, therefore, lower disparities among regions. While regional disparities of the original EC members were not striking (with the exception of Southern Italy), successive enlargements increased regional disparities with regard to per capita income, employment, education, productivity, and infrastructure. Regional differences led to a north-south divide, which motivated the development of EC structural policies. The election of Jacques Delors in 1985 as president of the Commission led to renewed efforts to address these imbalances. They culminated in the establishment of new cohesion policies that were enshrined in the 1986 Single European Act, which introduced new provisions making economic and social cohesion a new EU common policy. In this regard, the regional development policy emerged as an instrument of solidarity between some Europeans and others. Since the late 1980s the structural funds became the second largest budgetary item of the EU. These funds have had a significant impact in relationship to the investment needs of poorer EU countries (see table 1.3) and have made an impressive contribution to growth in aggregate demand in these countries (see table 1.4).

Indeed, the structural and cohesion funds have been the instruments designed by the EU to develop social and cohesion policy within the EU, in order to compensate for the efforts that countries with the lowest per capita

Table 1.3   Gross fixed capital formation versus community support frameworks

	Percent GFCF due to EU support		Percent of GFCF versus CSFs*	
	1989	1993	1989	1993
Spain	2.9	4.1	5.8	8.0

Note: *CSFs include the private sector expenditures entered into the financing plan of the CSF.
Source: Kesselman et al., *European Politics in Transition*. Data: EC Commission, *Fourth Annual Report on the Implementation of the Reform of the Structural Funds, 1992*, Com (93) 530, Brussels, October 29, 1993, 84.

Table 1.4   Estimated annual impact of structural funds (1989–93)

	Average annual growth rate (89–93)	Estimated impact
Spain	1.5	0.2

Source: Kesselman et al., *European Politics in Transition*. Data: EC Commission, *Fourth Annual Report on the Implementation of the Reform of the Structural Funds, 1992*, Com (93) 530, Brussels, October 29, 1993, 84.

income relative to the EU (Ireland, Greece, Portugal, and Spain) would need to make to comply with the nominal convergence criteria. These funds, which amount to just over one-third of the EU budget, have contributed significantly to reduce regional disparities and foster convergence within the EU. As a result major infrastructure shortcomings have been addressed and road and telecommunication networks have improved dramatically both in quantity and quality. In addition, increasing spending on education and training have contributed to the upgrading of the labor force. In sum, these funds have played a prominent role in developing the factors that improve the competitiveness and determine the potential growth of the least developed regions of the country (see Sebastián 2001, pp. 25–26).

During the 1994–99 period, EU aid accounted for 1.5 percent of GDP in Spain. EU funding has allowed rates of public investment to remain relatively stable since the mid-1980s. The percentage of public investment financed by EU funds has been rising since 1985, to reach average values of 15 percent for Spain (see figure 1.2). Moreover, the European Commission has estimated that the impact of EU structural funds on GDP growth and employment has been significant: GDP rose in 1999 by 3.1 percent in Spain. In the absence of these funds public investment would have been greatly affected.

Between 1986 and 2006 Spain received 118 billion euros from the EU (excluding the funds from the CAP). To put it in perspective Spain has received three times more funds than the total Marshall Plan. No wonder some refer to this as the "largest solidarity operation in world history."[12] Only in 2001 Spain was allocated nearly 63 percent of the EU's structural funds budget (US$27.8 billion). Overall in absolute terms Spain is the country that has benefited the most from the structural and cohesion funds. In 2005

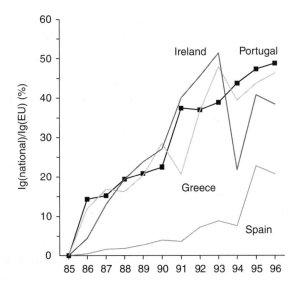

Figure 1.2   Percentage of public sector investment financed with EU funds
Source: Sebastián (2001, p. 28).

Spain received 7.878 billion euros from the structural and cohesion funds (24 percent of the total or 50 percent of the cohesion ones: 1.386 billion).

At the same time, Spain has benefited extensively from the agricultural, regional development, training, and cohesion programs. These funds have represented 24 percent of the annual agrarian income (80,000 million euros in 20 years). They have also contributed to the dramatic improvement of infrastructures (40,000 euros in 20 years): in 1986 Spain had 773 km of highways, in 2006 6,267 km, and 4 km of each 10 have been funded with European funds. In 1986 it did not have any high-speed trains; today it has 3 lines and for every 100 euros invested in trains, 38 have came from Europe. There are currently (2007) nine major ongoing infrastructure projects that will be partially funded with EU funds. Spain has also received 12,000 million euros from the cohesion funds that have helped fund projects such as the high-speed train from Madrid to Barcelona (3,518 million in EU funds). While these funds represent "only" 1 percent of the PIB, they have played a central role because they have generated opportunities that have led to initiatives and reforms that have been key for the modernization of the Spanish economy.

Moreover, EU funding has allowed rates of public investment to remain relatively stable since the mid-1980s. The European Commission has estimated that the impact of EU structural funds on GDP growth and employment has been significant: Overall, these funds, given their impact on the demand side (i.e., public works) and on the supply side (they have increased the productive capacity of the Spanish economy), have contributed to economic growth. It is estimated that on average these funds have added 0.4 percentage points to yearly economic growth during the 1989–2006 period, or the equivalent of 600 euros per habitant and per year.[13] The 2007–13 EU budget agreement guarantees that Spain will be a net recipient until that date, but the bulk of the funds will be channeled to the new member states (representing between 3 and 4 percent of their GDP, which will allow them to create 2.5 million jobs).

The combined impetuses of lowering trade barriers, the introduction of the VAT, the suppression of import tariffs, the adoption of economic policy rules (such as quality standards or the harmonization of indirect taxes), and the increasing mobility of goods and factors of production that comes with greater economic integration have boosted trade and enhanced the openness of the Spanish economy. After 1999, this development has been fostered by the lower cost of transactions and greater exchange rate stability associated with the single currency. For instance, imports of goods and services in real terms as a proportion of GDP rose sharply in Spain (from 9.6 percent in 1984 to 13.6 percent in 1987), while the share of exports shrank slightly (from 16.6 percent in 1984 to 15.8 percent of GDP and from 17.1 percent of real GDP in 1992 to 27 percent in 1997) (see table 1.5). As a result, the degree of openness of the Spanish economy has increased sharply over the last 21 years. Henceforth, changes to the production structure and in the structure of exports, indicators of the degree of competitiveness of the Spanish economy (i.e., in terms of human capital skills, stock of capital, technological capital) show important improvements, although significant differences remain in comparison to the leading developed economies (which confirms the need to press ahead with the structural reforms). These achievements verify that in terms of economic stability Spain is part of Europe's rich club. Its income levels, however, remain behind the EU average.

As chapter 2 examines in greater detail, this data shows that nominal convergence advanced at a faster pace than real convergence.

From a social standpoint, these were two decades of political stability, associated with an overall strengthening of the State's financial and budgetary capacity, and with a significant increase in social expenditures. The overall architecture of the system has been maintained but there has been a substantive growth of the amount of benefits, with a consequent upgrade of social standards, as well as a movement toward the institutionalization of social dialogue, with the signature of social pacts (see chapter 3). For instance, in

Table 1.5   Divergence of GDP per capita (1980–2000)

	1980	1985	1990	2000
EU Totals	100%	100%	100%	100%
Spain	74.2	72.5	77.8	81.0

Source: European Union.

1980 expenditure on social protection was 18.1 percent of GDP in Spain, a significantly lower level than the EU average at that time (24.3 percent) and only higher than that of Greece (9.7 percent). Since EU accession, despite an increase of 3.4 percent of the resources dedicated to social protection in Spain (the Spanish welfare state grew significantly in size during this period and expenditures on social protection over GDP increased by 50 percent), the differential with the EU average has not been reduced but has rather increased from 6.2 points in 1980 to 6.8 points in 1997. In the end, the Spanish welfare state has undergone a deep process of change in qualitative terms, entailing both the introduction of several universal polices and a broader extension of tax-funded noncontributory benefits and services. At the same time, the need to transpose EEC's regulatory framework, the *acquis communautaire* (i.e., in the fields of labor and working conditions, equality of treatment for women and men, free movement of workers and health, and safety at work), and the role played by the structural funds has contributed widely to this development.

Spanish Lessons[14]

The Spanish experience integration to the EU provides useful feedback for other countries.[15]

First, the democratic prerequirement for membership is a powerful incentive for democratization and institutional reform. European integration had a very important effect on the democratization processes. Europe had a symbolic impact (i.e., "the identification of EU with liberal democracy and political freedom"), and the pressures induced by the democratization prerequisite for membership, the effect of membership prospects on domestic policies and policy direction, and the involvement of political and economic elites in European institutions during negotiations as well as their participation in European transnational networks all had a very positive impact on the transitions to democracy (see Pridham 2002, pp. 185–186). Moreover, the EC had important indirect levers, particularly during the negotiations for accession, to influence the direction of events and the decisions of policy makers and economic actors (i.e., economic incentives). As a result Spain undertook deep processes of institutional, social, and cultural reforms. Hence, from a political standpoint EU integration has been an unmitigated success, as Spain has consolidated its democratic regime and institutions. The two processes—European integration and democratization—were thoroughly intertwined.

Second, EU membership paves the way for the complete incorporation of new member states into the major international structures of Europe and the West, as well as the normalization of their relations with their European partners. Spain has become, again, an important player in Europe and the world. More importantly, accession has allowed it to influence European policies from within as it now participates on decisions taken at the European level, which affect it, and over which before accession it had little influence, and in any case, no voting power. This is very important because some of the decisions adopted by the EU have an even greater impact over countries than some decisions of their national administrations.

Furthermore, the Spanish (and Portuguese) accession experience also illustrates that any negotiations within the EU should not be based on an "us against them" approach but on a "them versus them" stance. For instance, the new member states should take advantage of divisions among older member countries. The Iberian experience shows that despite similar interests and objectives, after 21 years there has not been a consistent approach to EU negotiations between Portugal and Spain. They have often cooperated, but they have also worked separately and with other EU members. Portugal and Spain choose alliances depending on the issue at stake. Hence, although the new members (such as Portugal and Spain before) will find themselves on the same side on many issues (e.g., social questions, EU structural funds, and the concept of cohesion), each new member should develop its own ad hoc coalitions with other members based on common interests.

Fourth, one of the most important lessons from the Spanish enlargement is that the terms of accession are not always final. Renegotiations after accession are possible and compensatory mechanisms can be developed. Therefore, whatever the accession terms for 2004–06, the focus of the new member states should be on 2006, when the EU will start its next seven-year budget period. The focal point should be accession economics and not development economics. The EU will pursue stability and homogenization, but the new member countries will want growth. In this regard, the Spanish experience shows that the aim of the new entrants should be to find the best ways to maximize the benefits of membership once they are in. A nakedly selfish strategy that satisfies only particular needs is also bound to fail. The new members also need to look at their potential contribution to the EU and the model of European integration they want to build. Paraphrasing President Kennedy, they should ponder, not only what the EU can do for them but also what they can do for the EU. This should not be a zero-sum game but instead a positive-sum game.

Spain also shows that EU membership has both benefits and costs. EU membership has improved the access to the European common policies and the EU budget. At the same time, Spain's trade with the Community has expanded dramatically over the past 21 years, and foreign investment has flooded in. One of the main consequences of these developments has been a reduction in the economic differentials that separated the country from the European average. Since 1986, Spain's average per capita income has grown to 98 percent. The culmination of this process has been the participation of Spain as original founder of EMU in 1999. EU integration, however, has also brought significant costs in terms of economic adjustment, loss of sovereignty, and cultural homogenization. In addition, accession has also brought more integration but also fears (exacerbated by issues such as size, culture, and nationalism).

Sixth, the Spanish experience also illustrates that economic success drives public opinion. The decision to join the EU was supported by practically all the main political parties. Furthermore, the *Eurobarometer* polls consistently indicate that the overwhelming majority of the Iberian people support the process of European integration. Originally, this support hinged largely on the expectation that EC membership would increase economic growth and standards of living. Subsequently these polls indicate that this support has remained largely instrumental because Spanish citizens have a very utilitarian concept of the EU—that is, they evaluate the consequences of membership in terms of costs and benefits. Up to this point since the membership benefits have been explicit (i.e., EU funds) and much larger than the costs, it is not surprising to find a comparatively high level of consistent support for the EU among Spanish citizens.

An additional lesson is that membership may give countries a better competitive position. Indeed, EU integration has been a catalyst for the final conversion of the Iberian countries into modern Western-type economies. The idea of Europe became a driving force that moved reforms forward and it was a fundamental factor for bringing together political stabilization and economic recovery. One of the key consequences of EU membership has been that it has facilitated the modernization of the Spanish economy, as well as the implementation of the micro- and macroeconomic reforms that successive Spanish governments undertook throughout the 1980s and 1990s (see Tovias 2002). In a context of strong support among Spanish citizens for integration, membership became a facilitating mechanism that allowed the governments to prioritize economic rather than social modernization and hence to pursue difficult economic and social policies, with short-term painful effects. Moreover, as a result of enlargement, Spanish producers gained access into the European and world markets, which provided additional incentives for investment and allowed for the development of economies of scale, resulting in increasing competitiveness. Furthermore, it gained access into the EC market, thus attracting investment that would help build these new industries. Finally, Spain also benefited from the EU financial assistance programs.

As we have seen, the economic record also shows that nominal convergence is faster but that real economic convergence is a slow process.[16] The process of financial liberalization, economic reforms, and the significant decline in real interest rates permitted Spain to meet the Maastricht convergence criteria. Therefore, on January 1, 1999 Spain became a founding member of the EMU and Spain, which as late as 1997 was considered an outside candidate for joining the Eurozone, fulfilled the inflation, interest rates, debt, exchange rate, and public deficit requirements established by the Maastricht Treaty. This development confirmed the nominal convergence with the rest of the EU. Yet, the data presented in this chapter show that nominal convergence advanced at a faster pace than real convergence. Indeed, 21 years have not been long enough. Spain's European integration has revealed both convergence and divergence, nominal and real.

As chapter 2 analyzes, the experience of Spain demonstrates the limits of peer pressure and the ability of the *acquis communautaire* to force change.

The EU Commission has pointed out in successive enlargement overviews the need for the new Eastern European member states to combat corruption and economic crime, strengthen independent judiciaries, and develop the capacity to implement the *acquis*. However, Spain as well as other member states have encountered (and still do) problems in all of these areas.

In addition, the Iberian enlargement also shows that patterns of migration can be reversed. Spain was made to wait for accession in the 1980s, partly over immigration fears that never materialized. As in 1986, the treaties of accession have established a period of seven years for the new member states of Central and Eastern Europe. Fears of uncontrolled migration were not substantiated after 1986 (or even after the seven-year transition period). On the contrary, as a result of improved economic conditions in Spain, one of the key results of EU access was that by 1995 there were 100,000 fewer Spaniards living in other EU member states than before enlargement. Furthermore, the reverse process took place, with thousands of Europeans (particularly from Germany and Britain) migrating to Spain. Such concerns are likely to prove to be unfounded again.

Indeed, the European Commission estimates that from 70,000 to 150,000 workers (of a population of 350 million) could migrate from Eastern Europe to the older member states. This is hardly a large number. The continuing existence of language, cultural, and structural barriers will most likely continue to hinder labor mobility in an enlarged Europe. In addition, the rapid economic growth of Eastern European countries (particularly compared with some of the EU's sclerotic members, such as Germany) is likely to have the same effect that it had on migration patterns in Spain after 1986. Finally, although it is likely that migration will cause difficulties in specific regions (especially on the eastern borders zones of Austria and Germany) and industries, the problem may not be excess migration from the east but too little migration. Given the EU's ageing population and its low fertility rates it will be important to facilitate the migration of young people from Eastern Europe. In the end, instead of displacing local people from the labor market or lowering wages, immigrants from the new members states should contribute to the host country's economy by adding value, creating jobs, and pushing up wages because they will be able to work legally (as several 100,000 workers are currently illegally in the EU).[17]

It is also necessary to note that the success of Spain was very influenced by the support that the country received from EU funds. As we have seen, during 1994–99, EU aid accounted for 1.5 percent of Spain's GDP. EU funding has allowed rates of public investment to remain relatively stable since the mid-1980s. The percentage of public investment financed by EU funds has been rising since 1985, reaching average values of 15 percent for Spain. These funds, which amount to just over one-third of the EU budget, have contributed significantly to reduce regional disparities and foster convergence within the EU. As a result, major infrastructure shortcomings have been addressed and road and telecommunications networks have improved dramatically both in quantity and quality. In addition, increased spending on education and training have contributed to upgrade the labor force. In sum, these funds have played a prominent role in developing the factors that improve the competitiveness and determine the potential growth of the least developed regions (see Sebastián 2001).

Nevertheless, while acknowledging the critical role played by EU funds in the success of Spain, it is also important to stress that successful integration is not only a budgetary issue. On the contrary, the Spanish experience demonstrates that the main benefits of integration derive from the opportunities it generates in terms of trade and foreign direct investment (FDI). Spain shows that a critical factor to determine the final outcome of integration will depend on the pattern of investment, which should bring about important *dynamic effects*. Dynamic effects should be more important than static ones. Indeed, the opening up to international trade improves the potential for growth, lowers production costs, and reduces the risk premium in response to a brighter macroeconomic outlook, which results from economic reforms. These developments help account for the increases in FDI in Spain (where it reached of 2.7 percent of GDP in 1990). FDI, in turn, has had very positive implications for the Spanish economy because it has facilitated the transmission of technology, has paved the way for advances in productivity, and has thereby fostered an increase in the potential GDP growth of both economies.

Indeed, receiving EU funds is by no means a guarantee of success. Ireland received a larger transfer per head than the other three cohesion countries (Greece, Portugal, and Spain). Yet its GDP per head grew only from 52 percent of the French levels to 60 percent in 1990. Then in 2000 it passed France. Why did it take two decades to accomplish this goal? The key was the process of reforms of the 1980s and 1990s. In Spain GDP per head grew from 62 to 74 percent, and in Portugal from 53 to 69 percent of the French levels from 1986 to 2001. Greece, for its part, received millions of Euros in EU funds but experienced more than a decade of decline after accession. While it had a higher GDP per head than Ireland until 1986 and a higher one than Portugal until 1987, by 2004 it was the EU's poorest country. This shows that what really matters is not so much how much money you receive but how you spend it. This evidence illustrates that success is contingent on the good use of regional projects and structural funds (i.e., transport projects). Spain is perceived as a case of success based on its regional policy and structural projects. Portugal, in contrast, has suffered from insufficient matching funds and implementation challenges. This will be particularly critical for the new member states because they will have fewer resources available: The EU has allocated only 10.3 billion euros for the new states the first 3 years in regional aid and farm subsidies, and Poland will receive 67 euros per capita and Hungary 49. In contrast, Greece received 437 per head and Ireland 418.[18]

The experience of member states also shows that while access to markets is important, EU membership is not enough. Success is not automatic. On the contrary, it is largely determined by how countries exploit the advantages of membership, namely, access to EU markets and free movement of labor and capital. For instance between 1985 and 2002 the ratio of the stock of inward

FDI to GDP grew in Spain from 5 to 33 percent; in Portugal from 19 to 36 percent; whereas in Greece it fell from 20 to 9 percent. In addition, fiscal and monetary discipline, planning, as well as reforms are also critical. The countries that have performed the best within the EU are the ones that have followed this policy mix. This is so because stability influences the rate of growth and gives confidence to investors. For instance, Greece, one of the worst performers, ran fiscal deficits close to 10 percent until 1996, and its public debt increased from 48 percent of GDP in 1986 to 111 percent in 1996. On the contrary, in Ireland—one of the best performers—, the debt fell from 112 percent in 1987 to 38 percent by 2000. It is also critical not to use funds to prevent economic reforms and to garner support for failing industries. The best models are Ireland with its investment in education (technical colleges), low corporate taxes, and flexible industrial relations; and Finland with its focus on innovation. Finally, it is also important to minimize expectations: Austria generated too many expectations to oversell EU membership to its citizens and when they failed to materialize, it created a backlash.

The economic difficulties Spain experienced in the early 1990s provide an additional lesson for new members, namely that "automatic pilots" do not work. The credibility of monetary and economic authorities cannot be built up by linking it to semirigid institutional mechanisms (as Spain tried to do in the late 1980s and early 1990s with EMS membership). On the contrary, it has to be earned through the adequate management of existing discretionary powers. Furthermore, the Spanish EMU integration shows that the consolidation of integration processes is contingent on the adequate coordination of macroeconomic policies among members prior to the (possible) adoption of a monetary currency. In Spain, EU integration required a set of measures including increased competition, the privatization of public enterprises, industrial restructuring, and deregulation. These measures translated into efficiency gains, which were reinforced by a more stable macroeconomic framework. At the same time, lower inflation and fiscal consolidation led to lower real (and nominal) interest rates, which, in turn, resulted in a higher sustainable growth. However, there have also been short-term costs associated with monetary integration. Indeed, the losses of the exchange rate and of monetary sovereignty require a process of nominal convergence and fiscal consolidation, as well as higher cyclical correlation, for Euro membership to be successful.

The Spanish experience in the EU also shows that prior to monetary integration, candidates must carry out a process of modernization and nominal convergence without fixing their exchange rate. As chapter 2 examines in detail, an additional lesson is that the reform of financial institutions does not necessarily bring about institutional changes in other areas (e.g., the labor market and fiscal policies). The virtual collapse of the EMS in 1992, caused in part by successive devaluations of the Spanish *peseta*, showed the limits of financial and monetary instruments to impose institutional reforms in other areas and to balance domestic and external economic objectives. Institutional reforms require active policies by the governments that are willing to pay the short-term political price for unpopular policies. The jury is still out regarding the domestic institutional impact of EMU.

Finally, while Spain had feverishly pursued their integration in the Community, the effects of EU integration have not always been favorable. As we have seen, in manufacturing and in agriculture, there has been both trade diversion and trade creation, implying further adjustment problems, since greater import penetration led to a contraction in domestic production. This was particularly true in the case of the manufacturing sector. Factors such as exchange rate movements and the strategies of multinational companies with subsidiaries in the country also played a critical role in the final outcome of integration. This analysis proves that the expected static effects, which were not always favorable to Spain, should not be the main economic expectation behind the ten countries' entry into the EU. Based on the Spanish experience, dynamic effects, on the contrary, provide an important rationale for supporting integration.[19] Over the long term, they will affect the new member states' rate of economic growth, which will be largely influenced by investment patterns, by the efficiency with which these resources are used and, finally, by their distributional effects among regions.

Conclusion

For Spain the EU symbolizes modernization and democracy. In Spain the European integration process has facilitated the reincorporation of the country to the international arena, contributed to the legitimacy of the new democratic regimes, acted as a buffer in controversial issues (such as decentralization in Spain and the implementation of economic reforms), and has facilitated and accelerated the process of convergence and modernization of financial, commercial, and manufacturing structures. The idea of Europe became a driving force that moved reforms forward and it was a fundamental factor for bringing together political stabilization, economic recovery, and democratic consolidation. As we look to future research agendas, it is important to stress that while the majority of the research in this chapter has focused on the policy effects and the influence of EU policies on the Iberian countries, it is also imperative to study the impact of EU membership on domestic institutions (Morlino 2002).

The examination of the Spanish experience in the EU leads to three main conclusions.

First, EU membership brings challenges and opportunities. While Spain has benefited enormously from EU membership, they have also had to implement painful reforms and some sectors of their economies (i.e., some Spanish agriculture and farms) have suffered.

Second, success is not automatic and there are no guarantees. For instance, despite joining the EU at the same time, the economic performance of the Spanish and Portuguese economies has diverged in the last seven years. While the Spanish economy is currently booming, driven by internal demand

and a bubble in the real state sector, Portugal is experiencing one of the worst recessions of the last two decades.

Finally, EU membership helps those who help themselves and are prepared to exploit the benefits of membership. The countries that have performed best (i.e., Ireland or Spain) are the ones that have used the EU funds wisely and have implemented the necessary economic reforms to take advantage of EU membership and attract FDI.

Yet, despite all the significant progress accomplished over one and a half decades, Spain still has considerable ground to cover. At a time in which the European Commission is reporting that the EU is "losing the battle on competitiveness," in a list of 44 indicators, including economic performance, reform, employment and research, among the EMU countries Spain (together with Portugal and Greece) is among the worst-performing countries in the majority of these areas.[20] Lack of political willingness to reform and sluggish growth will further hinder the convergence process. At the same time, differences in economic performance may be exacerbated within the EU by the accession of the Central and Eastern European states. Indeed, with the entry of the new member states, there is an increasing risk of a "two-tier" Europe, where some countries will do better than others. However, those who thought that EU/EMU membership would cure all the ills of the Spanish economy are bound to be surprised because the EU has limited direct powers to enforce outcomes.

Indeed the experience of Spain in the EU shows that the influence of indirect EU recommendations on policy and demonstration effects has been greater than direct action. Hence, it is not surprising that European states, and particularly Spain, are failing to live up to the ambitious targets established in the European Council of Lisbon in March of 2000, which aimed at making the EU more competitive. While EU membership will facilitate (and in many cases ameliorate) adjustment costs and will provide impetus for reforms, the experience of Spain shows that this is no substitute for the domestic implementation of reforms, which should proceed further in areas such as labor, product, and capital markets. The success of enlargement and institutional reforms will hinge to a considerable degree on the ability of European leaders to implement reforms in the face of domestic resistance and increasing skepticism about enlargement. We turn to this challenge in chapter 2.

Chapter 2

The Challenge of Economic Reforms

Introduction

In 2007 Spain commemorated 21 years of European Union (EU) membership.[1] As we have seen in chapter 1, EU integration was a catalyst for the final conversion of the Spanish economy into a modern Western-type economy. Indeed, one of the key consequences of its entry into Europe has been that membership has facilitated the modernization of its economy (Tovias 2002). Membership was not the only reason for this development. The economic liberalization, trade integration, and modernization of the Spanish economy started in the 1950s and 1960s and Spain became increasingly prosperous over the two decades prior to EU accession.

Indeed, the actual accession of Spain after 1986 forced the political and economic actors to adopt economic policies and business strategies consistent with membership and the *acquis communautaire*. EU membership also facilitated the micro- and macroeconomic reforms that successive Spanish governments undertook throughout the 1980s and 1990s.

The overall economic results have been very beneficial. Spain has closed the wealth gap with the European richest countries.[2] In 20 years per capita income has grown 20 points, 1 point per year, to reach close to 90 percent of the EU15 average. With the EU25 Spain has already reached the average. The country has grown on average 1.4 percentage points more than the EU since 1996 (see figure 2.1).

Furthermore, the Spanish economy has led an extraordinary process of convergence and has integrated into the international economy. The integration with Europe has deepened: 90 percent of the FDI, 87 percent of the tourists, 74 percent of the exports, and 66 percent of the imports come from the EU. European integration has also allowed Spanish companies and people to access international markets, expand internationally, and access capital abroad. One of the outcomes of this process has been the growing importance of Spanish multinational firms (such as Telefonica, Banco de Santander, and ACS), which have become leaders in their markets.

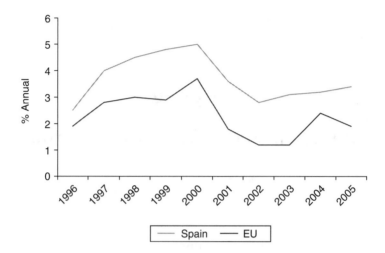

Figure 2.1   GDP growth
Source: EU Commission reports.

As we have seen, Spain has also benefited extensively from European funds: approximately 150,000 million euros from agricultural, regional development, training, and cohesion programs. Yet, the integration process also faced difficulties. The process of industrial restructuring was very painful and destroyed thousands of jobs (unemployment reached 23 percent in the early 1990s). The elimination of the corporate tax and the introduction of the VAT in the 1980s were also traumatic. EU integration also brought more controls and accountability on public financial accounts. Moreover, the 1992 crisis of the European Monetary System (EMS) was devastating for the Spanish economy: it led to three devaluations and the destruction of most of the jobs that had been created in the second half of the 1980s. Finally, the decision to join the EMU was also painful: it imposed fiscal consolidation.

Nonetheless, the overall effects of the EMU have also been positive for the country: it has contributed to macroeconomic stability, it has imposed fiscal discipline and central bank independence, and it has lowered dramatically the cost of capital. One of the key benefits has been the dramatic reduction in short-term and long-term nominal interest rates: from 13.3 percent and 11.7 percent in 1992, to 3.0 percent and 4.7 percent in 1999, and 2.2 percent and 3.4 percent in 2005.[3] The lower costs of capital led to an important surge in investment from families (in housing and consumer goods) and businesses (in employment and capital goods). Moreover, as we examine in this chapter, without the Euro the huge trade deficit would have already forced a devaluation of the peseta and the implementation of more restrictive fiscal policies.

Despite all these achievements the Spanish economy still faces serious competitive challenges. Indeed, the economic success has fostered a sense of complacency, which has allowed for a delay in the adoption of necessary structural reforms. Some economists have noted that "the Spanish economy is living on borrowed time."[4] Despite all the significant progress accomplished during the past two decades, Spain still has considerable ground to cover to catch up with the richer EU countries and to improve the competitiveness of its economy. Given the existing income and productivity differentials with the richer EU countries, Spain has to continue and intensify the reform process. Even the Spanish Minister of Finance, Pedro Solbes, has acknowledged that the current pattern of growth "is not sustainable."[5]

This chapter illustrates that EU and EMU membership have not led to the implementation of the structural reforms necessary to address these challenges. On the contrary, EMU has contributed to the economic boom and a real estate bubble (estimated at 30 percent real) fueled by increasing demand and record-low interest rates, thus facilitating the postponement of necessary economic reforms. However, Spain faces a competitiveness challenge that requires significant structural reforms. This challenge, however, is not a problem of European institutions, but of national policies. I conclude that the process of economic reforms has to be a domestic process led by domestic actors willing to implement them.

A central argument of this book is that both the transformation of the Spanish economy and the competitive challenges that it faces at the dawn of the new millennium have influenced the strategies of the economic actors, thus making it possible to develop new cooperative strategies to confront them. Hence, the importance in understanding the nature of these challenges.

The chapter is divided in three sections. The first one analyzes the economic convergence process and its challenges. The second section discusses the deterioration in the competitiveness of the Spanish economy and its symptoms. The final one explores the main shortcomings and challenges of the Spanish economy.

Convergence with the EU

Chapter 1 highlighted the benefits of EU and Euro membership on the Spanish economy, which have allowed the country to close the gap with the richest European countries. As we saw in the Introduction, from a nominal standpoint the Spanish economy has been performing even better than the European average (with the exception of inflation). Yet, the process of nominal convergence has advanced at a faster pace than real convergence. The country's income levels remain behind the EU average (see table 2.1).

Table 2.1 Divergence of GDP per capita (1990–2007)

	1990	2000	2006	2007
EU totals	100%	100%	100%*	100%*
Spain	77.8	81.0	97.2	98.0

Note: * EU25.
Source: European Union.

Indeed, 21 years have not been enough. While there is significant controversy over the definition of real convergence, most scholars agree that a per capita GDP is a valid reference to measure the living standards of a country. This variable, however, has experienced a cyclical evolution in Spain with significant increases during periods of economic expansion and decreases during economic recessions. Spain's European integration has revealed both convergence and divergence, nominal and real. As is seen later, since 1997, inflation in Spain has exceeded the EU average every year.

When discussing convergence, it is important to note that since the new EU member states that joined in 2004 are significantly poorer, enlargement has reduced the EU's average gross domestic product per capita by between 10 percent and 20 percent. This is the so-called statistical effect. Before enlargement (and the statistical effect) per capita income had increased "only" 16 percentage point in Spain since 1986. In Portugal the figure was 14.2 percent, and in Ireland, in contrast, it increased by 38 percent. Only Greece with an increase of 6.8 percent has had lower real convergence than Spain and Portugal. A possible explanation for this development has been the fact that while Spain grew between 1990 and 1998 an average of 2.1 percent, Portugal grew by 2.5 percent, and Ireland by 7.3 percent over the same period. This growth differential explains the divergences in real convergence.

Other explanations include the higher level of unemployment (on average 15 percent in Spain during the last decade); the low rate of labor participation (i.e., active population over total population, which currently stands at 61 percent; expanding the Spanish labor participation rate to the EU average would increase per capita income to 98.2 percent of the EU average); the inadequate education of the labor force (i.e., only 28 percent of the Spanish potential labor force has at least a high school diploma, in contrast with the EU average of 56 percent); low investment in R&D and information technology (the lowest in the EU, with Spain ranked 61—spending even less proportionally than many developing countries including Vietnam—in the World Economic Forum's *Global Report of Information Technologies 2002–2003*); and inadequate infrastructures (i.e., road mile per 1,000 inhabitants in Spain is 47 percent of the EU average and that of railroads is 73 percent). The inadequate structure of the labor market with high dismissal costs, a relatively centralized collective bargaining system, and a system of unemployment benefits that guarantees income instead of fostering job search, have also hindered the convergence process.[6]

An important factor in the convergence surge after 2000 was the substantive revision of the Spanish GDP data as a result of changes in the National Accounts from 1995 to 2000. These changes represented an increase in GPD per capita of 4 percent in real terms (the equivalent of Slovakia's GDP). This dramatic change was the result of the significant growth of the Spanish population since 1998 as a result of the surge in immigration (in 2003 population grew 2.1 percent). The inclusion of the new population data in the 2001 census resulted in the revision of all the macroeconomic data. As a result, Spain's per capita income has gotten closer to the EU average, growing from 73.7 percent in 1986 (the year of accession) to 79.1 percent in 1992 (the Single European Act, SEA), and 83.4 percent in 1999 (EMU). If we take into account the 25 member states the growth differential has also been positive increasing from 88.2 percent in 1996 to 97.2 percent in 2004 (or 89.7 percent in terms of the EU15). Between 2000 and 2004 the Spanish economy experienced a rapid process of convergence increasing by 4 points and reaching 97.2 percent. This development was the consequence of three factors: demographic (the percentage of the working-age population over total population), the participation rate (the percentage of people employed over the working-age population), and labor productivity (GDP/number of people employed) (see table 2.2).

The key factor in this acceleration of convergence, given the negative behavior of productivity (if productivity had grown at the EU average Spain would have surpassed the EU per capita average by 3 points), has been the important increase in the participation rate, which was the result of the reduction in unemployment, and the increase in the activity rate (proportion of people of working age who have a job or are actively seeking one) that followed the incorporation of female workers into the labor market and immigration growth. Indeed between 2000 and 2004 the immigration population has multiplied by threefold and has grown from 0.9 million to 2.8 million.[7] The Spanish government has estimated that if the Spanish economy grows at an average of 3 percent, per capita income in Spain will reach the European average in 2010.[8]

As is seen later, given the existing income and productivity differentials with the richer countries and regardless of enlargement, Spain has to continue raising their living standards to bring them closer to the current EU average. For this to happen, it is necessary for its economy to continue growing faster than the other rich European countries. This will require further liberalization of the labor structures (both internal and external), as well as increasing competition within the service markets and improving the utilization of their productive resources. Convergence will also demand institutional reforms in R&D policies, in education, improvement of civil infrastructures, as well as further innovation, an increase in business capabilities, more investment in information technology, and better and more efficient training systems. A successful convergence policy will also require a debate about the role of public investment and welfare programs in both countries. In the Spain,

Table 2.2 The determinants of real convergence in Spain 2000–04 (UE25 = 100)

	Per capita rent	Labor productivity	Participation rate	Demographic factor
2000	92.7	99.0	91.8	102.4
2004	97.2	96.8	98.5	102.8
Difference	+4.5	−2.2	+6.7	+0.4

Source: OEP (2005, p. 18).

increases in public expenditure to develop the welfare state have sometimes caused imbalances in the national accounts. Yet Spain still spends significantly less in this area than her European neighbors (i.e., Spain spends 6.3 points less in welfare policies than the EMU average). Effective real convergence would demand not only effective strategies and policies, but also a strong commitment on the part of Spanish citizens to achieve this objective.

The Loss of Competitiveness

During the last decade Spain has accumulated intense disequilibria. While the economy continues with robust growth (3.7 percent growth is expected in 2007, more than double the rate in the Eurozone area as a whole), economic success is on shaky ground because it is being driven by the construction industry and private consumption. Indeed, robust economic growth cannot mask worrying imbalances in the existing economic model in which growth is largely driven by domestic demand: strengths in consumption (domestic demand has increased at rates of 10 percent in 2005) and residential investment, combined with high indebtedness levels (110 percent of the available income), and the negative contribution of the external sector to growth (i.e., in 2005 it only allocated 2 points to growth). This pattern is not sustainable.

One of the consequences of EMU membership for Spain was the convergence of interest rates, which declined by more than 12 percentage points since 1996. As we have seen, this has led to record-low interest rates in the country (negative in real terms) and an explosion of credit and mortgages. Over the last decade and a half financial deregulation, rising incomes (linked to the lower unemployment rates), immigration growth, and strong demand from foreigners (it multiplied by six compared to the first half of the 1990s) who have been purchasing real estate in Spain have all led to an upsurge of real estate demand. Consequently prices have increased by 130 percent since 1997 (on average nominal prices went up by 17 percent annually over the last few years), and the ratio of average house prices to average incomes is comparatively much higher than in other countries. According to some estimates construction makes up almost 17 percent of GDP (between 1985 and 1995 it represented an average of 13.5 percent) and in 2004 residential construction reached 8.3 percent of GDP (between 1985 and 1995 it represented an average of 13.5 percent).[9] The bubble in the housing market has been estimated at 30 percent, and it has led to another bubble in the construction sector, which has generated 20 percent of all the employment created in Spain in the last ten years. The U.S. market has grown moderately in comparison. This situation has led some observers to talk about a "real estate bubble." While the empirical evidence is not conclusive, there is no question that this situation is risky. Since most mortgages have variable rates, the savings rate is very low, and the rate of indebtedness of Spanish families has increased (before 1990 it represented 60 percent of disposable income and since then it has grown to 110 percent); mortgage holders are very vulnerable to interest rate increases from the ECB.

The real estate boom has overshadowed the lack of competitiveness of the Spanish economy. But, the degree of competitiveness is a critical variable to establish the potential for growth and development of economies in the short- and medium terms because it helps determine the share of domestic demand that is satisfied with products from abroad and the share of external demand that is satisfied with internal production. In this regard, the loss of competitiveness of the Spanish economy is a very worrisome development. The current account deficit is a key symptom of Spain's loss of competitiveness.

The Trade Deficit

Spain has a very open economy: exports represented 25.7 percent of GDP in 2004 and imports 29.3 percent. Inflation has contributed to Spain's trade deficit, which has widened sharply and has caused a blowout in the current account shortfall, which reached 7.8 percent of GDP in 2005, the highest in the industrialized world. Indeed, Spain has developed a "dual economy" in which the manufacturing/industrial sector on the one hand and the service/construction one on the other have diverged in terms of performance. While the construction sector is booming (over 700,000 houses were built in Spain in 2004, more than the total of France, Germany, Belgium, Holland, and Luxembourg combined), manufacturing production regressed by 0.4 percent in 2005 (the automobile sector declined by almost 9 percent in 2005), with exports not experiencing almost any growth.

The pressure on the manufacturing sector has intensified in the last two decades. By the 1980s Spanish firms were already facing increasing competition in the area of their main exports—clothing, textiles, leather—from countries in the Far East and Latin America, which produced all these goods at cheaper costs, and thus were attracting foreign investment in sectors where traditionally Spain had been favored. These concerns intensified further due to increasing fears about new competition from the Central and Eastern European countries after the enlargement of the EU (Sebastián 2001, p. 22). The major source of concern was due to the fact that these countries specialize in labor-intensive and low-to-medium technology products (such as machinery, electrical equipment, textile goods and automobiles), sectors that make up a large proportion of Spanish trade (i.e., 7.4 percent, 7.3 percent, 4.5 percent, and 20 percent, respectively, of total Spanish exports to the EU-15), and in which competitiveness via prices is of particular importance. At the same time, in the Central and Eastern European countries labor costs are between 20 percent and 60 percent lower than those of the EU.

Furthermore, the increasing threat of outsourcing (i.e., companies such as Samsung, Philips, Panasonic, or Levi's have closed their plants in Catalonia in the last couple of years), and the worrisome pattern of decreasing FDI coming into Spain (it has fallen in half during the 2000–03 period, from 40,728 million euros in 2000 to 22,705 million in 2003), have intensified the pressure on manufacturing firms. In 2005 FDI started to recover with an increase of 71 percent or 17.3 billion euros.

The lack of competitiveness is reflected in the record trade deficit. Spain's current account deficit for the first 11 months of 2005 reached 7.35 percent of GDP (61 billion euros or $75 billion), increasing by almost 60 percent between January and November 2005, with exports up by 4.45 and imports up by 11.4 percent. To place this figure in perspective, in the United States the deficit was at that time 5.8 percent. This imbalance has been affected by the soaring cost of energy imports, which has risen by 40 percent since 2004. The current account deficit reached 8.3 percent in 2006 and according to the EU Commission it is expected to reach 9.1 percent in 2007. These deficits are not sustainable.

Several reasons that explain the evolution of the trade deficit are as follows:[10]

1. The decoupling between production and domestic demand: increasing internal demand has led to a growth in imports, while exports have been hindered by the appreciation of the Euro, the crisis in the larger European economies, and the growing competition from other countries.
2. The savings rate is insufficient to cover investment projects. The current account deficit shows the disequilibria between savings and private investment. While the public sector is no longer in deficit, the private one shows a large deficit (particularly the one from nonfinancial societies).
3. Spanish exports are concentrated in a few markets. Seventy percent of Spanish exports go to the EU-15. Yet, the average growth of Spanish markets in the last five years has been 4.5 percent, while global markets grew by 7 percent. The slow growth of European economies during the last few years has had a deleterious effect on Spanish exports.
4. The limited degree of technological sophistication of Spanish products has also been a problem because most Spanish exports are labor intensive, which make them very vulnerable to cost-based competition. Indeed, high-technology exports only represent 8 percent of the total (less than half of the EU-15 average).

The impact of trade deficits in the context of a monetary union is still a matter of debate. It could be argued that in the absence of currency risks, imbalances inside the *Eurozone* should be no different from the balance of payments between Madrid and Catalonia, for instance. Yet, as other scholars have noted, a large deficit may raise questions about the creditworthiness of the debtor country. In the case of Spain a downturn in the booming property market may affect the solvency of some debtors.[11] Lenders may then decide to withdraw credit, and in this way a currency crisis may become a credit crisis. Wages and prices are not very flexible, which would make the adjustment more difficult, and in general Spanish products, as we have seen, are not that competitive thus making it complicated to replace domestic demand with a foreign one, and preventing the implementation of an export-led recovery. According to Martin Wolf, several factors lead one to believe that a downturn in the construction sector may have dire consequences:

> First, Spain has suffered a sizeable loss of competitiveness; second the technological capacity of Spain's tradable good industries is weak on many dimensions; third much of Spain's recent investment effort has gone into the production of nontradables particularly buildings; fourth Spain's industries are relatively vulnerable to competition from cheaper wage producers in central and eastern Europe, and Asia; fifth, underlying productivity growth has been low, which will make it harder to restore competitiveness; finally, wage bargaining is quite rigid and, above all, unresponsive to conditions in the Eurozone.[12]

Challenges

One of the main lessons from EMU is that countries should join only when their economies are sufficiently flexible. Indeed in order to prosper in a monetary union, countries need a sufficient degree of wage and price flexibility. Unfortunately the Spanish successive governments have failed to implement the necessary reforms to increase the flexibility of the economy and consequently, as we have seen, Spain has gradually lost competitiveness against the rest of the EMU countries. At the root of this problem lie the following shortcomings.

Inflation

Inflation remains one of the main economic challenges for the Spanish economy. The Spanish inflation rate has exceeded that of the Eurozone by an average of more than 1 percentage point each year, and in 2004 the gap widened to 1.5 points. In 2005, once again, it finished the year with disappointing results. The Consumer Price Index (CPI) jumped to an annual 4.2 percent, almost doubling the government estimates for the year, and 1.8 points higher than that in the Eurozone as a whole (see table 2.3). This is the worst result since 2002, when it reached 4 percent. While this increase has been largely attributed to the oil and food (particularly olive oil) price increases, it further damages the already deteriorated competitiveness of the Spanish economy. The price differential between Spain and the Eurozone stood at the end of 2005 at 1.8 points (2.4 percent in the Eurozone), the highest among all the Eurozone members and the third largest of all the EU members (only

Table 2.3 CPI evolution in January

Year	1997	1998	1999	2000	2001	2002	2003	2004	2005	2006
Variation	2.8	1.9	1.5	2.9	2.9	3.1	3.8	2.3	3.1	4.2

Source: INE.

ahead of Slovakia and Lithonia). This is the highest differential since 2003 and unfortunately there are no signs that it of it abating. Indeed, it reached 4.2 percent in 2006 and it is expected to reach 4 percent by the end of 2007.[13]

Most observers attribute the growing differential in Spain's inflation rate with the Eurozone to the fact that there continue to be barriers to entry in the service sector, particularly in the gas and electricity sectors, as well as collusive practices, commercial restrictions, and inefficient productive and commercial structures.[14]

Persistent high inflation also undermines Spain's economic growth and undercuts the ability of Spanish exporters to compete with other European countries. A continuation of this pattern for a few more years would have a very negative impact on Spanish exports.

The Labor Market

Employment figures have been very positive: unemployment has fallen from 20 percent in the mid-1990s to 7.95 percent in the first half of 2007 (the lowest level since 1978), and Spain has become the second country in the EU (after Germany) that creates the most jobs (an average of 600,000 per year over the last decade).[15] For instance, employment grew in 2005 by over 3 percent (0.4 percent more than in 2004) and the participation rate has grown from 56.3 percent in 2000 to 61.1 percent in 2004, closing the gap with the EU average of 65 percent. In 2005 the Spanish economy created 894,000 jobs (4.9 percent more than in 2004); the total number of employed people reached 19,314,300, and unemployment declined to 8.7 percent, the lowest figure in decades. In 2006 employment grew by 4.1 percent and unemployment decreased to 8.5 percent of the active population (it is expected to go down to 8.3 percent in 2007), and the employment rate is now higher than the OECD average for the first time ever.[16] At the same time the participation rate (for people between 15 and 64 years of age), which was, in 1997, 5 percentage points lower than that of the EU's (62.4 percent vs. 67.7 percent respectively); it has now increased to 70 percent, reaching the EU average. Just in 2005 the active population increased by 3.5 percent, a rate unprecedented in Europe, led by the incorporation of women and immigrants to the labor market.

These impressive results, however, cannot mask the weakness of this development: the temporary rate has grown from 30.8 percent in 2004 to 33.7 percent in 2005, the highest by far in Europe; productivity rates have been negative (it declined 1.3 percent in 2005); and there are wide disparities in the quality of work between men and women. Indeed, according to the OECD women's wages are almost 20 percent lower than men's (in Europe the average is 16 percent), female unemployment is at 11.6 percent (twice as high as male unemployment), the "glass ceiling" is hard to break (more than two-thirds of Spain's top 35 listed companies have no female board directors, and only 6 percent of directorships are held by women), and female workers are more likely to be stuck in low-paid short-term work.[17]

These weaknesses have been compounded by the spectacular growth of temporary employment. From 1984 through 1997 the number of temporary contracts increased from 7.5 percent to 39 percent of the total. Henceforth the level of temporary work among new workers in Spain rose from 61 percent in 1987 to 81.5 percent in 1990, doubling the proportion of the active population on temporary contracts during that period from 15 percent to 30 percent (and accounting for 90 percent of all employment contracts). In addition, almost 50 percent of the staff is temporary in small firms (see Bentolila, Segura, and Toharia 1991, pp. 237–238; Richards and Polavieja 1997, pp. 13–23).[18] The temporary rate stands (in 2006) at 33.7 percent of the labor force, a level twice as high as the EU one (13.6 percent). Poland is the second country of the EU with the highest temporary rate (25.4 percent), followed by Portugal (19.2 percent), Slovenia (16.6 percent), the Netherlands (15.7 percent), Sweden (15.3 percent), Finland (14.4 percent), and Germany (14.2 percent). Malta (3.7 percent) and Ireland (3.6 percent) are the countries with the lowest temporary rates.[19]

With only 10 percent of the active working population, Spain accumulates 31 percent of the temporary workers in the Eurozone, and there are more temporary workers in Spain than in Italy, the United Kingdom, Belgium, and Sweden combined. Until the second half of 2006 (and largely as a result of a new tripartite agreement signed by the social actors, which is discussed in chapter 3), this problem did not abate. On the contrary, the current level of temporality is the highest one ever with the exception of the 1994–95 period.[20] Of the 900,000 new jobs created in Spain between June 2004 and June 2005, two-thirds carried contracts of six months or less. This is a particularly acute problem for young workers between 15 and 25 years of age: 65 percent of them have a temporary job.[21]

In addition, the industrial relations framework does not provide the necessary flexibility (either internal or external) to firms to deploy and organize their labor force.[22] A central challenge for Spanish firms and employers is to find a balance between the reduction of temporary levels and the rigidity of some contracts. In a context of relatively high dismissal costs (generally entitled to 45 days' pay for every year worked) and high employers' share of social security contributions as a percentage of wages (which is among the highest in Europe), employers have been using these contracts as instruments to introduce flexibility in their labor force in order to be able to adapt it to market conditions, technological change, and demand. They are often accused of abusing temporary contracts by hiring people until the end of July, the start of the holiday season in Spain, and then renewing them in September to avoid paying for holidays.

While temporary employment may have contributed to more than halve Spain's official unemployment rate since the 1993 recession to 8.7 percent, and to a 60 percent increase in the number of people in the workforce during the last decade, temporary work, however, limits the incentives of employers to invest in their workers, the commitment of employees to their firms, and hinders the development and implementation of training programs, with negative consequences on productivity. These contracts pay as little as 4 euros an hour and offer little, if any training. Furthermore, the trend toward temporary work is stifling innovation and worker mobility, and job insecurity leads to a lack of enterprise among young people with university degrees.[23] Employers are starting to recognize the perverse consequences of these developments (Jiménez Aguilar 1997, pp. 12–13) and demand a reduction in the costs of dismissals and social security contributions.[24] The generalization of this practice has led to the establishment and institutionalization of a model based on low costs that is no longer competitive.[25]

Rigidities in the labor market further hinder economic adjustment in cases of shocks and make it more difficult to adopt new technologies. Yet, according to several reports Spain remains among the least flexible economies: According to the *Euroíndice Laboral* published by the IESE for Adecco, which looks at three variables (contracts, working time, and dismissal restrictions) Spain is, only ahead of Greece, the country in the EU with most labor rigidities and one of the countries with the highest dismissal costs. According to this report, Spain exceeds the European average in those three variables. In the contract variable Spain has the highest score of the whole group (78 points against the 33 average in the EU), partly because of the maximum duration of a temporary contract (12 months, compared with 36 months in Sweden or Italy, and the absence of limits in Germany or the United Kingdom). Dismissal restrictions are also higher in Spain: it scores 50 points in the report compared with the EU average of 37 points (although Portugal with 60 points and Holland with 70 score higher). Finally, Spain is one of the countries with the highest dismissal costs in Europe with an average compensation of 56.3 weeks of salary as cost of dismissal (only Portugal with 98.7 weeks and Greece and Germany with 68.3 weeks are more expensive). If these differences were reduced, 175,000 people would find employment (thus unemployment would fall to 7.5 percent); and 375,000 temporary workers would become indefinite ones (thus the temporary rate would be reduced to 28 percent).[26] According to the World Bank it is three times more difficult to hire a worker in Spain than the OECD average, and twice as difficult to fire them (see Figure 2.2).[27] These difficulties are partly compounded by the quasi-federal system established in the country during the democratic transition, which decentralized many of these areas to the regional and local governments.

This problem has been compounded by the fact that Spain entered the Euro at undervalued exchange rate and subsequently it lost competitiveness against the Eurozone because of above-average wage increases and inflation. Unit labor costs have continued to rise, not so much because of higher nominal wages (which have grown moderately), but because of a fall in productivity.[28] As a matter of fact, real wages decreased in Spain two years in a row between 2004 and 2005 (see table 2.4 just for wages negotiated in collective agreements), and according to a the November 2007 IESE-Adecco ILCA report between 1997 and 2007 Spanish salaries have only increased 1.4 percent due to the poor performance of productivity growth.[29] This is a

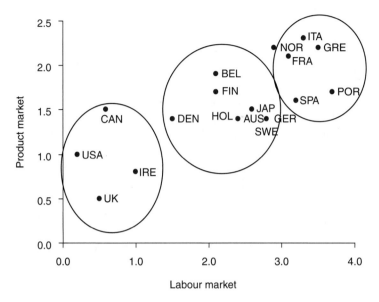

Figure 2.2   Index of product and labor market regulation (1998)

Table 2.4 Wage increases negotiated in collective agreements in Spain (2000–06)

Year	Wage increase, (in agreement)	Wage increase, (revised)	CPI real year, average	Purchasing, capacity
2000	3.1	3.7	4.0	−0.3
2001	3.5	3.7	2.7	1.0
2002	3.1	3.9	4.0	0.1
2003	3.5	3.7	2.6	1.1
2004	3.0	3.6	3.2	0.4
2005	3.2	4.1	3.7	0.4
2006	3.3	3.6	2.7	0.9

Source: MTAS: *Estadísticas de Convenios Colectivos.*

development similar to what has happened in Germany where yearly nominal wages dropped from 3 percent in 2000 to 0.5 percent in 2005, but with a different impact: in Germany it has contributed to improve its competitive position against all the Eurozone countries and the profitability of the corporate sector.[30]

Yet, the following graph shows that since 2000 unitary labor costs have increased over that of the EU-15, causing an important loss of competitiveness (see figure 2.3).

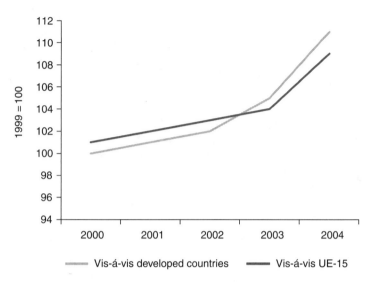

Figure 2.3 Competitiveness: Unit labor costs
Source: OEP (2005), p. 30.

Productivity

The unfavorable evolution of unitary labor costs is closely associated to the insufficient growth of productivity (see figure 2.4).

Productivity in Spain has only grown an average of 0.3 percent in the last 10 years, one whole point below the EU average, placing Spain at the bottom of the EU only ahead of Italy and Greece. The productivity of a Spanish worker is the equivalent of 75 percent of his U.S. counterpart (and it has worsened: it was the equivalent of 85 percent in 1995).[31] The most productive activities (energy, industry, and financial services) only contribute 11 percent of GDP growth.[32] According to the Conference Board, Spanish labor *productivity* suffered the biggest fall in 2005 among all the countries in the OECD, with a drop of 1.3 percent (in the EU it was up by 1.1 percent), and OECD data show that during the 1994–2003 period Spain was placed in the penultimate position among 30 developed countries. In 2007 the productivity of Spanish workers is 3.7 percent lower than it was in 1997. And this is still a persistent problem: while there has been some recent improvements, in 2006 productivity increased only by 0.7 percent, still among the lowest in the EU (only ahead of Italy's by 0.2 percent). It is expected to grow by 0.8 percent in 2007 (while real wages will increase by 0.9 percent).[33]

While we know little about what determines productivity growth in advanced economies, some of the reasons for the lackluster productivity performance of the Spanish economy may include heavy regulation, public spending (i.e., public sector productivity shows a decline), low rate of investment, low skill levels in human capital, poor infrastructure (e.g., congestion in

Productivity differential: 54%

Nominal wages differential: 46%

Figure 2.4 Determinants of loss of competitiveness of Spanish economy
Source: OEP (2005), p. 31.

roads, or problems in retail and wholesale distribution), mediocre performance in innovation and expenditure on R&D, poor intellectual property protection, poor science base (i.e., the reduced number of scientific publications), and weak presence in high-technology industries. Finally, this drop can also be explained by a massive wave of immigration, which in general has lower levels of education, and also increased the total working population (thus reducing average workers' contribution to GDP).[34]

The Economic Structure

An economic structure based on Small and Medium Enterprises (SMEs) with companies that have the capacity to adapt to changing environments has produced benefits such as flexibility, openness to innovation, fluid communication channels, and employment creation. However, the small dimension of these firms generates deficiencies that hinder their competitiveness. For instance, they have difficulties exporting and competing in international markets, they generally fail to use new technologies and managerial tools, they have problems raising capital and accessing public funds on research and development, they have little purchasing power and a tendency to underutilize their productive capacity, and they lack resources to train their workforce. More importantly, their size limits the possibility of economies of scale necessary to compete and improve productivity.

Moreover, the small dimension of Spanish companies makes it also difficult for them to generate the collective goods that these firms need to compete successfully. Most firms employ production strategies that rely on relatively skilled labor force. Yet, they do not have strong incentives to invest in their workers because they are vulnerable to "hold up" by their employees or the "poaching" of skilled workers by other firms. Employees, for their part, do not have strong incentives to share with management the information that they gain at work, because they would be open to exploitation. Finally, the dimension of Spanish firms hinders their options to raise capital to innovate and their ability to invest in new technologies. As is seen later in the book, these shortcomings have led the economic actors to support institutional mechanisms to help coordinate their activities and provide the necessary collective goods to succeed in the global economy.

The 2004 Enlargement

At the European Council meeting in Copenhagen on December 13, 2002, the EU threw open its doors to the East and concluded years of difficult negotiations with 10 candidates: Estonia, Latvia, Lithuania, Poland, the Czech Republic, Slovakia, Hungary, Slovenia, Malta, and Cyprus. This historical summit was the last act in the reunification of Eastern and Western Europe following the end of the Cold War, a process that culminated in 2007 when Romania and Bulgaria joined the EU. As a result, the EU now extends from Portugal to the borders of Russia (growing from 15 to 27 countries), with a population of 451 million, a GDP of US$8,800 billion, and a GDP per capita of US$21,410.[35] Not only was this enlargement process an historical event, but it was also unique. This was the largest single enlargement of the EU since it was established and, unlike the Greek or Iberian enlargements, it covered former communist and totalitarian states where a civil society, independent institutions, a free press, and an entrepreneurial class have been largely absent since the end of World War II. Since the collapse of the Soviet Union in 1991, these countries have built, virtually from scratch, new social, political, and economic institutions. This process, and the sacrifices involved, as in Spain, has been supported by the prospect of joining Europe. Enlargement will have a significant impact on the Iberian countries, raising a number of policy and research issues.

As we have seen in chapter 1, in 21 years Spain has been able to change the terms of accession and negotiate compensatory mechanisms to mitigate the negative consequences of unfavorable accession treaties. Ultimately, integration has had a very positive outcome and has benefited greatly from European funds and policies. However, this is about to change. Since Spain has been one of the major beneficiaries of the EU's redistributive funds, the entry of Central and Eastern European countries (some, such as Poland, with large agricultural sectors) has already resulted in a reduction of the resources currently received by Spain from European funds. A new scenario has opened, characterized by increasing competition for European funds, FDI, trade, and migration patterns. These developments as we will see have forced the Spanish government (as well as economic players) to reevaluate current strategies and policies. Furthermore, the new enlargement has generated new demands from the Eastern European members in a context in which the richer countries are committed to maintain (or even, if possible, reduce) their existing budget ceilings, which currently stand at 1.27 percent of EU GDP. This has resulted in a shift of resources to the East, implying that Spain will receive progressively less funds from the EU budget, and that it will, therefore, make a greater financial contribution to the EU.

Indeed, as we have seen in a previous section, since the new member states are significantly poorer, enlargement will reduce the EU's average gross domestic product per capita by between 10 percent and 20 percent. Hence, Spain's per capita income has gotten closer to the EU average (this is the so-called statistical effect). This means that many Spanish regions will no longer be eligible for aid, as funds are redirected toward new member states. Under existing rules, only the regions with an average per capita income of less that 75 percent of the EU average (which includes practically all the regions of the new member states) qualify to receive structural funds as regions classified as *Objective 1*. In addition, only the countries with an average income of less than 90 percent of the EU average have access to the Cohesion Fund that would include all the new member countries (e.g., Poland, at 40 percent, Lithuania, at 36 percent, and Cyprus, at 78 percent). Regional funds currently represent 34.5 percent of the EU's budget, and CAP funds 45 percent. Hence, as a result of enlargement there are three groups of countries. First, is a group of poorer countries formed by 10 of the 12 new members (except Cyprus and Slovenia), with average per capita incomes of 42 percent of the EU average and 21 percent of its population. A second group comprises five countries (Cyprus, Greece, Portugal, Slovenia) with an average per capita income of close to 90 percent of the EU average and 13 percent of its population. Spain at 98 percent would be part of that group as well. The last group is integrated by the richer countries of the Union, with 66 percent of its population and an income of 115 percent of the EU average.

Hence, many Spanish regions do no longer qualify for structural and cohesion funds. For instance, prior to 2004, 11 of Spain's 17 regions (Extremadura, Andalusia, Galicia, Asturias, Castile-León, Castile-La Mancha, Murcia, Valencia, Ceuta, Melilla and, under special conditions, Cantabria) received EU structural funds because their per capita incomes were below the 75 percent threshold and, hence, were considered *Objective 1* territories. After the 2004 enlargement, however, only four Spanish regions (Andalusia—67.4 percent, Extremadura—58.4 percent, Castile-La Mancha—73.6 percent, and Galicia—71.3 percent) remain below 75 percent of the EU average income, allowing them to qualify for European funds in the same conditions. In addition, the entry of Bulgaria and Romania in 2007 (the two poorest countries of the Union, with per capita incomes of 27 percent and 26 percent of the EU average, respectively) has raised further the average of the current members, enabling only one region to qualify (Extremadura).[36] Hence, the political, electoral, and budgetary implications of these developments are daunting and unprecedented. As we have seen, the European Commission has estimated that the impact of EU structural funds on GDP growth and employment has been significant: GDP rose in 1999 by 3.1 percent in Spain. In the absence of these funds public investment will be greatly affected.

The EU countries and the Commission discussed mechanisms to allow for a progressive phasing out of these funds to prevent their sudden cancelation as a result of the "statistical effect." The affected countries (including Spain) suggested proposals to raise the ceiling above 75 percent to have access to the funds, or to establish different access criteria for current and new members. In the end, as a result of the new agreement, Spain will shortly become a net contributor to the EU budget. According to the latest data, seven communities already exceed the European average (Madrid, Navarra, Basque Country, Catalonia, Baleares, La Rioja, and Aragón). The other 10 (with the exception of Extremadura) are below the average but still over 75 percent. Fortunately for some of these regions the budgetary perspectives for the 2007–13 period, approved by the EU in the Fall of 2005, were based on previous economic data from the 2000–02 period, according to which Extremadura (59.9 percent of GDP), Andalusia (69.3 percent), Galicia (73.4 percent), and Castile-La Mancha (74.7 percent) still qualify under the 75 percent criteria and will be included. On the contrary, Asturias, Murcia, Ceuta, and Melilla, all were left out because of the "statistical effect" and the Canary Islands, Castile-León, and the Comunidad Valenciana had already exceeded the 75 percent threshold.[37]

Moreover, the entry of the new member states has also affected Spanish firms. Spain has to further speed up the reform of its productive and economic structures to increase the productivity of its labor force—still significantly lower than the EU average. As a result of the enlargement process, Spain will face increasing competition for its main nonagricultural exports—such as clothing, textiles, and leather. Problems should be expected in labor-intensive industries given the relatively low wages in Central and Eastern European states, which produce all these goods at a cheaper cost and will attract foreign investment in sectors in which Spain has traditionally been favored. Moreover, since the 12 new members have lower labor costs, the manufacturing plants currently producing in Spain have been tempted to move to Eastern Europe (this started even earlier, e.g., car manufacturer Seat moved a plant from Pamplona, Spain, to Slovakia in 2001). According to *Eurostat* in 2005, in Spain, the average yearly salary was 13,009 euros higher than in the Czech Republic (5,016), Estonia (2,069), Lithuania (2,299), Hungary (3,082) or Bulgaria (1,176).[38] In this context, it will be important for the economic actors and leaders of the country to continue pushing for a shift toward more capital-intensive industries that require a more highly skilled labor force but that rely on standard technology (e.g., chemicals, vehicles, steel, and metal).

However, enlargement, paradoxically, may help in this process because it will also bring significant opportunities to Spain (and other EU members). Indeed, Spanish products will now have access to new markets, which will provide access to cheaper labor and may help improve competitiveness. This could also allow the development of more diversified investment patterns, thereby reducing risks. Spanish firms have invested very heavily in Latin America over the past decade. Current political and economic uncertainties in Latin America, however, suggest that diversification into Eastern and Central Europe might be the appropriate strategy for Spanish firms, which are still underrepresented vis-à-vis companies from the larger EU countries (Spanish investment in these countries currently stands at a mere €200 million).

In terms of the agricultural impact of enlargement, Spanish farmers should also expect to face serious adjustment problems, particularly as EU membership will imply the full applicability of the CAP to the 12 new members and considering that agricultural prices in Central and Eastern Europe (especially Poland) are generally lower than in Spain. Once the barriers for Eastern European agricultural produce come down, market prices in Spain might decline given the new entrants' lower prices and their potential for expanding production. Furthermore, for some agricultural products, EU membership is expected to provide incentives to increase production in the new member states. Finally, the new member states' markets will be opened to substitutes, thus resulting in surplus disposal that would have to be supported by the European budget.

In the next decade CAP funds will be redesigned and most likely reduced. The EU leaders agreed in October 2002 to effectively freeze CAP spending until 2013 (it is supposed to increase merely 1 percent after 2006, well below inflation levels). Furthermore, in order to facilitate enlargement (and the WTO Doha world trade round), the European Commission proposed a plan in January 2003 to reform EU farming, including the elimination of production-linked subsidies, the channeling of subsidies into rural development funds, the reduction of payments to big- and medium-sized farms to achieve a fairer distribution, the cutting of payments to farmers if they fail to follow new criteria on food safety, environment, and animal welfare and, finally, the lowering of prices at which the EU guarantees to buy up grain and dairy products. Spain (among others, particularly France, Ireland, Italy, Greece, and Austria) remain bitterly opposed to these plans. The reduction of the CAP's funds for many Spanish farmers will most likely result in the cofinancing of agricultural policies (something the Spanish governments have been unwilling to consider so far).

Finally, from a political standpoint, EU enlargement will likely result in a shift toward the north, and the so-called Mediterranean block (including Italy and Greece), which shares substantive similarities and interests, will carry less weight. Indeed, enlargement will shift the EU's center of gravity to the east and north, which will have economic and political implications for Spain, reducing the voting power of Spain (and the Mediterranean bloc in general), while changing the EU's cultural character. In a Europe of 27 members the institutional powers and influence of Spain will be further diluted. First, Spanish votes will be less decisive in European institutions such as the European Commission, the Council, and the Parliament. Second, pending the approval of a new Constitution or Treaty, enlargement is also likely to result in the extension of qualified majorities to additional policy areas that so far had to be decided by unanimity. Also, the shift in budgetary priorities and the limited resources will also mean that some of the policy priorities that Spain has defended within the EU, such as support for Latin America and North Africa-Maghreb, are likely to receive less attention and resources (and there is even the possibility that they may no longer be European policies).[39]

Other Indicators

Spain lags well behind in the following critical areas: since most employment is in sectors based on intensive- and low-qualified labor, only 36 percent of Spanish employees work with new technologies; the percentage of the population that participates in professional training programs is merely 5.8 percent, well below the 9 percent EU average; Spain is listed twentieth in the GCI in the area of innovation capacity and technological development of Spanish firms; and while investment in R&D has increased over the last 5 years (1998–2003) at an average of 7.6 percent, the percentage of investment in R&D (at 1.1 percent of the GDP) is still lagging behind the 1.93 percent EU average. This is reflected in the number of patents published (see table 2.5). The largest percentage of all patents published in Spain by sector is in chemicals, materials, and instrumentation (43 percent); followed by telecoms and electronics (16 percent), food and agriculture (12 percent), automotive and transport (11 percent), pharmaceutical and medical (10 percent), and energy and power (4 percent).

Productivity is also affected by capital stock deficiencies. Despite the spectacular improvement in infrastructures Spain still lags behind the EU (see table 2.6), and public investment, which had experiences rates over 9 percent in the 1990s, decelerated markedly between 2000 and 2003. This development is particularly worrisome in the context of the spectacular population growth of the last five years.

Table 2.5   Innovator indicator. Spain compared

Country	Patents published 2004	World rank
Germany	55,478	4
Italy	4,869	10
Australia	4,142	11
Spain	2,260	15
Mexico	308	29
Portugal	134	33

Source: Thomson Scientific. From *Financial Times*, Wednesday, October 26, 2005, p. 3 of Special Report: Investing in Spain, 3.

Table 2.6   The stock of infrastructure of the Spanish economy

Infrastructure Stock	2000	2001	2002	2003	2004
Public investment growth	−8.9	9.2	9.0	1.2	6.7
Infrastructure growth	3.3	3.6	3.4	3.6	3.6
Infrastructure growth per capita	2.5	2.0	1.7	1.4	2.5
Infrastructures per capita (UE-15 = 100)	84.2	84.1	82.3	79.4	80.0

Source: OEP (2005, p. 36).

This deficit in capital stock requires that the government continues investing in infrastructures to close the gap.

The quality of human capital is also deficient. While the quality of labor has improved, according to the International Program for Student Evaluations, Spanish students are below OECD averages in reading and comprehension, math, and sciences. Primary education in Spain has been recently declared "ridicule" by the governor of the Bank of Spain,[40] and according to the OECD the high level of student failure in secondary education (measured by the number of students who have to repeat a grade), which is one out of three students, is one of the most worrisome developments because these students do not recover the time lost and it costs additional money to educate them. Half of Spaniards do not complete secondary education, and 28 percent of the students have repeated a grade at least one time (the average in the OECD is 13 percent).[41] Moreover, according to an OECD report, between 1995 and 2004 the rate of students who obtained a secondary education diploma (high school and medium-level professional training) increased by 7 percent; yet only 64 percent of Spaniards between 25 and 34 years old of age have completed at least high school or professional training (compared with 77 percent in the OECD countries and 79 percent in the EU). Surprisingly expenditures in education decreased in Spain from 5.3 percent of GDP in 1995 to 4.7 percent in 2004 (the average in the OECD countries is 5.8 percent). But according to the OECD the issue is not just how much money is spent but also how it is spent: there is not a direct link between funds and results. Unfortunately, Spain is one of the most inefficient countries in terms of expenditure per student ($47,000 in 2002) and mathematical outcomes. In a standardized test, Spain is only ahead of Italy, Greece, and Portugal; yet nine other countries spend less than Spain.[42]

The data is a little better in higher education: Spain is one of the OECD countries with the highest proportion of people with a higher education degree (university and higher degree in professional training) with 40 percent of the people between 25 and 34 years old of age graduating, or 5 points above the OECD average. Among graduates of the high-level professional training system, which is very prestigious, the graduation rate is 17 percent, 8 points above the OECD average. The access ratio has increased in the last two decades; and while the education is not of high quality it is very egalitarian: Spain is the OECD country that has the highest number of blue-collar workers' children attending university, and their performance is very similar to that of the sons and daughters of wealthier people; and 70 percent of the university students complete their university degrees (32.7 percent of the total population).[43]

Yet, there are still important problems with the Spanish universities. For instance, no Spanish university is ranked in the top 200 in the Shanghai Jiang Tong University Ranking of World Universities (2006); Spain spends only 1.3 percent of GDP in higher education (or 1,700 euros per student); it has one of the most dense student populations in universities

(44,800 students on average) and the R&D and connection with the market are insufficient.[44]

Furthermore, Spain is the only OECD country in which an increase in the number of college graduates is no longer accompanied by significant benefits in the labor market. While the salaries of university graduates are still much higher (they earn on average 41 percent more than those who do not hold a college degree), this difference has been reduced by more than a third since 1997; and it no longer improves the perspective to find a job (particularly for men). The difference in employment rate has decreased from 19 points to 13 between 1997 and 2004 (85 percent of the males and 48 percent of the women who only have mandatory education have jobs versus 87 percent of the men and 79 percent of the women who have university degrees). Consequently, the percentage of university graduates have stagnated in the last few years: before 2000 it was above the OECD average, but in 2005 it was only 33 percent, 3 points below. The reason for this development is largely attributed to the lack of congruence between what university students learn in college versus what the labor market needs (see table 2.7).[45]

In addition, while changes to the production structure and in the structure of exports, indicators of the degree of competitiveness of the Spanish economy (i.e., in terms of human capital skills, stock of capital, technological capital), have shown some improvements, significant differences remain in comparison to the leading developed economies. According to the 2007 *Global Competitiveness Index* (GCI) Spain is placed twenty-nine in the world, and in some of the categories computed in the ranking (i.e., the quality of public institutions) Spain is even performing poorer than in previous years (it was ranked twenty-third in 2005 and twenty-fifth in 2007).

The country's poor record in innovation is also deteriorating even further. Although Spanish scientists account for 4 percent of the world's published research, the country lags behind other European countries in innovation league tables based on patent filing.[46] Data from the European Office of Patents indicates the level of patents in Spain is only 19 percent of the European average and 11 percent of the United States. Furthermore, according to the latest European Commission's *Innovation Scoreboard* Spain is "losing ground" and is placed sixteenth among EU countries. One of the central

Table 2.7 The education of the Spanish labor force

Level of education	2000	2001	2002	2003	2004
Illiterate	0.5	0.5	0.4	0.4	0.4
Primary education	25.2	23.5	22.2	20.4	18.9
Secondary education	46.5	47.4	48.1	49.5	49.9
University education	27.8	28.7	29.3	29.7	30.8

Source: OEP (2005, p. 37).

problems, according to the report, is the "very weak performance of entrepreneurial spirit." The rate of enterprise creation in Spain is merely 10 percent (11.2 percent in Europe), and out of the new companies created 70 percent do not have paid employees. This can be partly explained because of the precariousness of the job market, which leads youngsters to look for security above everything else and many look for jobs as civil servants. This problem is compounded by the fact that there are significant hurdles to opening a new business in Spain: according to the World Bank report *Doing Business 2008*, Spain is ranked thirty-eighth in the world in a ranking that examines how easy it is to open a business in 178 countries (on average it takes 47 days, against 6 days in the United States or Denmark).[47]

Other problems include the very low level of cooperation on innovation among small- and medium enterprises, which is only 38 percent of the European average; backward steps on key indicators that measure the resources devoted to information technologies and telecommunications, which have decreased from 85 percent to 83 percent of the EU average; and, while there has been significant progress on R&D expenditures in the public and private sectors, Spain is still lagging far behind the EU average (the expenditures in the public sector have increased from 64 percent to 70 percent of the EU average but only from 45 percent to 49 percent in the private sector). This is an endemic problem in Europe: Of the total investment in R&D, 75 percent of it comes from the private sector in Japan, 65 percent in China, 64 percent in the United States, and 54 percent in the EU.[48] Spain invested in R&D 1.05 percent of GDP in 2004 and 1.13 percent in 2005, still below the 1.81 percent average of the EU25. At the current pace it would take 20 years to get to the EU average. As is seen in later chapters, while the country has made a significant effort to invest in R&D in the last couple of years, it still lags well behind the leaders. In 2002 Spain spent 0.99 percent of its GDP in R&D, and in three years this proportion increased to 1.13 percent (or 10,000 million euros), still behind the EU (1.77 percent) and the OECD average (2.25 percent).[49] The government wants to reach the equivalent of 2 percent of GDP by 2015.

Finally, Spain also shows a significant deficit in relation to the information society and the use of electronic trade (the percentage of Spanish companies that buy and sell on the Internet is the lowest in Europe). High-technology exports are only 33 percent of the European average and have only increased 2 points (from 31 percent) since 2001.[50] Unfortunately not only is the country lagging behind in the adoption of new technologies, but according to recent data the situation is worsening. Spain is ranked twenty-sixth out of 69 countries in the last e-readiness ranking on the development of information society by *The Economist*, two positions behind the previous report (Italy and Malta have overtaken Spain). This outcome is largely the consequence of the poor quantity and quality of those infrastructures in the country (it received 6.7 points even lower than Italy and Portugal) that determine the possibility for people to connect to the Internet.[51]

Conclusions

European integration process has facilitated and accelerated the process of convergence and modernization of financial, commercial, and manufacturing structures in Spain. As we have seen, overall, the impact of membership has been very beneficial. While there have been painful changes (i.e., the process of industrial restructuring or fiscal reforms) with traumatic effects (unemployment levels reached over 20 percent in the early 1990s), these changes would have been necessary anyway. European integration accelerated the reforms but at the same time it allowed for an orderly implementation that benefited from the experiences and support of other European countries (and funds). The impressive rates of economic growth experienced by the country during the last 20 years are closely connected with EU membership. The sharp decline in interest rates that resulted from EMU integration, the transfer of European funds to Spain, the implementation of more orthodox fiscal policies, and the opening of the Spanish economy are all examples of outcomes associated with European membership. Finally, without the Euro, the huge trade deficit would have already forced a devaluation and the implementation of more restrictive fiscal policies.

The main economic lesson from the Spanish integration into Europe is that EU membership is no substitute for the domestic implementation of reforms. Successful convergence and increasing competitiveness will hinge to a considerable degree on the ability of Spanish leaders to implement reforms in the face of domestic resistance. Lack of progress will bring economic stagnation or worse. The economic actors have understood this predicament and have adopted new cooperative strategies to confront them. The following chapters discuss these strategies.

Chapter 3

Patterns of Labor Market Coordination in Spain

The Theoretical Framework Revisited

Basic factor endowments such as labor, land, or capital, influence economic and business strategies and condition managerial decisions. The role of these factors has been extensively analyzed in the literature (Porter 1990; Kotler et al. 1997; Fairbanks, Lindsay, and Porter 1997). At the same time, institutional factors also hinder or facilitate the strategies of governments and companies, and institutional theories have focused mainly on the analysis of organizational change (Powell and Dimaggio 1991). In this manner, institutional economists have attempted to explain the ways in which institutions and institutional change affect the performance of national economies (North 1990; Alston, Eggertsson, and North 1996).

Building on the new economics of organization, a group of scholars has developed a new theory of "comparative institutional advantage" that offers new explanations for the response of firms and nations to the challenges of globalization and economic integration (Hall 1999; Iversen 1999; Hall and Soskice 2001). They have attempted to explain cross-national patterns of economic policy and performance, and have argued that the institutional frameworks within which firms operate may condition what they can do. They challenge the thesis of convergence toward an Anglo-Saxon model and show that there is more than one path for economic success.

As we have seen in the Introduction, these authors focus on the *liberal* and *coordinated* industrialized economies of Western Europe, North America, and Asia. This book uses this theoretical framework and applies it to the case of Spain, which is a country that cannot be easily classified as either *liberal* or *coordinated* economy and defies easy classifications. While Spain is characterized by strong strategic coordination in financial markets, it is also perceived as lacking strong coordination in labor relations, an area in which there has been historically high levels of state intervention, (i.e., the minimum wage or the ability to translate a wage increase in a firm to the entire sector).[1] This has led some scholars to claim that it is in countries such as Spain "that the most pronounced movement away from strategic coordination toward the market modes characteristic of liberal market economies has taken place, as firms with limited capacities for strategic coordination of their own, have turned to market modes of coordination to replace the efforts of once-activist states" (Hall and Thelen 2005, p. 36).

There is evidence however, that contrary to this prediction Spanish economic institutions are not converging toward an Anglo-American model. In fact, as mentioned in the Introduction, in the realm of industrial relations the trajectory of chance in Spain parallels development in the CMEs more closely than those in the Liberal Market Economies (LMEs): there have been important elements of recentralization especially in wage bargaining (see table 3.1).

This book illustrates that outcome differences at the macro level reflect divergences at the micro level as the social actors pursue new strategies to respond to competitive pressures (Thelen 2001, p. 72). In Spain the decision by economic actors to develop coordination capacities has been influenced by the position of the country in the international division of labor. Indeed, the predominance of labor-intensive low value-added based firms in the country has influenced the choices of the economic actors and it has determined their policy preferences. As noted previously, Spanish firms derive their institutional competitive advantage from the capacity of their institutional framework to provide firms with weak collective goods, high versatility, and rapid adjustment to changing markets (Regini 2000). These firms base their competitiveness mainly on low costs, high versatility, and the ability to adjust rapidly to changing market conditions. Therefore, the priority for these firms has been to increase labor market flexibility. They have not focused so much on the development of a cooperative and highly educated labor force.

Table 3.1 Wage increases negotiated in collective agreements in Spain (1985–2000)

Year	Wage increase (1)	CPI real year average	IPC forecast december	Purchasing capacity
1992	7.3	5.9	5.0	1.4
1993	5.5	4.6	4.5	0.9
1994	3.6	4.7	3.5	−1.1
1995	3.9	4.7	3.5	−0.8
1996	3.8	3.6	3.5	0.2
1997	2.9	2.0	2.2	0.9
1998	2.6	1.8	2.1	0.8
1999	2.7	2.3	1.8	0.4
2000	3.6	3.4	2.0	0.2

Sources: CES: *España, Memoria Sobre la Situacion Socioeconómica y Laboral 2000*. Table II-34, p. 376. Data from MTAS: *Estadísticas de Convenios Colectivos*, and INE.

Furthermore, it shows that coordination is a political process. In a context of structural changes we have to examine the political settlements that motivate the social actors. I agree with Thelen (2001, p. 73) that the focus on the "political dynamics" helps to underline that coordination is not just a "thing that some countries have and others lack." This chapter shows that coordination has been possible in a county that "lacks" the presupposed appropriate institutional setting.

In Spain the social actors, have rejected the lower-cost alternative of pure deregulation and decentralization and instead, lacking the strong nonmarket coordination mechanisms that characterize CMEs, have developed innovative strategies to secure cooperation. This decision underlines a shift in power relations caused by structural changes that has resulted in a new dynamic equilibrium between union and employers.

Furthermore, this book is also rooted in the neocorporatist literature, which seemed to show in the 1970s that centralized social bargaining (or concertation) could mitigate the trade-offs between inflation and unemployment by allowing economic actors and governments to coordinate their actions and resolve certain collective-action problems (Schmitter 1981; Cameron 1984; Bruno and Sachs 1985). This early optimism was subsequently dispelled. Much of the literature of the 1980s argued that centralized bargaining could succeed only in countries that met certain institutional criteria: highly encompassing and cohesive business and labor organizations, coordinated collective bargaining, and Social Democratic parties in government. Changes in the world economy, however, led other scholars (Scharpf 1987; Iversen 1999) to argue that the decline of Fordism, the liberalization and integration of financial markets, and changes in sectoral and occupational structures had undermined the bases for centralized bargaining. This tendency, according to these authors, would be reinforced by events such as the European Monetary Union (EMU) that would further decouple the level at which macroeconomic policy was set (Iversen 1999). In other words, these developments would confirm the undoing of Schmitter's "Century of Corporatism" (1974) (Pérez 1998; Royo 2000). This conclusion, however, is challenged by the resurgence of national-level bargaining on income policy and other economic issues in a number of European states.

In the next sections I focus in particular on the role of social pacts in Spain. Since its typologies have not been adept at accommodating this phenomenon, the VoC literature has failed to contribute to the debate about the role of these pacts in the regulation of advanced economies. This is a glaring shortcoming. As some scholars have wondered, "If the crucial feature of coordinated market economies is the ability of employers to coordinate among themselves to produce collective goods, with the support of the social institutions present in those economies, is the concerted regulation of the economy envisaged by social pacts[2] simply the institutionalization of that capacity?" (Regini 2003, pp. 253–254). I contend that social pacts matter because they influence outcomes and public policies, which are the consequence of a concerted regulation of the economy. They are indeed the institutionalization of that coordination capacity.

This chapter proceeds in three steps. First it examines the development of social bargaining in Spain, with particular focus on the resurgence of social bargaining in the 1990s to illustrate the emergence of coordination mechanisms in the industrial and social policy realm. The second section analyzes the Spanish case in light of the literature and outlines the research puzzle. It shows that Spain does not fit into the categories proposed by the VoC literature. Yet coordination has flourished. The last section presents the Spanish case in comparative perspective.

Social Bargaining in Spain

Social bargaining in Spain emerged in the late 1970s, at the time of the transition to democracy.[3] The democratic transition took place in midst of one of the worst economic recessions experienced in Spain since the 1950s marked by the second oil crisis, the lack of competitiveness of the Spanish economy, a wages explosion, and the international economic crisis. This economic crisis resulted in a sharp increase in unemployment (14.6 percent by 1981), and inflation (15.2 percent by 1981). These developments provided the context for the emergence of social agreements to implement incomes policy between the social actors—business, unions, and the government. This process was known as "social concertation" and it began with the *Pactos de la Moncloa* of 1977, which were signed by all major political parties as part of the transition to democracy process. Originally, the purpose of these agreements was to define the new industrial relations setting, to restrain wage demands to control inflation and foster the recovery of business profits, and to contain labor militancy—which might pose a threat to the stability of the new regime by provoking the army and the extreme right (Royo 2000, p. 5). The social actors signed five additional major agreements in the late 1970s and mid-1980s (see Miguélez and Prieto 1999; Roca 1993; Solé 1985; Giner and Sevilla 1984). The government only signed two of them (the 1982 ANE and the 1984 AES). While concertation took place under conservative governments (1978–82 and again in 1997), the socialists were only able to reach two concertation agreements to cover three years (1983, 1985, and 1986). Tripartite bargaining collapsed after 1986 and reemerged in the mid-1990s. Table 3.2 includes the social pacts and the signatories.

Table 3.2 Social pacts in Spain (1977–86)

Social pacts	Years	Signatories
Pactos de La Moncloa	1977	Government and political parties
Acuerdo Básico Interconfederal (ABI)	1979	CEOE-UGT
Acuerdo Marco Interconfederal (AMI)	1980–81	CEOE-UGT-USO
Acuerdo Nacional de Empleo (ANE)	1982	CEOE-UGT-CCOO-Government
Acuerdo Interconfederal (AI)	1983	CEOE-UGT-CCOO
Acuerdo Económico y Social (AES)	1985–86	CEOE-UGT-Government
		CEOE-UGT

On balance, the final assessment of these agreements is very positive. By fostering consensus and facilitating agreements over the content of the new Constitution, the social concertation process provided the foundation on which the transition process was consolidated. In addition, concertation fostered the development of new laws regulating the industrial relations framework, helped mitigate industrial conflict, and contributed greatly to the institutional consolidation of the unions and employers' associations as well as their recognition as the legal representatives of workers and businesses.

From an economic standpoint, the main contribution of the social bargaining process was that for the first time it introduced macroeconomic considerations into collective bargaining. This development made enabled the wages to behave according to inflationary objectives. Hence inflation was reduced from 26.4 percent in 1977 to 8.8 percent in 1986. In addition, concertation fostered social peace and reduced industrial conflict, which resulted in a dramatic decline in the number of strikes during the concertation years (in 1977 there were 16,641 days lost by strikes, and 2,803 days were lost in 1985). The combination of social peace, wage moderation, and lower inflation increased the profitability of capital and contributed to higher business profits which, in turn, fostered confidence, investment, and jobs in the second half of the 1980s (i.e., starting in 1985 investment picked up and increased from 18.9 percent in 1985 to 24.4 percent in 1989, and employment grew by an average of 2.9 percent yearly in the second half of the 1980s).

In spite of its effectiveness, the concertation process broke down after 1986.[4] It would take almost a decade for social bargaining to resume. The electoral defeat of the Spanish Socialists in the 1996 general election and the victory of the conservative *Partido Popular* brought about an unanticipated development: the resurgence of national-level bargaining between the government, business, and labor unions on diverse regulatory items. This development further challenges the conventional wisdom about the undoing of Corporatist institutions by the pressures of international market competition and integration. This resurgence was particularly surprising given the perception of Spain as lacking encompassing labor market institutions. Although there has not been until recently a return to explicit incomes policy negotiated centrally at the national level,[5] there has been a return to national-level social bargaining (see table 3.3).

The process has continued under the Socialist government. Several agreements emerged from the tripartite agenda approved in 2004: The Regulations for the Foreigners Law; the Decree for the extraordinary regulation of immigrants; the rule for the extension of Collective Agreements, which gives capacity to collective bargaining to intervene in the area of early retirements, increases in the minimum wage (SMI) and minimum pensions; the establishment of a reference index (IPREM) for income and public services; the development of a Complimentary Social Provision; an agreement to guarantee the support to people with dependencies; and an agreement to renovate and develop Training for Employment.[6]

Indeed, since 1994 cooperation among the bargaining actors has been very significant. In 1994 the business confederation, *Confederación Española*

Table 3.3 Main social pacts, content, and leading signatories (1986–2007)

Agreement	Years	Signatories	Main content
Interconfederal Agreement to regulate labor ordinances	1994	CEOE, CCOO UGT	Labor regulations
Agreement to set up institutions to supervise the implementation of the 1994 pact	1996	CEOE, CCOO UGT	Implementation mechanisms
Agreement to increase risk prevention in the workplace	1996	CEOE, CCOO UGT	Safety rules
Agreement to boost social provisions for rural employment.	1996	CEOE, CCOO UGT	Employment in rural areas
Tripartite Agreement for the Extra- Judicial Resolution of Labor Conflicts (ASEC)	1996	CEOE, CCOO UGT	Resolution of labor disputes
Agreement on pension reform	1996	CCOO, UGT, and the government	Pension system
Tripartite Agreement on Professional Training and Continuing Education	1996	CEOE, CCOO UGT	Professional training
Interconfederal Agreement for Employment Stability (AIEE)	1997	CEOE, CCOO UGT	Reduction of temporary contracts
Interconfederal Agreement on Collective Bargaining (AINC)	1997	CEOE, CCOO UGT	Articulation of collective bargaining
Interconfederal Agreement on Coverage Gaps	1997	CEOE, CCOO UGT	Labor ordinances
Agreement over part-time work	1997	CCOO, UGT, and the government	Promotion of part-time contracts
Agreement to incentive stable labor contracts and penalize temporary ones	1998	CCOO and the government	Reduction of temporary contracts
Agreement to increase certain minimum Social Security pensions	1999	CCOO, UGT, and the government	Increase pensions
Pact to constitute the Foundation forthe Prevention of Labor Risks	1999	CCOO, UGT, and the government	Health and safety in the workplace
III Agreement on Continuous Training	2000	The government, CCOO, UGT, CIG, and CEOE	Training
II Agreement for the Extra-Judicial Resolution of Labor Conflicts (ASEC II)	2001	CEOE, CCOO, UGT	Resolution of labor disputes
New agreement on pensions and social protection	2001	CCOO, UGT, and the government	Pension system

Continued

Table 3.3 Continued

Agreement	Years	Signatories	Main content
Interconfederal Agreement for Collective Bargaining 2002	2001	CEOE, CCOO, UGT	Wage bargaining framework
Interconfederal Agreement for Collective Bargaining 2003	2003	CEOE, CCOO, UGT	Wage bargaining framework
Interconfederal Agreement for Collective Bargaining 2004	2004	CEOE, CCOO, UGT	Wage bargaining framework
Competitiveness, stable employment, and social cohesion (Joint Declaration)*	2004	Government, CEOE, CEPYME, CCOO, UGT	Framework for social dialogue
Interconfederal Agreement for Collective Bargaining 2005	2005	CEOE, CCOO, UGT	Wage bargaining framework
Agreement for Improvement in the Quality and Growth of Employment (AMCE)	2006	Government, COEO, CEPYME, UGT, CCOO	Reduction of temporary contracts and improvement of the quality of employment
Agreement to reform the social security system	2006	Government, CEOE, CEPYME, CCOO, UGT	Reform of the pension system
Interconfederal Agreement for Collective Bargaining 2007	2007	CEOE, CCOO, UGT	Wage bargaining framework
Agreement to Reform the Social Security Reserve Fund. This was the first concerted reform of the SS system since the transition. As a result the government increased to 15 years (from 12.5) the minimum required to receive a pension	2007	Government, CEOE, CEPYME, UGT, CCOO	Give more flexibility to SS reserve fund
Interconfederal Agreement for collective bargaining 2008	2008	CEOE, CCOO, UGT	Wage bargaining framework

Source: CEOE: *Confederación Española de Organizaciones Empresariales*, CCOO: *Comisiones Obreras*, UGT: *Unión General de Trabajadores*; CEPYME: *Confederación Española de Pequeñas y Medianas Empresas*.

de Organizaciones Empresariales (CEOE) (and the *Confederación Española de Pequeñas y Medianas Empresas* [CEPYME]), and the two major trade union confederations (CCOO and UGT) signed the "Interconfederal Agreement to Regulate Labor Ordinances and Labor Regulations." This pact sought to fill the gaps left by the repeal of the labor ordinances in 22 subsectors that still lacked a replacement agreement and to regulate the devolution of regulatory competencies to the collective bargaining process. The main objective of this agreement was to regulate the passing out of the old Labor Ordinances established during the Franco regime that governed the industrial relations system (including professional and wage structures and the disciplinary regime) for most economic activities.

The return to social bargaining at the national level on other key issues continued in 1996 when the same actors signed the "Tripartite Agreement for the Extra-Judicial Resolution of Labor Conflicts," which developed a new system to resolve labor conflicts that may emerge between workers and employers. The pact established mechanisms for mandatory mediation and voluntary arbitration of collective bargaining conflicts (including conflicts over labor mobility, minimum services prior to strikes, layoffs, and modifications of work conditions). The main goal of this agreement was to avoid the formalization of these kinds of conflicts in labor courts. Furthermore, in 1996 the unions and the conservative government negotiated an agreement on pension reform largely based on a previous agreement signed by the major political parties (the Toledo pact). This agreement aimed at improving the financial situation of the pension system and at making it more equitable. The CEOE refused to sign it because it did not include lower payroll taxes. This agreement was renewed in 2001 (UGT refused to sign it this time).

In 1997 the unions and business organizations signed a "Tripartite Agreement on Professional Training" to foster cooperation between unions and employers to train workers. One of the most significant agreements, however, was negotiated between the two largest confederations (UGT and CCOO) and the employers' association (CEOE) in 1997 to limit employers' liability to high redundancy costs and to restructure the collective bargaining system. The consequence of this negotiation was the signing of the 1997 "Interconfederal Accord for Employment Stability." The main goals of this agreement were to promote permanent employment by tightening the use of fixed-term contracts and shifting financial incentives, to improve the job prospects of certain categories of workers (i.e., it introduced a new indefinite contract with lower redundancy costs), and finally, to reform the legislation that regulates the termination of all contracts for objective reasons to facilitate its implementation by labor courts (Fraile 1999, pp. 269–311). As part of that negotiation, the social partners also reached another agreement, the 1997 "Interconfederal Agreement on Collective Bargaining and Coverage Gaps."

These agreements constituted an important milestone, not only because they were negotiated pacts (as opposed to the previous two reforms of 1984 and 1994 that were introduced by the socialist government) but also because dismissal costs were one of the most contentious issues between employers and the unions.[7] Finally, on December 2001, UGT, CCOO, and the CEOE signed an "Interconfederal Agreement on Collective Bargaining 2002." This was the first Interconfederal agreement signed by the social actors since 1984, but it set an important milestone, as it has been be renegotiated in subsequent years (see table 3.3). It includes wage policies guidelines. Although there has not been a return to incomes policy in Spain until 2001, wage demands have been moderate during the last decade and only slightly above expected inflation, and wage settlements have reflected this strategy (for current data see also table 2.4 in chapter 2). Indeed, between 1997 and 2007 Spanish salaries have increased only by 1.4 percent. This tendency has been corrected lately. According to the *Instituto Nacional de Estadística,* between September of 2006 and September of 2007 salaries have increased by 3.8 percent (and inflation by 2.36 percent) and unit labor costs have increased by 3.9 percent.[8]

This development had very positive consequences for the Spanish economy as we examined in chapter 2. Social peace and wage moderation fostered by the return of national social bargaining have contributed to a new virtuous circle characterized by sustained rapid growth, improving fiscal position, lower unemployment, and higher investment, which in turn, will promote rapid growth.[9]

Yet, the degree of temporary contracts remained very high during the past decade, despite the 1997 agreement. As indicated in chapter 2, the temporary rate grew from 30.8 percent in 2004 to 33.7 percent in 2005 and it stands (in 2006) at 33.7 percent of the labor force, a level twice as high as the EU one (13.6 percent). This problem let the social actors to reach a new agreement. On May 4, 2006 the Socialist government and the social actors (CEOE, CEPYME, UGT, and CCOO) signed a landmark pact, *Acuerdo Para la Mejora del Crecimiento y del Empleo* (the Agreement for Improvement in the Quality and Growth of Employment, AMCE) after 14 months of hard negotiations.

This agreement allows Spanish firms to convert their temporary workers into permanent ones through a contract of job promotion, with lower dismissal costs. It includes initiatives to reduce the temporary rate, such as a period of time (up to December 31 of 2007) during which existing temporary contracts can be converted into permanent ones using the so-called contract of promotion of stable employment, with a dismissal cost of 33 days per year of work (as opposed to the regular 45 days per year for regular permanent contracts). After that period the conversion will be extended to regular permanent contracts, which gives a powerful incentive to employers to convert their current temporary workers to indefinite ones.

The agreement also limits to 30 months the renewal of temporary contracts for one worker. Hence, those workers who have served for 30 months in the same position, through two or more temporary contracts, will be automatically converted to permanent contracts (with the exception of certain categories of contracts such as the training or interim ones). It also establishes a program of incentives to promote permanent employment, creating subsidies of between 500 and 3,200 euros per year (depending on the type of contract that is converted into a permanent one) for hiring certain categories of workers. These subsidies will last on average four years (as opposed to the previous two years). The groups included are young males between 16 and 30 years old (800 euros and 4 years), women (850 euros and 4 years), workers 45 years old and older, and women hired two years after having a child (1,200 euros and for the duration of the contract or 4 years, respectively), or long-term unemployed (600 euros and 4 years). The accord also includes the eventual elimination of subsidies for the conversion of temporary contracts into permanent ones: those contracts signed prior to June 1, 2006 that are transformed into permanent ones will have subsidies (800 euros for three years) only if they were converted before January 1, 2007.

The pact also includes a reduction of unemployment contributions for employers by 0.25 percent until 2008 and an additional 0.25 percent after that year (only for permanent contracts). At the same time, it established that employers' contribution to the *Fondo de Garantia Salarial* (Fogasa, the fund to guarantee salaries) will be reduced from the previous 0.4 percent to 0.2 percent. Unions were able to include an improvement of the coverage provisions for the Fogasa, as well as the unemployment protection system, which now extends unemployment benefits to 6 months for workers 45 years old and older without family who have exhausted their benefits. Finally, with the aim to limit the abusive use of subsidiary contracts, the agreement introduces new rules to regulate the use of third firms to provide services; it commits to the improvement of the labor inspection services, and establishes a new registry book for firms, which incorporates all the relevant data about the use of these third-party firms, all with the aim of limiting abuses.[10]

This landmark pact balanced the demands of employers for lower dismissal costs and social security contributions, with those of the unions for increased unemployment benefits and more incentives for permanent jobs. The results of this reform were quite immediate. Two months after it was approved the number of workers converted from temporary to permanent tripled compared with the previous year: 124,250 contracts were converted to permanent ones and 2453,637 new indefinite contracts (a 55 percent more) were created. Yet, the overall impact has been limited and the results somewhat disappointing: while the temporary rate has decreased to 31.9 percent by November of 2007 (a reduction of 2.5 points since the agreement was signed), it is still at the same level of 2004.[11]

The Empirical Puzzle

Spain lacks a tradition of social bargaining among democratic actors. In fact, it had no experience with the neocorporatist agreements that had been an integral part of the industrial relations setting in many other European nations. In Sweden, Austria, the Netherlands, Finland, and Belgium, among other countries, social bargaining had been the preferred mechanism to regulate relations among social actors after World War II. The success of this strategy, however, depends on unions' cooperation in implementing incomes policy and controlling inflation.

In these countries social democratic parties had remained in power for an extensive period of time and sought to implement traditional social democratic policies to achieve full employment. At the core of such policies lies a compromise between business, the state, and the organized working class in which all partners cooperate to promote what might be described as a virtuous circle of full employment, economic growth, and welfare state redistributive measures. Social concertation plays a critical role in such social democratic experiments because it is the institutional instrument that "delivers" incomes policy or the wage restraint that result from top-level negotiations between business organizations and trade unions. Under these agreements unions agree to wage moderation in exchange for material and political compensation from businesses and the state (Royo 2000, pp. 9–11). According to the corporatist literature, the organizational prerequisites for concertation were the presence of highly centralized and encompassing unions and employer associations, and a peak-level system of wage bargaining (Lehmbruch and Schmitter 1982; Goldthorpe 1984).

A comparison of these institutional factors across European countries suggests that Spain does not meet some of the institutional criteria advanced by the neocorporatist literature for the success of coordination schemes. The structure and organization of Spanish economic actors, especially its labor unions, did not foresee the successful implementation of social concertation agreements in this country. Union membership rates in Spain are among the lowest in the OECD, and they are far lower than the rates of unionization of traditional neocorporatist countries, such as Sweden. According to the EIRO (2003) "crude" union density figures in Spain stand at between 10 and 19 percent, the lowest in the EU with Estonia, Latvia, and Poland (see table 3.4)[12]

At the same time, Spain does not have the monopolistic and encompassing unions that exist in other countries such as Germany, Austria, or Sweden. In Spain the labor movement is dominated by two major confederations: UGT and CCOO, which compete for workers support. The number of workers covered by collective bargaining agreements is high (over 60 percent), and the industrial relations setting is characterized by three-tier bargaining, which occurs at the central, sectoral, and firm level. Most workers, however, are covered by agreements negotiated at the sectoral level (see Royo 2002, pp. 219–234). Therefore, Spain is often labeled as a country with an "intermediate" systems of wage bargaining, more centralized than the one existing in countries such as France or Britain, but less so than the system prevalent in Austria or Sweden (see table 3.5).

Furthermore, the institutional setting in Spain differs in several important respects from liberal and coordinated market economies common in other OECD countries. Like other European countries (such as France or Italy) Spain has transformed its economic management system over the last three decades through reforms that borrow from both models of capitalism, but

Table 3.4 Trade union membership in Spain (1993–2003)

Spain	1993	1998	2003	Change 1993–2003
CC.OO.	654,000	713,000	958,000	+46.9%
UGT	740,000	796,000	944,000	+27.6%
USO	Na	72,000	106,000	+47.2%*
CGT	Na	Na	100,000	
ELA-STV	Na	Na	103.596**	
Total	Na	Na	2,108,000	

Note: * Change from 1998 to 2003.
Source: EIRO. ** ELA.

Table 3.5 Coordination indexes

Country	1980–87	1988–95
Austria	3.00	3.00
West Germany	3.00	3.00
Denmark	2.40	2.26
Sweden	2.50	2.50
Finland	2.40	2.15
Switzerland	2.25	2.25
Belgium	2.00	2.00
Ireland	2.00	3.00
Netherlands	2.00	2.00
Spain	2.00	2.00
France	1.84	1.98
Italy	1.50	1.40
United Kingdom	1.40	1.15
United States	1.00	1.00

Note: The index ranges from 1—fragmented bargaining at the plant level and little coordination to 3—coordinated bargaining by the peak associations.
Source: Nickell (2003).

the state and state actors continue to play an important role. As mentioned in the Introduction, Spain conforms to a large extent to the so-called state capitalism model—or State Influenced Market Economies, SMEs (Schmidt 2002, pp. 141–146; Schmidt 2006), in which the government is still a major institutional actor and leads business-labor relations, even after the processes of liberalization and integration in the European Union (EU) in the 1980s and 1990s. According to Schmidt, in SMEs the state is defined as "influencing because it tends to intervene where it sees fit, either 'enhancing' business and labor activity because public intervention has a positive impact on economic actors' interactions and productive capabilities, or 'hindering' it in cases where it has a negative impact on economic actors; interactions and productive capacities" (Schmidt 2006, p. 7).

For its part, the Voc literature has also analyzed the relationship between production regimes and welfare systems in terms of institutional complementarities. As we saw in the Introduction, within each model (LMEs and CMEs) and each country, aspects of its welfare state and production regime "fit" each other. Moreover, the VoC approach is built around the concept of institutional complementarities. According to this concept institutions are complementary to one another when the presence of one raises the returns available from the other; therefore, economies that do not conform closely to either model (such as Spain) would underperform.

This "dysfunctionality" has been stressed by others authors such as Amable (2003) who has argued that the absence of the institutional preconditions in Mixed Markets Economies (MMEs), such as Spain, preclude them from benefiting from the complementarities and beneficial spillovers found in ideal cases. These countries have a pattern of specialization based on small firms that compete mostly on price. Therefore, he characterizes the Southern European model as one based on low social protection that hinders investment in specific skills; low skill levels that prevent engagement in high-technology activities; limited competition; underdeveloped financial markets; and strong state intervention that help account for the underdevelopment of financial markets. These factors make it difficult for these countries to move toward a higher value-added and higher-technology path (see Molina and Rhodes 2005, p. 5). Others, however, have suggested that complementarities can also be found in hybrid countries (Crouch 2005).

While this literature is ideal to define categories for empirical work it is not clear how countries that do not fit easily into either category, such as Spain, should be classified Molina and Rhodes (2005) have developed a third category: "Mixed Market Economies" (MMEs). These economies (such as Italy and Spain) "occupy an intermediate position. While unions and employers have stronger organizational structures than in LMEs, they are more fragmented and less well articulated than in CMEs" (p. 6). Therefore, these economies cannot generate the same collective goods, and neither can they develop the same frameworks of coordination. However, the economic actors do have sufficient veto power to block change and MMEs provide few incentives for economic actors to invest in long-term specific assets. They argue that the process of adjustment hinge on state action and the capacities of interest organizations. The role of the state in these countries is stressed by other authors, such as Schmidt (2006) who has created a similar typology to integrate these countries: State-Influenced Market Economies (SMEs).

In sum, Spain is characterized in the literature as a country with limited strategic coordination on labor relations. Yet this unpropitious institutional setting has not precluded the development of coordination mechanisms among economic actors in Spain over the last decade. On the contrary, as we have seen coordination among economic actors has flourished in Spain as the social actors have developed distinctive processes of tripartite bargaining to reform social policies and regulate the labor market. Globalization, structural pressures by employers for more flexibility to respond to changing market conditions, and a shift in the content of bargaining toward production issues (such as working times or work organization) have not resulted in a move on the part of employers to deregulate labor relations. On the contrary, Spanish firms seeking greater flexibility in personal and wage policy at the plant level have supported cooperative processes that have involved the collective management of industrial relations above the plant level.

The renewal of tripartite bargaining in Spain in the 1990s illustrates that the trend has been toward greater coordination and centralization, not decentralization. Lacking the nonmarket coordination mechanisms that support the high-quality/value added model of the CMEs, Spanish employers supported the renewal of social pacts in the second half of the 1990s as a mechanism for securing labor cooperation and peace. This strategic shift challenges the conventional wisdom that explains changes in industrial relation systems as a universal move on the parts of employers to deregulate labor relations and a movement along a continuum in which deregulation culminates in convergence toward a LME model. On the contrary, reforms in Spain went in the opposite direction, recentralizing bargaining, clarifying the links between central- and plant-level bargaining (i.e., the 1997 AINC), and strengthening the most representative unions against growing challenges to give employers a reliable interlocutor at the plant level. This development has to be explained.

This is the central puzzle of this book: *How can we account for such development?* While the VoC approach has theorized extensively on the different forms by which change occurs, it does not sufficiently explain why (or how) it occurs. Institutions are used by economic actors as resources to achieve their goals, yet actors are not only defined by their institutions (Schmidt 2006, pp. 17–18). The central argument of the book is that successful coordination depends not only on the institutional framework and the organization of the social actors but also on their interests and strategies. Social bargaining is a political process, and, therefore, it is necessary to examine the political settlements that motivate the social actors.

In Spain structural fragmentation has been mitigated by factors such as the centralization of the business sector around the *Confederación Española de Organizaciones Empresariales* (CEOE) or the strategic unity of action between the two leading confederations (CCOO and UGT), which have promoted the development of alternative logics of interaction and coordination among economic actors. They have been able to accommodate different demands from their affiliates and articulate them in effective ways in order to be able to deliver collective goods in the industrial relations realm. At the same time, the state has played a central role, but increasingly more often as facilitator rather than as provider of resources and income. Finally, despite Molina and Rhodes's (2005, p. 17) contention that "the absence of foundations for coordination at the micro and meso-levels impedes the formation of stable cross-alliances either across or within specific sectors," we will show that the quasi-federal structure of the Spanish state has also played a facilitating role by allowing regional governments to play a key role to facilitate the emergence of coordination mechanisms at the micro levels.

The next chapters examine the evolving interests of capital and labor, and the structural and political constraints within which they define and defend their interests.

The Spanish Case in Comparative Perspective

The trajectory of reform in Spain toward a CMEs model and the return of social bargaining has not been a unique development. On the contrary, throughout the 1980s and 1990s social bargaining resumed in countries, such as Ireland, Italy, and Portugal, that also lacked a strong democratic corporatist tradition. These countries had a tradition of corporatism derived in part from Roman Catholic social teachings. In these countries, like in

Spain, the "inadequate" structure, strength, and organization of the economic actors; the lack of a tradition of Social Democratic government; and the relatively decentralized structure of wage bargaining did not preclude the emergence of tripartite bargaining. In all cases unions agreed to participate in social bargaining and entered social pacts for reasons of convenience. Indeed, the EMU process, changes in the balance of power among the actors involved, transformations in the economic structure, the inability to curve inflation, or the convergence toward an intermediate model, led the social actors to the social bargaining table to confront these challenges (Regini 2000; Rhodes 1998).

In Portugal social bargaining surged in the mid-1980s and was sustained during the last decade (Royo 2002, pp. 89–112). There were three main periods. The first one was from 1986 to 1995. This was a decade dominated by the Prime Minister Anibal Cavaco Silva, leader of the conservative Social Democratic Party (PSD). His governments conducted an aggressive policy of economic liberalization, privatization, and deregulation of the labor market. Dr. Cavaco Silva, however, was also a strong believer in the social concertation process, and starting in 1986 he negotiated landmark agreements between the unions (mainly UGT) and employers' associations. His last agreement was the 1992 "Agreement on Incomes Policy." The electoral victory of the Portuguese Socialist Party (PS) in the 1995 general election marked the beginning of a new political cycle and a new phase of social dialogue. The new government vowed to develop and implement its policies with the participation of the social actors. The result of this approach was the signing of two agreements in 1996, one a short-term pact and the other a strategic agreement that covered the last three years of the legislature (1997–99). The PS government was reelected in 1999 and it continued its negotiations with the social partners within the Permanent Council for Social Concertation (CPCS). In 2001 the government and the social actors signed two new agreements on professional training and work safety. These were the last agreements.

Ireland also provides an interesting case marked by a tendency to deal with industrial relations issues (including wages) in a centralized way. Since the 1970s almost all pay agreements have been either negotiated centrally or have followed a general norm. However, the basic relationship between trade unions and employers has been an antagonistic one, and the industrial relations system has been characterized by widespread restrictive practices. Large general unions dominate the labor movement, and the Irish industrial relations system had historical roots in the British model (although current trends are moving it away from this source). Following difficulties reaching and implementing national collective agreements in the 1940s, 1950s, and 1960s, yearly national wage agreements started in 1971 and continued through 1978. Over the last three decades the corporatist trend has been reinforced. The "National Understanding for Economic and Social Development" was signed in 1979 covering such issues as wages, taxation, employment, social welfare, and health. This agreement marked a significant departure: for the first time the government became directly involved in national negotiations with the social partners.

A second "National Understanding" followed it but from 1981 through 1987 there were no centralized agreements. Social bargaining resumed in October of 1987 with the "Program for National Recovery" covering the period to the end of 1990, which included industrial relations, social and economic issues, and continued in 1990 with the "Program for Economic and Social Progress," which also included specific macroeconomic and industrial policies. Social bargaining continued throughout the 1990s. In 1996 the social partners signed the "Partnership 2000 for Inclusion, Employment and Competitiveness," a program of economic and social policy that also included a pay agreement. This agreement consolidated the pattern of agreed national programs and extended their scope with the new emphasis on inclusion and employment (Von Prodynski 1999, pp. 63–69).

In Italy social bargaining has proceeded intermittently. There were incomes policy agreements in 1977 and 1983. In 1984, however, disagreements among the main trade union confederations brought the process to an end. Following a period of fragmentation that led to bargaining decentralization, national-level negotiations resumed in 1992 when the unions agreed to abolish the *scala mobile* and freeze company-level bargaining for two years to support the government austerity program. In 1993 they signed a new agreement establishing an incomes policy framework based on a two-level bargaining structure. In 1998 the *Patto di Natale* reaffirmed this framework and introduced European inflation as a referent (Pérez 2002; Regini and Regalia 1997; Rhodes 1998).

From a theoretical and comparative standpoint what is interesting about these countries is that generally speaking they all lacked the kind of encompassing bargaining organizations and centralized systems of wage bargaining that characterize successful efforts at centralized social bargaining in traditional neocorporatist countries. In this regard, the Spanish case is attractive as a microcosmic example of the dynamics that follow from Europeanization and the attempt to impose monetary discipline in a fragmenting bargaining context. It helps illustrate ways in which these pressures influence the preferences of the social actors.

Yet, the following features differentiate the Spanish experience from that of other countries (and from the first phase of social concertation in Spain):

1. The length of the process: social bargaining resumed in 1993, has extended over a decade, and continues into the new millennium.
2. The scope: since 1994 there have been more than two dozen agreements.
3. The content: these agreements have been very ambitious and have covered multiple issues from pensions and social policies, to wages, to labor market regulations and industrial relations issues.
4. The commitment to social bargaining across the partisan divide is as follows: social dialogue started under a Socialist government in 1993 and continued with a conservative party in power. The new socialist government elected in 2004 reaffirmed its commitment to this approach and has been an active participant in the process.

5. The endurance: despite setbacks (i.e., the general strike of 2002 over labor market reform) social bargaining has continued and new agreements have been signed.
6. The increasing autonomy of the social actors in the realm of industrial relations: while the government played a central role during the first phase of social concertation, during the last decade trade unions and employers associations have been the central actors of this process and have reaffirmed their autonomy from the government, which has played a more limited role.
7. The Spanish model of social bargaining has superseded the traditional corporatist exchange based on the extension of social rights in return for wage moderation and cooperative industrial relations. These pacts have also included other issues such as internal and external flexibility, and welfare policies.
8. Starting in 2001 the tripartite agreements have included, again, wage bargaining.

Indeed, the Spanish case illustrates that the economic pressures that are eroding the coordination mechanisms of *Coordinated Market Economies* (CMEs) are offering incentives to the Spanish social actors to address new challenges through social pacts. Spanish governments are also trying to make labor markets more flexible, but distributional conflicts are not necessarily leading to a neoliberal solution. In Spain the main forces of change—namely, increasing competition, financial integration, difficult macroeconomic circumstances, technological changes, the transformation in the nature of business, and new demands on educational and professional training systems—have led the social actors to work together to implement significant changes in the Spanish system of industrial relations. In addition, fiscal decentralization, little labor mobility, EMU, and relatively inflexible labor markets are also exerting particular pressures on the Spanish economy.

The Spanish case is also interesting from a comparative perspective because the tripartite bargaining agreements conform to a mixed (mid-pluralist) model of corporatism that is rather different in form from the traditional Social Democratic (SD) corporatism of the Scandinavian countries (Rhodes 1998).[13] This new form of neocorporatism focuses on reduced labor costs and competitiveness (Hassel and Ebbinghaus 2000), and it is characterized by concertation among weaker organizations (as opposed to the centralized peak organizations with a monopoly of representation that characterize the Scandinavian countries), with governments acting as instigators of social pacts to reform labor legislation or social programs (Rhodes 1998, p. 183; Hassel and Ebbinghaus 2000, p. 80). These scholars have noted that the main problem with the new form of corporatist pacts is that the political exchange is far less certain and predictable. Fiscal, economic, and competitive pressures prevent governments from compensating unions with an expansion of social and welfare programs. In this new economic environment, the rewards and incentives of social bargaining are not as immediate and evident as they used to be.

Consequently, the terms of the bargain are likely to change from one set of negotiations to the next, and the social actors have fewer incentives to engage in this political exchange. Hence, these arrangements are more likely to be less stable and subject to periodic breakdown.[14]

The chapters that follow examine the reasons that led the social actors to modify their strategies and pursue social bargaining.

Chapter 4

Business and the Politics of Coordination

Introduction

Chapter 3 showed that in Spain globalization and economic integration have promoted rather than undermined the development of cooperative institutional settings and "institutional complementarities." Unable to escape from economic interdependence Spain has developed coordination mechanisms at the micro- and macro level as a means to address and resolve tensions between economic interdependence and political sovereignty, and between monetary and exchange rate policies (see Cameron 1998).

This chapter examines the evolving interests of capital and the structural and political constraints within which employers define and defend their interests.[1] The analysis of the Spanish case confirms the thesis that strategic actors with their own interests design institutions (Thelen 2004). In Spain previous rounds of institutional innovation (particularly the introduction of temporary contracts in the 1980s) have produced effects (uncertainty), which in a context of competitive challenges have reshaped employers' interests and promoted coordination.

This is the central puzzle of this chapter: *How can we account for such development?* The central argument is that successful coordination depends not only on the organization of the social actors but also on their interests and strategies. Social bargaining is a political process, and, therefore, it is necessary to examine the political settlements that motivate the social actors. The next sections examine the evolving interests of capital and the structural and political constraints within which employers define and defend their interests.

In order to understand this outcome it is important not only to identify the set of actors that push for institutional change, but also to ascertain the structural constraints that influence the range of options available to these actors (Hacker and Pierson 2002), and the ways in which previous policies shape the "distribution of preferences" (Huber and Stephens 2001).

Business Organizations in Spain[2]

The authoritarian corporatist legacy of the Francoist regime left an important imprint in the configuration of employers' associations in Spain. Both workers and unions were integrated into the authoritarian corporatist vertical unions. Following Franco's death and in response to the growing union activity four preexisting businesses merged in 1977 to create a single national peak employers' organization, CEOE (the *Confederación Española de Organizaciones Empresariales*), which claimed monopoly representation of employers after the integration in March 1980 of the confederation of small- and medium-sized firms, CEPYME (*Confederación Española de la Pequeña y Mediana Empresa*). About 90 percent of all firms are members (Van der Meer 2000, p. 578). The CEOE represents businesses from all sectors of the economy: agriculture, industry, services, and finance (Pardo Avellaneda and Fernández Castro 1995, p. 157). It has over 1,350,000 businesses affiliates, which employed three-fourths of the Spanish workers in the early 1980s and up to 95 percent of the employers by 1987. The other three major business associations represent small- and medium-sized firms and are all now part of the CEOE.[3]

The CEOE has a double structure; it is organized by territories and sectors, with membership defined by inclusion in both structures. Voting weight is determined by the size of the firm, with the sectoral structure having a greater weight.[4] The peak-level confederation has the power to sign its own wage agreements, participates in demand formulation, and assists in bargaining at lower levels. This representative monopoly of the CEOE has favored the social bargaining process.

Despite a long history of confrontation between unions and employers, the advent and consolidation of a new democratic regime in the 1970s changed this dynamic, and fostered more cooperation between the social actors, which facilitated the development of social bargaining. Indeed, the new democratic regime encouraged the development of institutions and processes that supported cooperative links between business and labor. Despite the fact that during the dictatorship the "vertical unions" had attempted to go beyond the class struggle, business and labor interests remained distant.

The beginning of the transition, however, did not foreshadow that a cooperative relationship would develop between the CEOE and the unions. The first years after Franco died were characterized by a very high level of disputes. The CEOE, worried about the growing industrial conflict and in agreement with the conservative government, refused to strengthen the unions' role in the system. Its stance toward them was clearly antagonistic. The CEOE blamed the political instability on the unions, and accused them of supporting revolutionary strategies that were resulting in the worsening of economic conditions. It was also particularly concerned about the strength of the communist union, CCOO, and focused its actions on trying to weaken the latter's position among workers.

In this regard, the CEOE and the conservative government took specific steps to consolidate the UGT when its leaders came back from exile. They viewed this strategy as means of dividing and weakening of the union movement. Consequently, they opposed the CCOO's attempts to develop a unitary labor organization that would integrate all unions. At this time, union representatives in firms suffered constant discrimination, and in most cases, they operated underground to avoid reprisals. Employers even tried to develop a Christian democratic-oriented union that might balance the strength of the CCOO and the UGT. This attempt failed (Führer 1996, p. 233). The CEOE was able to prevent the legal recognition of union activities at the firm level until the Union Freedom Act was approved in 1985, and argued against the return of the unions' wealth confiscated by the dictatorship.[5]

The event that triggered a shift in this confrontational strategy was the 1978 election of representatives to the work councils. These elections clarified the union landscape and confirmed the supremacy of the CCOO and the UGT in the labor movement. The CEOE was forced to acknowledge these results and reassess its strategy toward unions. It began to recognize unions as valid intermediaries for the workers, and realized that the development of a new industrial relations setting had to be negotiated. The organization's preference, however, was for moderate unions, and, therefore, it started a process of rapprochement with the UGT—which they considered more moderate than CCOO. The CEOE started this new strategy in 1978 with negotiations at the highest level with UGT. The consequence was the signing of the ABE that same year (see chapter 3), the first of five centralized agreements signed by the employers association and the UGT between 1979 and 1986 (and with the participation of the government and CCOO in two of them). The CEOE viewed the concertation process as a way to consolidate its position in the system. It also sought to "reward" the moderate union. When it reached agreements with UGT in 1978 and 1980, it intensified its attacks against CCOO and accused that union of radicalization and irresponsible demands.[6]

Cooperation resulted in the institutionalization of the role of unions and business associations. Their representative position was accepted by the government, and they became recognized in the boards of several public institutions. The capstone of this process was the creation of the *Consejo Económico y Social* (CES, the Economic and Social Council) in 1991—an advisory board recognized by the Constitution (Royo 2000, 2002).

Explaining Business Strategies

During the last decade Spanish employers have realized that in order to improve the competitiveness and productivity of their firms and to be able to adapt to changing market conditions, they need increasing cooperation from workers and unions. They have understood the benefits of coordination, which facilitates agreements with labor on production issues and the implementation of reforms that allow firms to adjust more flexibly to technological changes and demand. This new approach has signaled a strategic shift on the part of employers in favor of further coordination and cooperative relations with unions. They are now willing to accept greater employment stability in exchange for more internal flexibility in the organization and deployment of labor within the workplace. In order to understand this development it is necessary to examine the link between employer strategies and macro-structural changes (Thelen 2001, p. 77). Several factors contributed to this development and these are discussed in the following paragraphs.

Changes in the Environment and the Character of Business

The Shifting Balance of Power

Changes in the environment can shift the balance of power of the social actors and can also influence their strategic outlook. Indeed, the balance of power among the social actors is variable and depends not only on structural factors but also on specific junctures and shifting circumstances (Regini 1999, p. 20; Salvati 1995). In this regard, increasing cooperation in the industrial relations realm in Spain in the 1990s can be partly understood as a result of the weakening of its social actors, who needed to rely on each other to address new mounting economic and social challenges.

In Spain the economic transformations of the 1980–90s strengthened the position of employers' vis-à-vis unions. Increasing labor market segmentation and the individualization of labor relations contributed to the weakening of trade union organizations at the firm level in Spain, as manifested in the relative decline in union density, which hindered unions' capacity to mobilize workers in a response to manpower policies to liberalize the labor market (Royo 2002).

At the same time, the economic crisis of the early 1990s, labor rigidities, and the opening of the Spanish economy to external competition has forced Spanish firms to build new competitive strategies, seeking greater flexibility, mobility, and the externalization of production to small nonunionized firms. Product decentralization was reflected in the growth in the number of small firms (under 50 workers), which increased from 95.1 percent of firms in 1978 to 98.1 percent in 1989, and their share of employment, which grew from 38.4 percent to 52.2 percent during the same period in Spain (Fraile 1999, p. 280; Richards and Polavieja 1997, p. 31). Most of the SMEs operate in the service and commerce sectors (real estate, tourism, minority trade, food, social services, education, health, and beverages). In these sectors the level of unionization was only half of that in all manufacturing, reflecting the small size of most firms and the prominence of professional and technical staff (in 2001 31.7 percent of Spanish worked in management positions classified as technical managers and medium-level professionals, while only 11.2 percent were classified as working in positions that did not require qualifications). The combination of all of these factors led to the increasing individualization of labor relations, lower labor costs, and gave firms more flexibility in the organization of work and in the deployment of labor through mobility, overtime,[7] rotation, and part-time work. This structure based on small firms presents particular challenges resolving collective-action problems; hence the pressure for Spanish employers to seek further coordination.

In addition, as we saw in chapter 2, this individualization of employment relations was further hastened by the spectacular growth of temporary employment. Employers, who have blamed high dismissals costs and their contributions to social security (both are among the highest in Europe: 45 days' pay for every day worked compared with a maximum of 8 days in the United Kingdom) have used temporary contracts as a form to limit such costs. As a result, from 1984 through 1997 the number of temporary contracts increased from 7.5 percent to 39 percent of the total. Henceforth, the level of temporary work among new workers in Spain rose from 61 percent in 1987 to 81.5 percent in 1990, doubling the proportion of the active population on temporary contracts during that period from 15 percent to 30 percent (and accounting for 90 percent of all employment contracts). This development has further weakened unions (see Richards and Polavieja 1997, pp. 13–23).

Finally, the existing collective bargaining system in which collective agreements and most wages are set at the sectoral level has also been a traditional source of frustration for employers who have sought greater flexibility and to negotiate agreements at the firm level. Pressures to seek a new articulation of the collective bargaining system were hastened by the passing out of the remaining labor ordinances in the early 1990s. The 1994 Labour Reform, which also broadened the content of collective bargaining, repealed the Labor Ordinances and gave the social actors freedom to negotiate new terms of employment (e.g., work shifts, labor mobility, wages, working conditions, training, functional mobility, job classifications, promotions, and technological innovations and changes in the organizations of work) previously regulated by law, within certain limits. In other words, the reform shifted powers to the market. In a competitive context marked by intensive firm restructuring in which issues of work flexibility played a critical role, some employers pushed for a legal framework that would facilitate the individualization of employment relations and the marginalization of work councils.[8]

Yet, labor weakness has not led to a shift toward a Liberal Market Economy (LME). While these changes have provided greater flexibility to employers and have weakened labor, they have not led to a deregulation of the industrial relations system or the establishment of a LME model in this realm. On the contrary, in a context of increasing deterioration of competitiveness, non-coordination and conflictive relations with labor presents serious challenges problems for Spanish firms. In the end, for the reasons that we examine next, the shift in the balance of power in favor of capital has led to further cooperation.

New Competitive Challenges

As we examined in earlier chapters, by the 1980s Spanish firms were already facing increasing competition for their main exports from countries in the Far East and Latin America, which produced all these goods at cheaper costs, thus attracting investment. These concerns intensified further due to increasing fears about new competition from the new Central and Eastern European EU member states, which like Spain also specialize in labor-intensive and low-to-medium technology products, and in which labor costs are between 20 and 60 percent lower than those of the EU average.

In addition, there are still significant differences in the production structure and in the structure of exports, in comparison to the leading developed economies. The balance of payments deficit currently represents 7.8 percent of GDP, a dire reflection of the lack of competitiveness of the Spanish economy, and at a time in which the EU, and Spain in particular, seem to be "losing the battle on competitiveness"[9] and the country is ranked twenty-ninth in the 2007 *Global Competitiveness Index* (GCI). Furthermore, as we examined in chapter 2, the increasing threat of outsourcing and the worrisome pattern of decreasing Foreign Direct Investment (FDI) coming into Spain have intensified the pressure on employers for change.[10] The problem is particularly acute in labor-intensive sectors, such as the textile industry, which closed the 2006 year with a reduction in production by 15 percent and the loss of almost 20,000 jobs. And the crisis is not abating: as recently as the spring of 2007 two new textile firms in Catalonia (*Fluinsa* and *Textil Abadesses*) were forced to close their plants and dismiss 100 employees, as a result of growing competition from Asia and the lack of competitiveness in the sector.[11] These competitive pressures and a shifting competitive environment have convinced Spanish companies that they need to move toward a new model based on value added and that they need the cooperation of unions and workers to do so; hence their support for social bargaining in the last 10 years.

Industrial Relations and the Labor Market

Furthermore, the industrial relations framework does not provide the necessary flexibility (either internal or external) to firms to deploy and organize their labor force.[12] A central challenge for Spanish firms and employers is to find a balance between the reduction of temporary levels and the rigidity of some contracts. As we have seen earlier, in a context of relatively high dismissal costs, employers have been using these contracts as instruments to introduce flexibility in their labor force in order to be able to adapt it to market conditions, technological change, and demand. As a result, almost 50 percent of the staff is temporary in small firms, and the country has the highest level of temporary work in the EU (see Bentolila, Segura, and Toharia 1991, pp. 237–238 and Richards and Polavieja 1997, pp. 13–23).[13] The temporary rate stood (in 2007) at 31.9 percent of the labor force, a level twice as high as the EU one (13.6 percent).[14] Only the 2006 labor reform is shifting this tendency as we will see below.

The widespread use of these contracts may have contributed to halve its unemployment rate since the 1993 recession, to 7.95 percent in 2007 (the lowest level since 1978) and has helped to bringing the underground job market into the open (there was a 60 percent increase in the number of people in the workforce between 1993 and 2005).

Yet, as noted before temporary work limits the incentives of employers to invest in their workers, stifles innovation, reduces the commitment of employees to their firms, and hinders the development and implementation of training programs. Indeed, these developments foster a sense of insecurity and distrust, which undermine the concept of the breadwinner protecting his or her nuclear family, that have deleterious effects on productivity.[15] Employers recognize the perverse consequences of these developments (Jiménez Aguilar 1997, pp. 12–13) and there is growing consensus on the fact that higher productivity has to be based on better education and training, and it requires more coordination.[16]

Indeed, there is growing agreement among employers (and economic actors in general) that Spain faces an uncertain future if it does not address the problem of labor precariousness. As we have seen in chapter 2, in 2007, 5.5 million workers, more than a third of the active population, have temporary contracts, and this in a country that had created 10 million jobs in the previous 10 years. Moreover, most of them are young people and women. In fact, among workers between 16 and 24 years of age, 6 out of 10 have temporary contracts (double the rate in the OECD countries), and 65 percent of those aged 15–25 years have a temporary job.[17]

It also affects those with college education (18.9 percent of male college graduates have temporary contracts and 34.5 percent of the female ones, compared with the EU average of 6.8 percent and 12.7 percent, respectively).[18] In addition, according to the OECD the so-called "trash contracts" are one of the reasons for the stagnation in the number of college graduates and their salaries (see chapter 2).[19]

This development has very dire consequences. On the one hand, young people lack the resources to leave their parents' homes (the emancipation rate has been reduced by 25 percent in the last 20 years). This problem is aggravated by the high prices of housing (see chapter 2). On the other, they do not have incentives to complete their studies because they perceive that with an undergraduate degree they will not make much more money and they will have a temporary job. What is, hence, the point of studying? As Marcos Peña, president of the tripartite advisory body Economic and Social Council (CES), has stated, "If young workers, who are the ones responsible for the articulation of our future, are in a precarious situation, we face the risk that our future will also be precarious."[20]

According to a recent OECD report the main reasons for the high rate of temporary contracts are rooted in the deficiencies of the educational system and its distance vis-à-vis the labor market, and the excessive protection differential between temporary and indefinite workers. Therefore, the solution will involve increasing cooperation between the educational system and the business sector to facilitate internships and practical training in firms, and to reduce the differences in the cost of dismissals between temporary and indefinite workers.[21] Companies have to invest more in training as well because Spanish workers are at the bottom of the EU in professional training: according to the EU only 25 percent of the Spanish population between 25 and 64 had participated in any training activity during the previous year, compared with 42 percent in the EU (70 percent in Finland or Sweden, 80 percent in Denmark). It is also essential to develop a competitive and prestigious vocational training system linked with the business sector, a particular challenge in a country where the so-called *Formación Profesional* (professional training) has been traditionally reserved to school dropouts and has been largely associated with academic failure.

In Spain 62 percent of the students go to high school and 38 percent attend professional training (in Europe this proportion is reversed: 37 percent go to high school and 63 percent attend professional training). This imbalance not only affects the ability of firms to recruit workers with appropriate training and skills, but also contributes to the high rate of unemployment among college graduates (11.5 percent one of the highest in the EU—with an average of 6.2 percent), and to the relative poor quality of jobs available to them (only 40 percent of college graduates have jobs commensurate with their academic qualifications, 10 percentage points below the EU average).[22] This need is particularly pressing because according to demographic estimates Spain will lose between 20 and 35 percent of its university graduates in the next 10 years. Fortunately, employers understand the significance of these issues and they are working on these areas: as we will see in chapter 6, employers are working closely with schools, universities, and regional/local governments to align the educational system with employers' needs.

In the end, the generalization of the practice to hire temporary workers has led to the establishment and institutionalization of a model based on low costs and low value-added that is no longer competitive.[23] Hence employers now agree that Spain has to make a significant effort to reduce the temporary rate, which results in low salaries but also in low productivity, and have made this a priority in their negotiations with unions.[24] Indeed there is growing consensus among employers that in order for workers to perform better and to be more productive it is critical to reduce the actual precariousness, improve the educational system, and make the industrial relations framework more flexible to facilitate the migration of workers to the most dynamic sectors of the economy. There is also growing agreement that the employment that is being created is not of sufficient quality. In a context in which the economy has been growing at rates above 3.5 percent, and employment at 4.1 percent, there are no excuses not to address this problem.

The decision by the social actors to sign a new agreement in 2006 (the *Acuerdo Para la Mejora del Crecimiento y del Empleo*, the Agreement for Improvement in the Quality and Growth of Employment, AMCE) to reduce the temporary rate with the unions and the government (see chapter 3) was the confirmation of these objectives. The main goal of this agreement is to improve the stability of employment, which was stated explicitly by the signatories of the agreement as a necessary factor in the establishment of a new model of growth based on the improvement of businesses' competitiveness and increases in productivity. This agreement seeks to trade-off lower dismissal costs (something that unions have historically opposed) in exchange for a reduction of temporary contracts and improving conditions for those in temporary jobs.[25] In the signing of the agreement in May of 2006, the [then] secretary general of the CEOE, José María Cuevas, and the secretary general of the CEPYME, Jesús Barcenas, both praised the benefits of indefinite jobs and recognized the need to find the right balance between labor flexibility and worker incentives to foster productivity. The president of the government, José Luís Rodríguez Zapatero, declared this agreement "historic" and stated that it had the strategic objective to reduce the level of temporary work in order to improve productivity "by facilitating human capital accumulation, as well as improve labor insertion and commitment to the enterprise."[26]

Wage Moderation

Employers have also sought wage moderation. Indeed, one of the keys for the economic success of the country in the last decade has been wage moderation, which has been one of the outcomes of the social bargaining process. While confrontation in the late 1980s and early 1990s resulted in wage increases (Royo 2002, pp. 177–182); social bargaining has produced on average wage increases of 0.5 percent, as average real wages decreased by 4 percent between 1995 and 2005 according to the OECD, and this despite the rapid economic growth and the surge in business profits (which increased by 73 percent between 1999 and 2006). The *Acuerdos Interconfederales para La Negocicón Colectiva* (the Interconfederal Agreements for Collective Bargaining) that unions and employers have signed between 2002 and 2008 have contributed to wage moderation. According to the *Encuesta de Convenios Colectivos* (Survey of Collective Agreements), the purchasing capacity of salaries during that period only increased by 2.5 percentage points compared with inflation, but according to the *Instituto Nacional de Estadística* (INE, National Institute of Statistics) salaries lost purchasing capacity in three of those years (2002, 2005, and 2006).[27] These agreements have been very important because they enshrined a common objective between employers and unions: to develop a productive system based on competitiveness, value-added, and productivity (instead of low costs). They included clauses to guarantee the purchasing capacity of salaries, but also productivity clauses.[28]

Indeed, Spain is the only 1 of the 30 OECD members in which the purchasing capacity of salaries has decreased between 1995 and 2005 (in the previous decade, between 1990 and 1995, real wages increased by 1.9 percent annually). This development was accompanied by a surge in employment that led to a dramatic decline in unemployment (unemployment reached 8.5 percent of the active population in 2006), and the employment rate is now higher than the OECD average for the first time on record. However, most of this employment is in low skills and low wages (thus explaining why salaries have not decreased for most Spaniards),[29] which has contributed to widening the income gap between the wealthiest 20 percent and the poorest 20 percent (in 2002 the top 20 percent earned 5.1 percent more than the bottom 20 percent, and in 2005 the former earned 5.4 percent more), and has increased the number of Spaniards who live below the poverty line (around 2 million workers in 2005, or one in every five in 2005, up by 19 percent in 1995, and well over the 16 percent EU average). This has resulted in more inequality, which has not been compensated by a comparable redistributive effort (while European countries invest on average 28 percent of their GDP in social protection, Spain only invests 20 percent—only up by 19.5 percent in 1995). In other words, the growth of the Spanish economy has been supported by the creation of low-skilled and low-wage jobs (particularly in sectors such as construction).[30] This development does not bore well for the sustainability of the model and employers have come to understand this.

Collective-Action Challenges for Small Firms

According to the central Directory of Enterprises (DIRCE) as of January 1, 2003 there were in Spain 2,808,385 small and medium enterprises (SMEs) (defined as enterprises that employ between 0 and 249 workers). This represents 99.87 percent of the business census in Spain (a total of 2,813,120 enterprises excluding agriculture and fisheries). According to the European Observatory of SMEs, in 2000 the average size of the Spanish enterprises, which represent around 13.5 percent of the total European enterprises, was five workers (in Europe the average is six, and only Italy with three and Greece with two have lower averages). Since 1985, the first year that the National Statistic Institute (INE) started to compile the DIRCE, the number of SMEs has increased by 511,688 productive units, and between 1995 and 2003 the number has grown by 22 percent. The most productive period has been between 2001 and 2003 when 167,626 new SMEs were created (a 6 percent growth). In 2004 there were 6.7 SMEs per 100 inhabitants. According to the INE almost eight out of 10 Spanish firms (79.1 percent) have two or less workers and more than half do not have any (51.4 percent). In 2005, 138,333 new enterprises opened in Spain (6,155 more than in 2004), and the overwhelming majority of them were SMEs (and this despite the fact that Spain has been ranked as the fourth OECD country in which it is most difficult to start a company, only behind Portugal, Greece, and Italy: on average it takes 47 days and 10 procedures compared with the OECD average of 16.6 and 6.2, respectively).[31] Companies have sprung up in areas such as daily life (child care or home services); the improvement of the quality of life (security, or collective public local transportation); the organization of cultural activities, sports, and entertainment; and environmental services (such as waste, energy, and water management).[32]

As noted in chapter 2, an economic structure based on SMEs with the capacity to adapt to changing environments has produced benefits such as flexibility and openness to innovation. Yet, the small dimension of these firms presents challenges when they try to export and compete in international markets because they lack the necessary economies of scale. At the same time, generally these small companies lack the capacity to use new technologies and managerial tools, they have difficulties raising capital and accessing public funds on research and development; they have little purchasing power and a tendency to underutilize their productive capacity; and they lack resources to train their workforce.

From a competitive standpoint, as is examined later, the small dimension of Spanish companies makes it also difficult for them to generate the collective goods that they need to be competitive. Furthermore, most of these firms employ production strategies that rely on a relatively low-skilled labor force, and they do not have strong incentives to invest in their workers because they are vulnerable to "hold up" by their employees or the "poaching" of skilled workers by other firms.

In this context employers are increasingly recognizing that one of the keys to improve competitiveness will be to develop processes that allow the incorporation of knowledge to all the sectors of the productive system. This, in a context of SMEs, requires additional coordination and cooperation among all the economic actors.

Not surprisingly the mortality rate among SMEs is extremely high: between 65 and 85 percent of the SMEs disappear within the first four years after they start their operations, and only in the first year about half of them disappear for reason that include insufficient funding, poorly developed projects, poor management, or inadequate utilization of the opportunities offered by new technologies.[33] In the end, these shortcomings have led firms to support the development of institutional mechanisms to help provide the necessary collective goods to compete in the global markets.

Consequently, there has been new initiatives to help SMEs, like the *Red PIDI*, an information network with information points throughout Spain to advise potential entrepreneurs about public resources, which was initiated by the *Centro Para el Desarrollo Tecnológico Industrial* (CDTI), an institution that is part of the Ministry of Industry, Tourism and Commerce; or *Redepyme* a project to train and advise entrepreneurs that was created by the *Escuela de Organización Industrial* (EOI), which is part of the "*Programa Crece*" (Program Grow) of the Ministry of Industry and has received funds from the European Social Fund.

The Failure of Government Imposed Reforms
The support for coordination has been further hastened by the relative failure of government-imposed labor market reforms throughout the second half of the 1980s and the first half of the 1990s (Royo 2002), which convinced Spanish firms of the need to develop a partnership with unions (and the government) in order to address common challenges, reform the regulatory framework, and change the economic model. Their return to social bargaining that I described in chapter 3 reflects this commitment. In this regard, the 1997 *Interconfederal Agreement for Employment Stability* (AIEE) was a direct

response to the dramatic increase of temporary workers in Spain since the 1984 reform of the Workers' Statute.[34] In this agreement the unions agreed to reduce dismissal costs for certain categories of workers (one of the most contentious issues in Spanish industrial relations because employers claimed that uncertainties over the costs of dismissals, which are subject to judicial review, raised the average price paid for redundancies and thus kept them from hiring workers under indefinite contracts) in exchange for a commitment from employers to reduce the proportion of temporary contracts (Royo 2002, pp. 66–68).[35] Along the same lines, the 1997 *Interconfederal Agreement on Collective Bargaining* (AINC) attempted to rationalize the existing collective bargaining system. It called for a clearer articulation of the levels of collective bargaining, stipulating that it would be desirable to reserve some items for national-level sectoral bargaining: wage structure, professional classifications, the regulation of temporary contracts, information rights of work councils, and the maximum work-time and its distribution—remitting to lower levels (i.e., for provincial- or firm-level collective bargaining) issues such as specific wage settlements, rest periods, vacations, special work-time arrangements, and so forth (Royo 2002, pp. 64–70; Fraile 1999, pp. 299–300). Finally, the 2006 agreement (AMCE) to reduce the temporary rate (see chapter 3) further pushes in this direction by allowing Spanish firms to convert their temporary workers into permanent ones through a contract of job promotion, with lower dismissal costs.

The results of this latest reform have been moderately satisfactory: indefinite contracts increased by 40 percent in the first year. In the first six months that followed the reform (signed in May of 2006, and approved by the government the following month) the ambitious program of incentives included in the reform led to a surge in the conversion of temporary contracts into indefinite ones (which grew by 108 percent, reaching 670,000 contracts). In the first 11 months of the reform 2.2 new indefinite contracts have been signed (an increase of 41.4 percent) and half of them have been with workers 30 years or younger. While the original incentives were phased out after six months, employers can still take advantage of the contract to promote indefinite employment, which has reduced dismissal costs (33 days per year worked, as opposed to the regular 45 days). As a result of this shift the temporary rate has decreased to 31.95 percent, which is still too high.[36]

These agreements have become a reference. In Catalonia the social actors have negotiated an agreement on competitiveness that exchanges more labor flexibility on mobility and computing of working hours for employment stability, and includes the creation of industrial observatories, 10 technological centers, 12 training centers, and investment agencies.

Shortcomings of the Existing Model

In the end, the current industrial relations model does not generate the trust between employers and workers that fosters cooperative relations and promotes higher productivity. According to recent data 45 percent of Spanish workers are not satisfied with their jobs and Spain is one of the European countries with the lowest level of job satisfaction among workers (55 percent), only lagging behind Turkey (50 percent), and well behind the leaders: Belgium (77 percent), Slovakia (71 percent), the Czech Republic (66 percent), and France (64 percent). Spanish workers mostly complain about their working conditions, their salaries, the number of hours that they work, and the precariousness of their jobs. One of the main concerns, however, is the lack of investment by firms in their education and training: 92 percent think that this should be the responsibility of firms, and 52 percent of them think that it should be a priority. Consequently 45 percent consider changing their jobs (51 percent in the private sector).[37]

These results highlight the negative consequences of a model based on precariousness and limited investment in workers. The lack of loyalty of workers is not conductive to higher productivity and further hinders the competitiveness of Spanish firms. Indeed, employees do not have strong incentives to share with management their ideas and initiatives, because given the precariousness of their labor situation when they work under temporary contract, they would be subject to exploitation. This problem is compounded by the fact that more than half of college graduates accept jobs below their qualifications. Indeed, while the Spanish college population is among the highest in Europe (1.5 million) Spanish universities have in general a very weak connection with the business world and there is a gap between the universities and the economic reality of the country.[38] Fortunately, as we will see in chapter 5, the system of professional training has experienced significant improvements (largely as a result of the cooperation between regional governments, employers, and unions at the regional level) and there is growing demand for these graduates.

Indeed, the productivity challenge (see chapter 2) is not merely one of temporary versus indefinite work or insufficient investment in R&D, but of culture and trust. Low productivity rates are also related to the Spanish economic development model based on the entrenched belief that the more hours that workers work in the office the more productive they are. Recent data shows, however, that this is an incorrect assumption: Spanish productivity has increased only by 0.09 percent between 1996 and 2006 (16 points below the OECD average), despite the fact that Spain is the fifth country in the world in which workers spend the most hours at work (an average of 1,780 in 2006 with 15 percent of the active population spending more than 50 hours per week working without counting extra hours or the time devoted to lunch or going to work). Spanish firms still largely reward the physical presence of workers in the company. This results in higher levels of stress, which contributes to lower productivity and less value added from workers. According to the International Labor Organization, stress causes the equivalent of between 0.5 and 3.5 percent of GDP in economic losses.[39] This is a cultural challenge and is rooted on trust (or lack thereof). It can only be addressed and resolved through increasing coordination and cooperation at the firm level.

Indeed, these developments have convinced Spanish firms that the country has to shift toward more capital-intensive industries that require greater skills in the labor force and rely on standard technology—e.g., chemicals, vehicles, steel and metal manufacturers. Hence, they are increasingly committed to the need to change the existing growth model (based on relatively low production costs, and domestic demand largely driven by the construction boom and a real estate bubble) in order to build a new framework based on innovation, specialization, quality, value-added, brand recognition, and productivity. The goal is to increase productivity by increasing the capital intensity of production. Hence employers understand that innovation and higher productivity require the following four main conditions:

1. Investment in capital technology (i.e., information systems and telecommunications);
2. A new culture of innovation and risk;
3. Human capital with strong skills and the flexibility to adapt to new technologies and processes, based on a model of continuous training; and
4. A flexible and adaptable industrial relations framework.

As we saw in chapter 2, however, Spain is still lagging well behind in all these areas: with most employment in sectors based on intensive- and low-qualified labor; only a third of the workers use new technologies and 5.8 percent of them participate in professional training programs (well below the 9 percent EU average). Furthermore, Spain invested in 2002 the equivalent of 2.8 percent of GDP in the knowledge economy (as opposed to 6.6 percent in the United States, or 3.9 percent in Germany), and it is listed next to last in the EU-15 in a study that measures high-level universities; graduates in sciences, technology, and math; and capacity to attract foreign students. While 4 out of 10 EU-15 workers work in knowledge-based areas, in Spain the figure is 1 in every three.[40] The Spanish government has set the ambitious goal to invest 2 percent of GDP by 2010, but the investment shortage is particularly acute in the private sector (it currently represents 47 percent of the total effort in R&D, and it should go up to 66 percent). A report from the European Commission about innovation in Europe highlights the low level of cooperation for innovation among Spanish SMEs: despite the fact that it has increased from 2.7 to 4.4 points, it is still only at 38 percent of the EU average.[41] Spanish firms are finally realizing that the only way to improve competitiveness and confront the competitive pressures that originate from the globalization process is through productivity increases that will largely be the result of investment in R&D.[42]

Macroeconomic Considerations

The combined processes of economic liberalization, privatization, and European integration further hastened the employers' strategic shift in favor of coordination (see Royo 2002, pp. 177–182). These developments had a significant impact in the industrial relations setting. At the micro level these processes have intensified competitive pressures and firms in Spain have been forced to design new strategies to confront these competitive challenges. At the same time, firms have been forced to accept new pressures to adjust working conditions and wages to the level of more advanced countries in order to increase competitiveness and create new jobs. In addition, Spanish firms' efforts to improve their competitiveness through further rationalization and labor market flexibility have led to tremendous changes in the business landscape. Restructuring and the privatization of publicly held companies have also influenced the strategies of Spanish firms. Outsourcing, downsizing, and reengineering have provoked significant changes in Fordist large-scale companies that used to be labor fortresses. Finally, European integration has forced the social actors to address the discrepancies between Spanish laws regulating the labor market and collective bargaining, and those prevailing in other EU countries.

At the macroeconomic level, the drive to prepare Spain for full integration within EMU influenced the government's anti-inflationary stance. Since wages are such an important component of unit costs, wage bargaining became a cornerstone of the government' anti-inflation policies (and the prospect to meet the EMU criteria), therefore enhancing the political function of the unions and the social bargaining process. Employers agreed with the EMU objective and supported wage moderation as an instrument to achieve it.[43] Indeed, some observers of the industrial relations' scene have emphasized the inability of employers and the government to impose wage moderation and curb inflationary expectations in the absence of centralized bargaining as a reason for the return of social bargaining in Spain (Pérez 1998, pp. 13–23). Pérez argues that this development reflects the inability of Spanish producers to control costs, and the failure of their governments to achieve macroeconomic policy objectives in the 1980s. According to her argument, the Spanish government failed to restrain wages by relying on a tight monetary policy and a strong currency stance because employers could not control costs in a fragmented and decentralized bargaining context in which inflation was exacerbated by the overvaluation of the currency.[44] Therefore, government and businesses were interested in the return to national bargaining as a way to achieve their goals.[45]

The empirical evidence seems to support this argument. One of the most important consequences of the social concertation process in Spain had been the decline of real wages in the context of incomes policy agreements signed by the unions and employers' associations in the 1980s (Royo 2000, pp. 98–99). This development contributed to a significant lowering of inflation, which decreased from 19.8 percent in 1978 to 8.8 percent in 1986, the last year covered by a framework wage agreement. The collapse of concertation resulted in the acceleration of real wage growth, particularly after the definitive breakdown of negotiations in 1988. Furthermore, this acceleration in real wage growth took place in a context of a very tight monetary policy stance to strengthen the value of the peseta. The combination of high interest rates and a strong currency strategy, however, failed to bring down consumer prices and unions were able to extract high real wage concessions from employers (wage increases averaged 8.3 percent in 1990, 8.1 percent in 1991, and 7.2 percent in 1992; see Royo [2000, p. 221]). In other words, high interest rates and the reliance on the external rate anchor of the ERM failed to impose wage discipline in the context of a relative decentralized bargaining structure (Pérez 1998, pp. 14–15). What explains the failure of this strategy?

Some authors have explained this development using the insider/outsider argument, according to which excessive job protection limits the responsiveness of wages to higher unemployment (Blanchard et al. 1995). According to Pérez (1998, p. 15), however, this argument is not convincing because this "insider" effect on wages in Spain is considerably lower than that estimated for Japan, Germany, and the United Kingdom. Moreover, Spain has higher levels of wage flexibility than either Germany or the United Kingdom (Jimeno and Toharia 1993, pp. 78–79).

Other authors have attributed the failure of the strong currency/high interest rates strategy to institutional features of wage bargaining, particularly the widespread practice of indexation clauses in collective agreements (Jimeno 1997, p. 83). This argument, however, is not particularly persuasive. As I have shown elsewhere (Royo 2000, pp. 135–139), disinflation was possible in Spain from 1978 to 1986 in spite of these institutional aspects of wage bargaining, and real wage declined in that period. Pérez (1998, pp. 16–17) has argued that the failure of the strong currency/high interest rates strategy in Spain was the consequence of two other factors. The first one was the limited effectiveness of monetary policy in the context of fixed exchange rates and increasing capital mobility, which resulted in massive inflows of short-term speculative capital that sought to take advantage of the high interest rates' differentials. These massive inflows had a strong inflationary impact, which forced the central bank to tighten credit and raise interest rates to compensate for the inflow of external liquidity, thus encouraging further short-term capital inflows and promoting a vicious circle that culminated with the restriction of capital inflows in 1989.

The second factor that contributed to reversing the Spanish disinflation process at the end of the 1980s, according to Pérez (1998, p. 16), involved shifts in the sectoral dynamics of prices and wages. According to this argument, massive capital inflows produced a significant appreciation of the currency over the period 1987–92, which sought to discipline wage growth by forcing employers exposed to external competition to resist excessive wage demands from unions. Pérez shows, however, that these expectations were undermined by a shift of resources from the competitive sector of the economy toward the sheltered one, encouraged by the better ability of the latter to pass on additional costs to consumers. This development resulted in widening differences between consumer and producer prices and the increase in the CPI (see figure 5.1).[46]

The consequences of these developments were that monetary authorities were unable to control domestic liquidity and also that they limited the role of the exposed sectors of the economy to set wage standards.[47] Both factors intensified the inflation proneness of the Spanish economy. This tendency was only reversed after the 1992 ERM crisis that forced the devaluation of the currencies and made possible a resumption of the disinflation process. According to this analysis, the failure of this policy course helps explain why governments and employers sought a return to social bargaining incomes policy in the 1990s (Pérez 1998, p. 18).[48]

The Economic Structure

The strategies of Spanish firms were also influenced by the position of their country in the international division of labor and by the economic structure (see Royo 2002, pp. 174–176). Regini (2000, p. 18) has contended that the predominance of high-skilled based firms in some countries over labor-intensive low value-added ones (and vice versa) influences the preferences of the social actors and determines their strategies. This is so because in countries with a predominance of high value-added firms (e.g., Germany or France) there is a lesser need for generalized labor market flexibility, and a greater one for the development of a highly educated and cooperative labor force. Using this interpretation some scholars (Regini 1997a; Regini and Regalia 1997; Rhodes 1997) have developed a microeconomically centered analysis to explain the return to national social bargaining in Italy in the 1990s. According to them this development reflects an attempt by employers to reconcile the need to control costs through more flexibility in hiring practices and the need for cooperative relations at the firm level in order to remain competitive. In other words, these arrangements constitute an institutional mechanism to support business competitiveness through consultative practices.[49]

Other scholars (Garrett 1998; and Soskice 1999) have developed further this analysis. They have argued that in social democratic corporatist countries, organized business has sought regulation (instead of deregulation) to confront more effectively the new challenges posed by globalization, seeking to preserve for their companies the financial systems, training frameworks, and research networks that allow them to remain competitive in international markets. According to this view, competitiveness depends not only on greater flexibility of firms but also on the ability of the national system in which they operate to provide them with collective goods (e.g., labor force cooperation, wage coordination, and highly skilled labor resources). In countries such as Austria or Norway, social bargaining has been successful because unions have contributed to overall wage moderation, have generated stable and productive environments, and have promoted the development of collective goods that are undersupplied by the markets (e.g., training, education, and infrastructure).

According to this argument, the economic structure influences the interests and strategies of the social actors. What is interesting according to Regini (2000, pp. 18–20) is that "the needs of actors sometimes seem antithetical to

those arising from the traditional working of their economic systems."
Indeed, in countries such as Italy or Germany, their employers' associations
are not seeking the reinforcement of their competitive advantages (i.e., in the
case of Germany the ability of the institutional framework to provide firms
with collective goods, and in the case of Italy the high versatility and rapid
adjustment of Italian small firms to changing markets). On the contrary, they
are pursuing the opposite priorities. In Germany, employers are seeking to
make the country's economy more flexible, whereas in Italy employers are
trying to institutionalize the production of collective goods (Regini 2000a,
pp. 18–20).

This argument can be applied to Spain. The Spanish production system,
with a predominance of small firms, bases its competitiveness mainly on low
costs, high versatility, and the ability to adjust rapidly to changing market
conditions. As in Italy, this competitive advantage is predicated on "weak
institutional regulation and effective but unstable voluntaristic regulation"
(Regini 1999, 21; Regini 1997). Yet the principal concern of Spanish firms
has not been the reinforcement of the institutional and structural conditions
that would promote generalized labor market flexibility. Indeed, within the
business sector there has been a main dilemma: whether to support strategies
that would individualize further labor relations or whether to build cooperative
relations with union. Supporters of the former strategy see the individualization of labor relations as an instrument to further flexibility, which helps
reduce costs and improve competitiveness. On the contrary, the supporters of
cooperative strategies have focused on the problem of governability and
the need to improve the provision of collective goods that would enhance the
competitive position of Iberian firms. The latter group seeks to eliminate
uncertainties in the markets and industrial relations by developing cooperative
relations with unions.

Spanish firms have come to recognize that the minimization of uncertainties
in the labor market increases "trust" among the social and economic actors
over the capacity of the system to address new challenges. At the same time,
they acknowledge the need to improve the ability of the national system in
which they operate to provide collective goods—namely, education, training,
wage coordination, and labor cooperation—that are essential to enhance
their competitiveness (Jiménez Aguilar 1997, pp. 10–16). This is particularly
true in the context of SMEs, which lack the resources and economies of scale
to train their employees in the use of new technologies. Finally, they value the
contribution of social cohesion and social peace—which generate confidence
among employers and further investment—to economic expectations.[50] Over
the last decade, this position has been gaining adepts among Spanish businesses (Espina 1999, pp. 389–390).[51] This analysis has led employers' associations and firms to decide that while both competitiveness and costs rely on
the increasing flexibility of labor and firms, they also depend on the ability of
the system to provide collective goods. Hence, they acknowledge that the
crucial problem for Iberian firms is the need to further institutionalize the
production of collective goods.[52]

Consequently, Spanish firms have given priority to develop further coordination and during the last decade there have been notable cases of cooperation among firms, unions, and regional governments.[53] For instance, in Valencia the industrial structure, based on a very uneven territorial distribution of SMEs with low technological intensity of production, offered an ideal profile for the development of cooperation and innovation processes. The combined pressure of technological change and the incorporation of Spain to the European Single Market pushed firms to develop dynamic interfirm cooperation mechanisms that have resulted in successful models, such as the ceramic tile industrial district located in Castellón (see Camisón and Molina 1998). In the Basque Country the cooperation of the regional government, firms, employers' association, and unions has led to the development of industrial clusters in sectors such as machine tools. There are also interesting examples in Catalonia and Madrid.[54] I turn to these cases in chapter 6.

Conclusion

This chapter has attempted to shed further light on the debate of how institutions evolve over time (Pierson 2004; Thelen 2004). In Spain institutional evolution has been the result of the actions from actors with particular interests that have been influenced by "changes in the broader social environment and the character of [the] actors themselves" (Pierson 2004, p. 108) and by coalition shifts.

It challenges traditional interpretations that view institutional change as a consequence of exogenous shocks (Olson 1982) and reaffirms the interpretation according to which institutional change is a dynamic process that can develop as part of an incremental but cumulative transformative process (Streeck and Thelen 2005). A period of uncertainty and competitive challenges has provided pressures on the Spanish social actors to experiment within the existing institutions. They have added new elements that have altered the institutions' overall trajectory and shifted them toward new goals and functions. This is another instance of institutional adaptation in which institutions that were created for a set of purposes have been redirected to serve different goals (Thelen 2004, pp. 292–294). For instance, an institutional mechanism that originated with the goal to control wages has become an instrument of coordination aimed at changing the prevalent economic model based on low wages.

In addition, the chapter examined the ways in which exogenous factors induce the social partners to review their positions and strategies vis-à-vis existing arrangements. It stresses the need to complement neoinstitutional explanations with a new set of hypotheses concerning actors' behavior (see Regini 2000, p. 9). The institutional structure of the Spanish economy combined with the competitive challenges faced by Spanish firms has made it more advantageous for them to support a CME model. This strategic shift on the part of firms constitutes an institutional mechanism to support business competitiveness through coordination and social bargaining. It is a refection of the interest of Spanish firms to reconcile the need to control costs through more flexibility in hiring practices and the need for cooperative relations at the firm level in order to remain competitive. The Spanish case thus confirms that "responses by the European economies differ according to the trade-off for their firms between deregulation and concertation, between more market and more adequate supply of collective goods" (Regini 2000, p. 19).

Spanish firms have decided that while competitiveness was contingent on the increasing flexibility of labor and firms, it also depended on the ability of the national system in which they operate to provide collective goods—namely, education, training, wage coordination, and labor cooperation. Hence, they have acknowledged that the crucial problem for their firms was the need to institutionalize further the production of collective goods. Consequently, firms have given priority to continuing social concertation and have supported cooperative strategies as instruments to further competitiveness. They understand that the most effective way to achieve wage moderation, increase competitiveness, and liberalize the labor market is through the acquiescence of unions.[55] Confrontation led to higher wages and the partial paralysis of the reform and liberalization processes in the second half of the 1980s and first half of the 1990s because unions mobilized in opposition to these reforms and were able to exercise a de facto veto power. Coordination, on the other hand, has resulted in wage moderation and has offered a gradual and stable path toward reform and liberalization of the labor market (Royo 2002, pp. 176–177). The state has played a crucial role in these processes facilitating (and participating in) the bargaining process, providing incentives to the actors and enacting legislation to implement the agreed reforms.

Developments within the international economic environment and within the domestic structure have changed the balance of power among the social actors. These changes have facilitated the emergence of new strategies among the social actors and have influenced their predisposition to negotiate and settle their differences through social bargaining. Preexisting institutions did not condition as much the choices made by the social actors. On the contrary, new emerging constraints and incentives to change have determined their interaction and strategies. In this regard, social bargaining is part of a "repertoire policy" available to social actors to respond to critical junctures, not merely the fixed mode of policy making underscored by the neocorporatist literature.[56]

As we will see in the next chapter, in a new economic and political context, trade union organizations have supported tripartite bargaining as a defensive strategy to retake the initiative and influence policy outcomes.

The analysis of the Spanish case confirms the thesis that in the context of structural constraints that influence the range of option available to them, strategic actors with their own interests design institutions. It shows that countries are not stuck in a particular pattern of labor relations and practices, thus rejecting institutional deterministic approaches and illustrating that although institutions are path dependent, they still offer constraints and opportunities for change. Indeed, institutions were still the object of political contestation and the industrial relations arena Spain is moving from "state capitalism" to "managed capitalism." Existing institutions affected the interests and strategic options available to the social actors and coalition shifts influenced institutional design.

Chapter 5

Unions and Economic Adjustment

Introduction

As we examined in chapter 3, the neocorporatist literature seemed to show in the 1970s that centralized social bargaining could mitigate the trade-offs between inflation and unemployment because it allows economic actors and governments to work together to resolve certain collective-action problems (Schmitter 1981; Cameron 1984; Bruno and Sachs 1985).[1] However, changes in the world economy have led other scholars to argue that the decline of Fordism and the liberalization and integration of financial markets have undermined the bases for social bargaining, thus confirming the undoing of Schmitter's "Century of Corporatism" (1974) (Pérez 1998; Royo 2000; Scharpf 1987; Iversen 1999). Yet this conclusion is challenged by the resurgence of national-level bargaining in a number of European states such as, Spain during the 1980s and 1990s.

This chapter analyses the resurgence of national-level social bargaining in Spain from the unions' perspective. As noted in the previous chapters social bargaining emerged in the 1970s, and after a breakdown in the second half of the 1980s, it resurfaced in the mid-1990s. While chapter 3 examined the question of how national-level social bargaining reemerged in Spain during the last decade despite unpropitious institutional and structural conditions from the business perspective; this chapter seeks to analyze why unions supported this development.[2]

The resurgence of social concertation in Spain has also been the result of the reorientation of the strategies of the unions. In the new context of the 1980s and 1990s, trade union organizations have supported tripartite bargaining as a defensive strategy to retake the initiative and influence policy outcomes. In addition, the resurgence of social bargaining has been fostered by a process of institutional learning, which led union leaders to conclude that previous confrontational strategies were detrimental to the interest of their constituencies, and threatened their own survival.

As we have seen, Spain offers an ideal venue for examining the relationship between corporatist arrangements and globalization because it is one of the few instances in which social bargaining emerged in an institutional and structural context markedly different from that of the small European states of Northern and Central Europe. The study of the Spanish case will confirm that the link between changes in the international economic environment and the process of domestic policy making also depends on domestic political and economic factors. They provide their own set of incentives for domestic actors to entertain certain political strategies.

Trade Unions in Spain[3]

Conflicts among unions during the transition to democracy in the late 1970s, rooted on historical factors, determined that there would be a pluralistic and competitive industrial relations setting in Spain.[4] In April of 1977 the Spanish Parliament approved the Free Union Association Act that recognized union freedoms.[5] When the government opened the Register of Union Organizations in 1977, *Comisiones Obreras* (CCOO), *Unión General de Trabajadores* (UGT), Unión Sindical Obrera (USO), and the Basque union *Euzko Langillen Alkartasuna-Solidaridad de Trabajadores Vascos* ELA-STV were all legalized. The government, following the Italian and French concept of "most representative union," developed mechanisms to guarantee the predominance of majority unions and established elections to work councils as the instrument to determine the representativeness of unions.[6] The approval of the Spanish Constitution in December of 1978 formalized the legal situation of unions and strengthened union and workers' rights (Arts. 7 and 28). In addition, the 1980 Workers' Statute established a system of dual representation based on trade unions' sections and work councils.[7] Finally, the new Organic Law on Trade Union Freedom, passed in 1985, established that union "representativity" would be determined in work council elections instead of membership.[8]

The 1978 election to the work councils established the superiority of the CCOO, closely followed by the UGT and distantly by the USO (see table 5.1). The ELA-STV received 11.6 percent of the vote in the Basque country and the CNT refused to participate in the elections. These elections confirmed a new landscape based on the existence of a pluralistic union setting dominated

Table 5.1 Elections to the work councils (1978–99)

Unions	1978	1980	1982	1986	1990	1995	1999
CCOO	34.57	30.86	33.40	34.54	36.9	37.79	37.68
UGT	21.70	29.27	36.70	40.92	42.0	34.92	36.76
USO	3.77	8.68	4.6	3.80	2.9	3.68	—
ELA-STV	0.90	2.20	3.30	2.92	3.2	3.62	—
INTG/CIG	—	1.20	1.20	1.20	1.5	1.76	—
Other unions	20.80	12.20	8.70	9.95	7.1	—	—
Nonunion	18.13	14.60	12.10	7.6	3.8	3.27	—

Sources: Data from the *Ministerio de Trabajo and Seguridad Social* and *Confederación de CC.OO.*

by two major confederations. This system resulted in what has been called a "representative duopoly" (Escobar 1995, p. 155), with the CCOO and UGT dominating the labor relations' landscape.[9] The practical consequence of these legal provisions has been the emergence of a semiduopolist structure with intense interunion competition.[10] In the nationwide elections to work councils, only UGT and CCOO have received more than 80 percent of the vote. Subsequent elections to the work councils confirmed the supremacy of the CCOO and UGT.[11] By 1982 UGT had surpassed CCOO in the number of representatives elected in work council elections (see table 5.1).[12]

In Spain unionism is still marked by a legacy of deep political, ideological, and geographical cleavages. These factors account for the trade unions' differing levels of development and strength across autonomous regions, which in turn affect internal decision-making and collective bargaining. For UGT and CCOO, the four largest regions of Andalusia, Catalonia, Madrid, and Valencia contribute the largest share of membership (Van der Meer 2000, pp. 583–585).

UGT and CCOO have a double representation structure by sectors (the "vertical structure" or "professional structure") and by areas (the "horizontal" or "territorial" structure). These structures are then merged into the union leadership (named the Union or Confederation). At the firm level, union action is implemented by the union section (the *sección sindical*), which is elected by the union members in the workplace. Beyond the firm, the local level of the vertical structure is formed by the federation and the horizontal structure by the area union (the *unión comarcal*). This organization is replicated at higher levels—region, province, autonomous region (the top level for unions operating within an autonomous region), and nation (Führer 1996, p. 151; Royo 2000, pp. 125–128). Representatives at all levels are chosen in elections that take place in assemblies and congresses. At a national level, 50 percent of the delegates come from the federations and the other 50 percent from the regions. The executive committees are elected by delegates from the autonomous regions in national congresses that take place every four years[13] (for a detailed analysis of the internal organization of unions see Cabrero Morán 1997).

In Spain there are also independent trade union organizations, particularly in the service sector (i.e., in the medical sector, air, railway, technical professions, public sector, and urban transport). Many of them are organized at the peak level by CSI-CSIF (*Confederación Sindical Independiente de Funcionarios*, the Independent Syndical Confederation of Civil Servants). Within the autonomous communities only ELA-STV (*Euzko Langillen Alkartasuna-Solidaridad de Trabajadores Vascos*, the Solidarity of Basque Workers) in the Basque Country and CIG (*Confederación Intersindical Gallega*), which is strong in Galicia, have surpassed the 15 percent threshold established by law to be considered representative unions.

The emergence and unraveling of the first phase of neocorporatist concertation (1977–86) culminated in the general strike of December 14, 1988, when the unions jointly took a stand against the economic policies of the

PSOE government (see chapter 2). During those years CCOO and UGT competed fiercely for dominance of the labor movement. Whereas UGT, which emerged very weak from the dictatorship, embraced concertation as a strategy for building up union organizational power and gaining the support from less militant workers. CCOO clung to the model of union as a social movement, and only signed two of the agreements (the ANE and the AI). The unraveling of concertation after 1986 (see chapter 2, and Royo 2000) culminated in a dramatic divorce of the Socialist government from the UGT, which marked a major shift in union strategies. The general strike of 1988 signaled a new strategic shift on the part of the unions. It confirmed unions' autonomy from political parties and their commitment to "unity of action." This new approach has diminished the level of competition between UGT and CCOO, which henceforth worked together to advance their objectives. This strategy crystallized into the Priority Union Proposal (*Plataforma Sindical Prioritaria*), a joint platform in which the unions set their agenda for the 1990s. This document articulated a list of demands around five encompassing themes: employment, welfare, income redistribution, participatory rights, and industrial relations. They sustained this unitary strategy throughout the 1990s and the first seven years of the new century and have signed new tripartite agreements with the government and employers. As a matter of fact, at the dawn of the new millennium there are many more things that bring together both unions than separate them. Despite differences over the years, their leaders have expressed that the unity of action strategy is irreversible and even talk about a future merging of the two main confederations.[14]

During the dictatorship, membership in the "vertical" unions was compulsory in Spain, except in those sectors, such as the civil service, in which union organizations were illegal. Hence, the collapse of the authoritarian regime allowed unions to "inherit" a large number of members. In addition, the disappearance of the official unions, which motivated workers to join new unions that could articulate their demands, coupled with the euphoria associated with the transition to democracy and the wish by Spanish workers to participate in public life and contribute to the democratization processes, fostered the high levels of union affiliation (see Fishman 1990; Miguélez 1995). Consequently, during the first years of the transition process, affiliation was high. In Spain at the peak of this period, UGT and CCOO claimed to have organized around 2 million supporters each, or one-third of all Spanish workers (Van der Meer 2000, p. 587).

This development, however, proved short-lived. The political and economic conditions for union participation deteriorated sharply in the second half of the 1970s. After the height of the transition period, unions failed to live up to the expectations of their affiliates and were not able to achieve outcomes favorable to their members. They also failed to develop services to affiliates that would have made membership more attractive. Therefore, once the transition euphoria dissipated, workers decided to cancel their memberships.

The economic crisis of the late 1970s and early 1980s, which resulted in increasing unemployment, the significant rise in temporary work, and informal employment in the black economy, coupled with the growth of the service sector and the underground economy, as well as the emergence of new forms of business organizations wherein traditional blue-collar unskilled workers were no longer dominant, have also been mentioned as some of the reasons for the sharp decline in union membership during those years. Other explanations for falling membership include poor member services, interunion competition, union politicization, and employers' pressures. Finally, other authors have stressed the impact of the statutory extension of collective agreements to nonmembers. Since all workers benefit from the agreements, they have little incentive to join trade unions and pay union fees (Malo 2001; Bover, García Perea, and Portugal, 1997).

As a result of these developments, trade union density in Spain is even lower at 18.6 percent after a sharp decline throughout the 1980s (ILO, 1997). In Spain the dramatic decline in union membership (see table 5.2) was accelerated by legal provisions that allow nonunion members to profit from *erga omnes* extension of collective bargaining.

As I indicated before, since all workers benefit from the agreements, they have little incentive to join trade unions and pay unions fees. By 1980 unions reported figures showing that less than one-tenth of Spanish workers paid dues to either confederation. This downward tendency, however, was reversed in Spain in the 1990s. The success of the general strike of 1988, coupled with the economic recovery of the mid-1980s, ignited new affiliations with unions in Spain.[15] Between 1986 and 1989 affiliation increased by 44 percent for the UGT and by 33 percent for the CCOO (Escobar 1995, p. 158; Pérez-Díaz 1985; Führer 1996; Moscoso 1995). According to unions' figures, union density in Spain rose from 16.1 percent in 1991 to 19.8 percent in 1998 before declining again to 17.8 percent in 1997 (see table 5.2). Overall the union membership trend for the 1990s stagnated or slightly receded. About one-fifth of Spanish workers are union members, thus making Spain (after France) the Western European country with the lowest rate of union organization when measured in terms of dues-paying members (Van der Meer 2000, p. 587). Finally, it is important to emphasize that although overall membership has increased in recent years, membership levels and union resources remain comparatively low. Union density is still higher in the larger industrial firms and public services, and it is lower in small

Table 5.2   Reported membership by selected unions in Spain (1981–97) (000)

	1981	1985	1989	1991	1993	1995	1997
CC.OO	389.2	356.1	439.4	579.8	648.9	661.9	698.2
UGT	208.2	345.3	494.3	669.3	750.4	655.3	672.2
USO	—	—	—	74.7	76.7	78.7	79.8
CSI-CSIF	—	—	—	109.7	141.1	134.9	149.6
ELA-STV	—	—	—	—	83.2	88.7	86.5
Union Density %	—	—	—	16.1	19.8	18.2	17.8

Source: Van der Meer (2000), Table SP.D, p. 588 and Table SP.19, pp. 602–603.

Table 5.3   Union bargaining coverage in Spain (1992–2006)

	1992	1993	1994	1995	1996	1997	1998	1999	2006
Firm level	15.0	13.5	13.65	13.7	13.1	11.9	11.9	11.1	11.9
Other levels	85.0	86.5	86.4	86.3	86.9	88.1	88.1	88.9	88.1

Source: MTAS, *Estadísticas de Convenios Colectivos.*

private industries and in the service sector. Unions have particular difficulties organizing new workers, the unemployed, unskilled workers, and those under temporary contracts (Richards and Polavieja 1997).

It is important to stress, however, that affiliation is quite irrelevant in determining the strength of Spanish unions. Since the conditions agreed upon in collective agreements are legally binding, as a minimum, for all workers in the appropriate economic and geographical domain and occupation regardless of union affiliation, the advantages of being a union member are scant. Hence, according to most scholars, a better proxy for union power is the coverage of collective bargaining as a percentage of the total number of employees in a sector (or *union coverage*), which has been increasing steadily since the mid-1980s (see table 5.3) (see Royo 2000, p. 120; Bover, Bentolila, and Arellano 2000).

Explaining Labor's Return to Social Bargaining

The decision by Spanish unions to return to the bargaining table can be seen, for the most part, as a defensive strategy motivated by their weakening at the firm level as a result of structural and political changes. It was also motivated by their failure to translate their capacity to effectively mobilize workers in a response to manpower policies to liberalize the labor market into legislation or government action from 1989 to 1993. In Spain, the labor movement failed to translate its unity into effective power as manifested in their inability to resist legal reform initiatives aimed at liberalizing the labor markets (i.e., the 1994 *Reforma Laboral*). In other words, with its support for tripartite concertation agreements, labor sought to mitigate the decline in its bargaining power at the firm- and enterprise levels. This section argues that the changing balance of power affected the predisposition of the unions to pursue their strategies through a new set of institutions.[16]

The Increasing Labor Market Segmentation and Individualization of Labor Relations

In Spain following the unraveling of social concertation in 1987 (see Royo 2000), unions found themselves in a weak position, with very low membership concentrated in declining industries, dependant on state funding, and with low contractual powers. The weakening of trade union organizations at the firm level in Spain is manifested in the relative decline in union density, which hindered unions' capacity to mobilize workers in a response to manpower policies to liberalize the labor market. The proportion of union members in the labor force in Spain declined sharply following the transition to democracy. Since the early 1980s trade union membership has remained low and changes in membership have been mostly caused by structural changes in certain sectors. This downward tendency, however, was reversed in Spain in the 1990s. The net union density rate in Spain rose from 13.32 percent in 1990 to 16.38 percent in 1993 (before falling to 15.82 percent in 1994), challenging the thesis of union decline in the Spanish context (see Jordana 1996). A detailed analysis of this trend, however, reinforces the thesis of this chapter that trade unions' weaknesses forced them to seek the support from new constituencies through the return to national social bargaining.

First, the economic crisis of the early 1990s, and increasing competition forced Spanish firms to develop new strategies, seeking greater flexibility, mobility, and the externalization of production to small nonunionized firms. As we saw in chapter 4, product decentralization was reflected in the growth in the number of small firms (under 50 workers), and their share of employment (Fraile 1999, p. 280; Richards and Polavieja 1997, p. 31). In these sectors the level of unionization was only half of that in all manufacturing. In addition, most of the new jobs have been created in the service sector (employment in the service sector grew from 7.4 million people in 1991 to over 10.5 million people in 2003), and construction (from 1.3 million in 1991 to 2 million in 2003) (see figure 5.1).

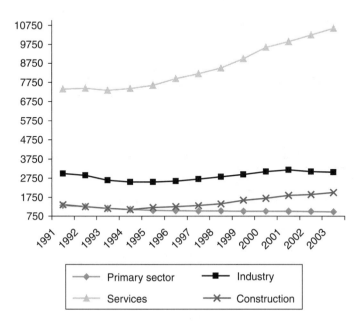

Figure 5.1   Evolution of employment by economic sectors, 1991–2003 (000, annual average)
Source: INE, *Encuesta de Población Activa*.

These are sectors in which unions have had difficulties increasing affiliation (see table 5.4).

The combination of all of these factors weakened unions because it led to the increasing individualization of labor relations, and gave firms more flexibility in the deployment of labor through mobility, overtime,[17] rotation, and part-time work. (see table 5.5).

At the same time, in the last three years, the proportion of workers working part-time has increased notably, reaching 12 percent in 2006.[18] Most of them are women (80 percent), and the large majority work part-time because they have not been able to find another job (31.9 percent) or they are studying (24.7) (CES 2006, pp. 310–311).

In addition, the weakening of unions caused by the increasing individualization of employment relations was further hastened by the spectacular growth of temporary employment. As we saw in chapter 2, from 1984 through 1997 the number of temporary contracts increased from 7.5 percent

Table 5.4   Union density (%) by sector (1991–97)

Sector	1997	1992	1993	1994	1995	1996	1997
Agriculture	9.4	12.6	12.6	13.6	11.8	12.0	11.3
Mining, manufacturing, utilities	21.8	23.4	27.4	27.3	25.6	25.2	24.3
Construction	9.6	11.7	13.8	13.6	11.5	11.3	10.7
Commerce	6.3	7.7	7.8	7.4	6.7	6.5	6.4
Transport and communications	31.9	36.3	38.4	38.0	34.6	33.3	31.9
Finance and business services	20.0	22.1	23.0	23.7	20.5	19.9	20.2
Public and private services	10.0	11.2	12.6	13.1	13.5	13.6	13.7
Total	16.1	18.1	19.8	19.5	18.2	17.8	17.8

Source: Van Der Meer (2000). Data from UGT, CCOO, CSI-CSIF, ELA-STV, and CIG.

Table 5.5   Wage earners and occupied in part-time work

Year	Occupied		Wage earners	
	Thousands	% of Total	Thousands	% of Total
1996	982.8	7.7	709.6	7.3
1997	1,050.7	7.9	794.7	7.8
1998	1,074.5	7.8	838.9	7.9
1999	1,158.6	8.0	928.7	8.1
2000	1,214.8	7.9	986.9	8.0
2001	1,266.6	7.9	1,036.8	8.1
2002	1,277.8	7.9	1,077.3	8.2
2003	1,336.4	8.0	1,129.3	8.3

Source: INE, *Encuesta de Población Activa*.

to 39 percent of the total and although there has been a small decrease in recent years it still stands at 31.8 percent in 2007. (see table 5.6). In addition, almost 50 percent of the staff is temporary in small firms, and the country has the highest level of temporary work in the EU—currently 33.69 percent of the salaried workforce (see Bentolila, Segura, and Toharia 1991, pp. 237–238; Richards and Polavieja 1997, pp. 13–23).[19]

The increasing level of temporality has clear effects on workers' involvement with the unions and it has profound consequences on the structure of the labor market, leading to a growing segmentation of workers between insiders (workers on permanent contracts with more stable, secure, and long-term prospects) and the unemployed and outsiders (workers on temporary contracts in a more precarious situation) (Richards and Polavieja 1997, pp. 32–39).[20] Labor segmentation provided a buffer that insulated permanent workers from layoffs, allowing them to bargain for higher wages, and led to the dualization of the labor force, thus accentuating the insider-outsider division within the national workforce. In addition, increasing segmentation was accentuated by industrial restructuring, which led to the closure of large plants and caused massive layoffs, thus shrinking further the manufacturing sector—traditionally the source of union strength (i.e., in 1995 only 18 percent of CCOO's members were temporary workers at a time when 34 percent of Spanish workers were temporary; see Jordana 1996, pp. 21–22).

These developments were particularly worrisome for unions because they constrained their bargaining strength and deprived them of members. The unions eventually realized that a continuation of this pattern threatened their survival, and decided that they had to counter them. In the end, the combination of high unemployment and the large number of temporary workers, coupled with changes in the occupational structure and the individualization of employment relations, forced Spanish unions to reassess their approaches. Union leaders realized that if they wanted to bridge the divide between insiders and outsiders and extend their influence beyond their core constituency, they had to develop a new strategy with a general commitment to the reduction of unemployment and the promotion of greater job security. In other words, with these new agreements unions sought to counter the conventional wisdom that views them as entrenched institutions that promote

Table 5.6 Workers by contract type (1996–2006) (000)

Type	1996	1998	2000	2001	2002	2003	2005	2006
Indefinite	6,383.5	7,125.7	8,354.7	8,735.4	9,066.7	9.637,7	10,333.1	10,691.4
Temporary	3,273.4	3,525.6	3,931.1	4,051.4	4,075.1	4,489.7	5,169.0	5,516.7
Temporary rate*	33.9	33.1	32.0	31.7	31.0	31.8	33.3	34.0

Note: * Temporary level as a percentage of temporary workers of all workers.
Source: INE, *Encuesta de Población Activa*.

the interests of insiders (see Jimeno and Toharia 1993; Bentolila and Dolado 1994), while helping to improve macroeconomic conditions that would contribute to economic recovery. This led them to develop a broader strategy with which to tackle unemployment and promote job stability through national social bargaining with the government and/or employers.

In order to achieve these objectives, unions refocused their attention on the firms to increase membership. They also developed unitary bargaining platforms that focused on certain strategic areas—temporary contracts, unemployment, work organization, training, information rights, and health and safety—aimed at bridging the divide between insiders and outsiders. These platforms would be the objective of national bargaining with employers and/or the government and would lead to the reemergence of national social bargaining. This new approach signaled a strategic shift on the part of the unions, which were now willing to accept more internal flexibility in the organization and deployment of labor within the workplace, in exchange for greater employment stability (Fraile 1999, pp. 297–299).[21]

In this regard the 1997 *Interconfederal Agreement for Employment Stability* (AIEE) was a direct response to the dramatic increase of temporary workers in Spain since the 1984 reform of the Workers' Statute.[22] As we examined in chapter 4, in a context of relatively high dismissal costs, employers have been using these contracts as instruments to introduce more flexibility in their labor force. They are increasingly recognizing, however, the perverse consequences of this development (Jiménez Aguilar 1997, 12–13).[23] Hence, the view that a new regulation of permanent contracts was needed in order to increase employment stability and minimize the increasing segmentation of the labor market gained adepts among employer and union leaders. Although at the beginning of the bargaining process the negotiating platform introduced by the unions did not include this new approach, the negotiating process and the final agreement demonstrated the unions' new strategic outlook. In reference to this new strategy CCOO stated that

> Bargaining with the CEOE, on the one hand, and with the Government, on the other, appears from the outset as a strategic challenge for the future of the syndical movement. To be able to respond to workers' demands, and to do so guaranteeing that the union gains contractual capabilities, are essential questions. Therefore the first task, chronologically and quantitatively, was to give impetus to a multidimensional bargaining process. A process born out of the syndical initiative, which responds to the need to address the problems of the less favored groups, and that at the same time, reinforces the strategy of unity of action with UGT.
>
> This process was born on May 9th of 1996 in response to the directives from the 6th Congress, which led the union to focus on the improvement of employment conditions and collective bargaining as priority objectives, and also as part of the campaign "For stable employment and with rights" launched in the first months of that year. In sum, [we developed this process] with the objective to influence employment conditions, which currently due to the high levels unemployment, temporality, and turnout deepen the differences in working

conditions among different collectives, provoke a social cohesion deficit, fragment industrial relations, promote disloyal business competition based in lower labor costs, and relegate quality as a secondary source of competitiveness. (CCOO 2000, pp. 24–25)

The same strategic approach applied to the negotiation and signing of the 2006 *Agreement for Improvement in the Quality and Growth of Employment* (AMCE). With this agreement the unions sought to reduce the number of temporary contracts (as a result of the agreement, the Workers' Statute established a provision according to which contracts of any employee who has been the subject of two or more temporary contracts that add up to more than two years during a two-and-half-year span will automatically become indefinite contracts). The union leaders attribute the high levels "of investment in sectors with intensive labor work and low productivity" to the high level of temporary work, and with this agreement they seek to contribute to a shift away from the predominant low-cost and low-productivity model.[24]

Pressures to Articulate Further the Collective Bargaining System

Management recourse to manpower policies based upon unstable, fixed-term contracts led to the appearance of contradictory tendencies in the labor market. While average real wages grew moderately (see chapters 2 and 4), a tight labor market in some areas of rapid employment growth (particularly in the case of services, banking, and insurance) led to increasing bargaining power in favor of certain workers who were willing to negotiate away from the collective bargaining process (Stoleroff 1992, p. 138). At the same time, it was also very significant that the sectors that came to take much of the lead in wage-setting were ones over which the national unions had lower levels of control. (i.e., the service and construction sectors) (Pérez 1998, p. 17). In addition, as we have seen, in the service sector the level of unionization was only half of that in all manufacturing, reflecting the small size of most firms (see Richards and Polavieja 1997). These developments were reinforced by the economic crisis of the early 1990s, which resulted in sharp increases in unemployment, and further eroded labor's capacity at the level of firm and branch collective bargaining. All these changes increased pressures on unions to seek a new articulation of collective bargaining that would allow them to retake the initiative in the wage setting process.

Pressures to seek a new articulation of the collective bargaining system were hastened by the passing out of the remaining Labor Ordinances. As noted in chapter 4, the 1994 Labor Reform, which also broadened the content of collective bargaining, shifted powers to the market because it repealed the labor ordinances and gave the social actors freedom to negotiate new terms of employment previously regulated by law, thus allowing employers to push for a new legal framework that would facilitate the individualization of employment relations and the marginalization of work councils (see figure 5.2).[25]

- — Monitor the implementation of labor law, social security, employment and health and safety regulations, and conditions of work established by agreement or custom and practice, to see that they are applied correctly;
- — Take the appropriate legal steps in pertinent cases;
- — Participate in welfare measures for workers and their families organized by the company based on collective agreements;
- — Work together with management to ensure the fulfillment of productivity targets;
- — Inform the workforce of changes or developments might that may affect them;
- — Conclude company or workplace agreements;
- — Call a strike in the establishment in which they operate.

Figure 5.2   The role of works councils in Spain according to the Workers' Statute
Source: EIRO.

This development put pressure on unions to get back to the bargaining table to stem this threat. With their support for these macro agreements, labor sought to relieve the decline in its bargaining power at the workplace level, and to regain the initiative in the collective bargaining process, while mitigating the difficulties that they were facing in organizing workers in the workplace. With the agreement of 1997, the union leaders supported publicly the need to strengthen the collective bargaining system and to foster collective bargaining within the enterprises.[26] CCOO included this goal as part of its rational to pursue social bargaining: ". . . with the objective to influence the collective bargaining system debilitated due to the existing coverage gaps, as well as the excessive atomization, and the disarticulation that currently exist" (CCOO 2000, p. 25).

The Failure of Confrontational Strategies

The strategic shift in favor of centralized social bargaining was also motivated by the unions' failure to translate their unity into effective power as manifested in their inability to resist legal reform initiatives aimed at liberalizing the labor market. Union leaders came to the conclusion that their confrontational strategies were eroding their influence in the policy-making process and the support from their constituencies.

With the organization (and the massive success) of the 1988 general strike, the two main confederations (UGT and CCOO) solidified a new strategy based on three pillars: unity of action, the abandonment of social concertation, and the appeal to new constituencies to broaden their bases of support (see Fraile 1999, pp. 286–287). The Socialist government shocked by the success of the strike reacted by shelving the youth employment plan that had triggered the strike, increasing wages for public sector employees and pensioners to compensate for the 1988 deviation in targeted inflation, and signing an agreement with the unions in 1990 on pensions, unemployment benefits, public sector wages, minimum wages, and bargaining rights for public sector workers. The success of the strike allowed unions to regain a role in the political arena, which helped them to reverse their organizational decline. They were unable, however, to reverse the government's manpower policy initiatives.

In the early 1990s, the struggle between the unions and the government centered on the ways to achieve the Maastricth criteria for EMU membership. The Socialists' convergence plan led to two more general strikes. The first one, which occurred in May 1992, took place over the so-called *decretazo*—a government decree establishing cuts in unemployment coverage by reducing the amount and length of benefits, tightening eligibility conditions, and increasing the required period of work to collect benefits from six months to one year. The second one took place in January 1994 over a government proposal to reform labor laws that sought to make working conditions flexible and increase the scope of collective bargaining. The 1994 reform removed restrictions on mobility, decentralized collective bargaining, eased dismissals (it broadened the dismissal causes to include organizational, technological, and productive reasons), legalized temp agencies, repealed the remaining labor ordinances by 1995, and expanded the types of temporary contracts (it introduced a new "apprenticeship contract" for youth under 25, and a new flexible part-time contract free of payroll taxes). The reaction of the unions to the unilateral reforms of the government was to force its hand through the intensification of industrial conflict and the increasing politicization of unions' strategies. At the same time, they attempted to derail the implementation of the reforms during collective bargaining, intensified industrial conflict, and organized general strikes. Although the general strikes were successful (e.g., between 3 and 5 million workers supported the January 1994 strike in Spain) and the unions demonstrated, once again, their mobilization capacity, they did have limited political impact and the government reforms were finally enacted. Indeed, increasing mobilization and union unity in Spain did not lead to labor victories (see table 5.7)

Unions also tried to influence the electoral process. In successive elections union leaders, who felt they had a responsibility to alter the parliamentary balance, called for a punishing vote against the government to pressurize it to give in to their demands (see Espina 1999). This strategy, however, was not translated into political successes in the electoral arena. On the contrary, the parliamentary elections that followed the general strikes in the 1980s led to the reelection of the incumbent government up to 1996 (the PSOE won twice—in 1989 and 1993). The failure of this strategy demonstrated that manifestations of opposition against specific governmental policies on the parts of the citizens were not incompatible with electoral support to the government that has adopted these policies.[27]

In the end, this confrontational strategy failed to influence policy outcomes, and higher wage demands and industrial conflict contributed to deteriorating economic conditions and higher unemployment. At the same time, such confrontational strategies left unions virtually outside of the policy-making process, with little influence over the course of the reforms. The failure of the Spanish unions to stop labor law reform and force a political

Table 5.7 Industrial conflict in Spain (1990–2006)

Year	Number of strikes	Number of participants (000)	Days lost (000)
1990	1,231	864	2,442
1991	1,552	1,944	4,421
1992	1,296	5,169	6,247
1993	1,131	997	2,013
1994*	890	5,428	6,255
1995	866	570	1,443
1996	807	1,078	1,553
1997	670	577	1,529
1998	618	672	1,264
1999	739	1,125	1,477
2000	727	2,061	3,577
2002*	729	1,242	1,917
2002	684	4,528	4,938
2003	674	728.4	789
2004	707	555.8	4,472
2005	669	331.3	758
2006	664	437.2	691

Note: * Includes general strikes.
Sources: CES: *España, Memoria Sobre la Situación Socioeconómica y Laboral.* Various years. Data from MTSS: *Estadísticas de Huelgas y Cierres Patronales,* and MTAS: *Boletín de Estadísticas Laborales.*

crisis through continued social mobilization forced them to reevaluate their strategies and adopt a more conciliatory stance that included resuming partial tripartite agreements with the government and the CEOE. The CCOO's leader recognized the limits of confrontational strategies when he stated that general strikes "are very extreme instruments of syndical action, very strong, as well as very difficult to manage, and to follow up the day after."[28] By promoting centralized bargaining and a new articulation of the collective bargaining system, they were making sure that peak confederations would remain significant players. José María Fidalgo, CCOO leader, confirmed,

> We are coming from a very conflictive period in which we have achieved very few of our objectives despite successive general strikes. From CCOO's perspective we are interested in social bargaining because imposed reforms erode the power and influence of the union. They also eliminate rights that later on are very difficult to recover. Therefore, we do not want to be spectators, but instead "jump into the airplane cabin," and participate in the changes. We want to participate and fulfill a social function that will legitimate our role.[29]

Antonio Ferrer, member of UGT's Executive Committee, confirmed, "We want to participate in the policy-making process and influence labor and socio-political issues."[30]

Internal Changes within Unions

This strategic shift was further hastened by the internal changes experienced by the two main confederations, with UGT attempting to turn the page on the union involvement in a corruption scandal, and CCOO trying to overcome internal ideological differences. These problems led to the emergence of new leadership in both unions that sought to strengthen the unity of action strategy while resuming partial agreements with the government and the employers' association. Between 1994 and 1996 there was a dramatic transformation of the union landscape motivated by the results of the work council elections and internal changes within each major trade union confederation.

As we have seen, following the general strike of 1988, Nicolás Redondo, UGT's secretary general, and the group of leaders that supported him, decided to pursue a confrontational strategy against the government. This decision was motivated by their disenchantment with the Socialist government policies and their conviction that their previous moderate stance has not benefited workers (Royo 2000). This strategic shift coincided with the election of Antonio Gutiérrez as secretary general of CCOO in the Congress that took place in November of 1987. As a result of his election, the more radical sector led by Antonio Moreno, lost the hegemony within the union. This sector, however, retained significant power until the 1992 Congress, because it still controlled secretariats such as employment, institutional relations, and collective bargaining. Gutiérrez, who represented a more modern and moderating outlook, came to power with the commitment to reestablish the "unity of action" with UGT. Consequently, between 1988 and 1991, coinciding with a period of economic expansion, the unions followed a confrontational stance and refused to negotiate centralized agreements, giving instead the initiative in wage negotiations to their sectoral federations.

One of the main consequences of these developments was the increasing autonomy of unions from the political parties. While UGT had followed the Socialist Party, PSOE's strategic lead after the party's victory in the 1982 elections (some of UGT's leaders had even been elected to Congress under the PSOE lists) and had subordinated the interests of the union to the party's, the general strike of December of 1998 drove a wedge between the party and the union that culminated with the final breakdown in the relationship (Gillespie 1990). The Communist Party, PCE (and later on *Izquierda Unida* a collation of leftists' parties that included the PCE), still exercised considerable influence within CCOO. The election of Gutiérrez, who supported an autonomous stance from the PCE/IU, would start to change this dynamic. By the mid-1990s, the process of separation between the unions and the political parties was a reality (Royo 2000).

The unwillingness of the union to negotiate with the government during the economic crisis of 1992–93 led the socialist government to issue a unilateral labor reform in 1994 motivated by the need to confront that dramatic surge in unemployment (over 20 percent). The reaction of the trade unions to the unilateral labor reform of 1994 illustrates the micro debates that took place within the labor movement. Within CCOO the confrontational group led by Moreno presented a report (supported by *Izquierda Unida*) to the Confederal Council of the union on February 1994 in which they proposed an all-out confrontation with the socialist government. This report concluded that the alliance between the socialists and the nationalist parties had led to conservative policies that had to be confronted head-on by the union in order to fulfill its mission. This was a continuation of the confrontational stance of the previous years. With this strategy they sought to complement the political opposition of *Izquierda Unida* (now led by Julio Anguita) against the socialists. Gutiérrez, who was becoming increasingly convinced of the futility of this strategy, and wanted to strengthen the autonomy of the union vis-à-vis *IU*, opposed this view. The defeat of CCOO in the 1986 and 1990 syndical elections had already given him the opportunity to advance more moderating positions within the union,[31] and he had initiated the strategic shift in favor of social bargaining during the CCOO Congress of 1992, when the minority sector (which supported the confrontational stance advocated by UGT) lost further weight within the union.

The results of the 1994–95 syndical elections however, provoked a cataclysm within both unions. In Spain the work council elections determine the representativeness of unions, which happen to be the only institutions with the legal capacity to bargain at levels above the firm. This system provides a great deal of autonomy to the union confederations because their strength is not determined by the number of affiliates but, instead, by the number of votes that they receive in these elections. These elections provided a test of workers' support for the confrontational unitary strategies that unions had started in 1988. The results of the 1994–95 syndical elections, however, showed workers' discontent with this strategy: UGT and CCOO lost almost 40,000 work council delegates (out of the 186,500 delegates that had been elected from both unions in 1990, or 6.5 percent percentage points compared with the elections of 1990). In addition, UGT, which had been the winner of the previous syndical elections in 1986 and 1990 (at a time when the union supported a more moderate strategy), lost its dominant position in favor of CCOO, which emerged as the victor (CCOO won 37.8 percent of the delegates, and UGT, losing 7.3 percentage points from the previous elections, won 34.7 percent). Another worrisome development for the unions was the fact that only 203,002 syndical delegates were actually elected, out of a possible 433,946 (see table 5.8). This meant that the number of workers' representatives elected was below 50 percent and that more than half of the enterprises (particularly small- and medium-enterprises) would not have workers' representatives.[32] Finally, and this may be the most significant factor, in large companies with more than 250 workers, nonsyndical candidates registered a spectacular advance (a 20 percent gain) with 15,708 delegates (UGT won 11,204 and descended 19.3 percent, and CCOO 14,912, and descended 8.6 percent). As Espina (1999, pp. 386–387) indicates, the workers' message was obvious: they opposed the confrontational strategy of the main labor confederations, and by voting for nonsyndical candidates,

Table 5.8 Results of trade union elections, number of delegates elected (1978–2003)

Unions	1978	1980	1982	1986	1990	1995*	1999	2003
CCOO	66,540	50,817	47,016	56,965	87,738	77,348	81,314	81,314
UGT	41,897	48,194	51,672	66,411	99,737	77,112	76,382	110,495
ELA-STV	1,931	4,024	4,642	5,372	7,488	7,146	7,267	9,035
INTG/CIG	—	—	—	—	—	—	—	4,595
Other unions	25,953	22,053	25,058	28,726	33,901	42,351	49,739	46,073
Small unions	58,725	43,553	17,024	12,408	8,407	6,631	8,969	8,337

Note: * Since 1994 the elections do not take place during a three-month period like before. Instead it is an open process, although most of the elections take place during the last three months of the four-year period. There are new elections in 2007.
Sources: Data from the *Ministerio de Trabajo and Seguridad Social* and *EIRE*.

Spanish workers supported a strategy more centered on the specific problems of the firms.[33] These surprising results raised the potential of an alternative to the traditional unions, which provoked a serious alarm in the union leadership and led them to reconsider their strategies.

The results of the 1994–95 syndical elections proved that the confrontational strategy would not pay off electorally and also that the unions risked further erosion if they continued in this path. They validated the position of moderating groups with both trade unions and gave them the opportunity to seize the initiative and change the policy stance. In this new context, the leadership of CCOO, led by Gutiérrez, which had been pushing for a more moderate stance in the 1987 and 1992 union congresses, used these electoral results in the 1996 CCOO's Congress as evidence of the need to shift the union strategy in support of a more consensus-based strategy that would focus on labor and industrial problems and leave behind a political agenda (see Espina 1999, pp. 386–387). This push allowed Gutiérrez to marginalize the minority sector within the union, which still supported a confrontational strategy (they had the support of about 30 percent of the union), and to leave it out of the main executive positions within the union.[34] The defeat of this faction led to the new strategic shift in favor of social bargaining and the resurgence of social pacts.

In UGT this debate took place at a time when Nicolás Redondo was planning to retire from UGT as a result of internal problems, a development that would present an opportunity for the more moderate faction within UGT to take control. The 1995 Congress elected as a new more moderate leader Cándido Méndez, who had not been directly involved in the confrontation between the UGT and the PSOE's leaderships. This Congress witnessed a confrontation between the supporters of the ongoing confrontational strategy and other sectors of the union, led by the industry federations, which supported a more constructive and pragmatist strategy. This internal struggle finished with the incorporation of a significant number of delegates from the latter sectors, which shifted the balance of power within the executive bodies in favor of moderation.[35]

The debate within CCOO about social bargaining and the strategic direction of the union ragged on into the new millennium. CCOO held its seventh Congress in April 2000 and elected José María Fidalgo as Gutiérrez's successor (he could not run for reelection after 12 years at the helm due to term limits). The selection of Fidalgo with Gutiérrez's support was not without controversy. The secretary of the metalworkers' federation, Ignacio Fernández Toxo, had also wished to present his candidacy. Fidalgo won with 70 percent of the votes but was unable to win the support of the minority group that still supported a more radical strategy and did not want Fidalgo to continue the policies of his predecessor. The minority faction obtained 30 percent of the executive posts, but once again, it failed to win any secretariats and was not represented in the day-to-day management of the union.[36] Despite Fidalgo's pledge to work for the integration of the minority faction, his decision to negotiate new agreements with the conservative Popular Party's government exacerbated tensions with Moreno's faction.

The absolute majority of the PP government from 2000 to 2004 led to a more complicated context that hindered the relationship with the government. UGT and CCOO tried to negotiate unsuccessfully some form of regulation to provide greater protection for temporary workers and to penalize the abuse of temporary contracts. The government unilateral labor market reform of May 2002 met with the opposition from the unions and a general strike on June 20, 2002. The success of this strike led the government to withdraw its proposals and repeal the law.

This period also witnessed increasing turbulences between the two leading confederations. UGT refused to accept the agreement that CCOO reached with the government and employers in 2001 to reform the state pension system,[37] and CCOO refused to support a two-hour general strike organized by UGT in April 2003 to oppose the involvement of Spain in the war in Iraq.

While UGT has remained quite stable internally, the situation has deteriorated further within CCOO. The confederation held its eighth Congress in April 1994 and this time there were three groups among the delegates: Fidalgo's group with 60 percent of the delegates, Moreno's with 23 percent, and a new group led by Rodolfo Benito (a former member of Fidalgo's team who had left in 2002 due to differences of opinion) with 17 percent of the delegates. Differences among these groups revolved around the distribution of power within the union and accusations about the lack of respect to opinions from minorities and regional federations (in which the minority tendencies are in the majority, such as Madrid). The most important debate, however, was, once again, about the bargaining stance of the union. The critics accused Fidalgo of being too keen on reaching agreements and to accept pacts that are very detrimental to workers (like the one on pensions that was opposed by UGT). Indeed, there is a clear divide between the minority groups who seek to use conflict as a bargaining tool to achieve benefits to workers, and the majority one, which views negotiations and social bargaining as a way to achieve favorable outcomes for workers. In addition, the majority rejects the overly political outlook about the role of the union of the minority. These positions have widened the differences about the strategic orientation of the union. In the end Fidalgo was reelected with 59 percent of the vote against the 29 percent obtained by Moreno. The program of action for the next four years, however, received 78 percent of the votes. This program emphasizes the need to improve employment and maintain the system of social protection.

In the end, the failure of labor confrontational strategies of the late 1980s and early 1990s, which contributed to the deterioration of economic conditions and aggravated the employment crisis of the early 1990s, led Spanish unions to reevaluate their strategies and complete a learning process that transformed their politics, strategies, and organizations in a radical way.

Liberalization and European Integration

The unions' strategic shift was accelerated as a result of the combined processes of economic liberalization, privatization, and European integration. As noted in chapter 4, these developments had a significant impact in the industrial relations setting because the prospect to meet the EMU criteria influenced the government's anti-inflationary stance, and wage bargaining became a cornerstone of the government's anti-inflation policies, therefore enhancing the political function of the unions and the concertation process. In the end unions supported wage moderation as an instrument to achieve the EMU criteria.[38]

At the micro level these processes have intensified competitive pressures and contributed to a shift in the balance of forces away from labor. Indeed, restructuring and the privatization of publicly held companies outsourcing, downsizing, and reengineering have provoked significant changes in Fordist large-scale companies that used to be labor fortresses, reducing employment in sectors and companies in which unions have been traditionally strong, and hence forcing them to reconsider their strategic outlook.[39]

To sum up, the combination of these developments resulted in a learning process on the part of the unions' leadership, who became convinced of the limits of a confrontational strategy, and led to new pragmatic and constructive strategies that facilitated their return to the bargaining table and thus the resurgence of social concertation in Spain (Espina 1999).[40] This new strategy was reinforced by the increasing autonomy of the unions from political parties.[41] The first result of this new approach was the signing of the bipartite agreement to resolve labor conflicts outside of the courts. This agreement signaled the beginning of a new phase marked by the resurgence of social bargaining. This new process was facilitated by the electoral victory in 1996 of the conservative Popular Party. This victory, by a very slim margin, had a dual effect. On the one hand, the government, which had included in the electoral program the need to negotiate with the unions, promoted social bargaining as an instrument of legitimization to dissipate fears about the course of its policies. On the other hand, the unions, which have had a sanguine breakdown with the Socialist government that had affected their outlook and made any agreement virtually impossible, took advantage of this new political environment to retake the initiative and play a role in the policy-making process. At the same time, the strategy to establish independent negotiating tables (in a way in which disagreements in one table would not hinder advances in others) and to start negotiating the issues over which the level of consensus among the social actors was greater facilitated the development of this bargaining process. This new dynamic facilitated bargaining, fostered consensus building among the social actors, and promoted the institutionalization of the process.

In a changing environment unions took advantage of a new political context that provided opportunities for political exchange at the national level. This process was facilitated by the emergence of new institutions that fostered consensus among the social actors. In the end, economic restructuring and the relative weakening of trade unionism may have—and this is the paradox—contributed to the institutionalization of industrial relations.

Conclusion

This chapter stresses the need to explain the social actors' attempts to develop new solutions and change outcomes. Spain lacks encompassing labor market institutions, yet social concertation flourished in the 1980s–1990s. Hence, the institutional context is not able per se to explain the behavior of Spanish actors. The analysis of this case confirms that the consolidation of concertation does not depend solely on the organization of the actors, but also on the interests and strategies of the social actors themselves. This chapter examined the ways in which exogenous factors induce the social partners to review their positions and strategies vis-à-vis existing arrangements. It stresses, again, the need to complement neoinstitutional explanations with a new set of hypotheses concerning actors' behavior (see Regini 2000, p. 9).

This chapter confirms the conclusion that the resurgence of social concertation in Spain has been the result of the reorientation of the strategies of the social actors. Developments within the international economic environment and within the domestic structure have changed the balance of power among the social actors. Economic and institutional changes have facilitated the emergence of new strategies among the social actors and influenced their predisposition to negotiate and settle their differences through social bargaining.

As we have seen, in a new economic and political context, trade union organizations have supported tripartite bargaining as a defensive strategy to influence policy outcomes. The decision by the unions to return to the bargaining table was for the most part a defensive one, motivated by their weakening at the firm level (evidenced by the relative decline in union density[42]) and their incapacity to effectively mobilize workers in a response to manpower policies to liberalize the labor market. Unions offered wage bargaining and social peace in exchange for participation in the decision-making process and benefits at the decentralized level. In other words, with their support for these macroeconomic agreements, labor sought to mitigate the decline in its bargaining power at the workplace level. With these pacts they have also tried to counteract the reduction in their capacity for collective action, which was a consequence of being sidelined by employers and governments, as well as the erosion of their influence in the policy-making process.

In addition, the resurgence of social bargaining has been fostered by a process of institutional learning and increasing autonomy by unions from political parties. This development also reflects an attempt by the social actors to reconcile the need to control costs through more flexibility in hiring practices and the need for cooperative relations at the firm level in order to remain competitive. In other words, these agreements have constituted an institutional mechanism to support business competitiveness through consultative practices (see Regini 2000).

Spanish unions did not face the same levels of resistance against these agreements (and particularly toward wage moderation) than unions in the Netherlands and other countries faced. First, the levels of membership were already very low and, therefore, they did not have much to lose. In addition, since the main trade-off (lower dismissals costs) did not affect older workers with permanent contracts (the core support of unions) the risk of further defections was very low. On the contrary, by addressing the main concern of temporary workers (more stable contracts) these agreements helped unions to build support from a younger generation of workers, women, and unemployed.

Chapter 6

Linking the Macro and the Micro: The Politics of Coordination and Institutional Reform at the Regional Level—The Basque Country

The Puzzle of Cooperation at the Regional Level

The previous chapters highlight how changing economic conditions, as well as the shifting interests of the economic actors, have promoted institutional changes at the national level that have promoted further coordination. They support the view that economic and institutional change is also the product of policy choices (Locke 1995). Indeed, political struggles have impacted policy choices.

The focus so far has been in developments at the macro level. Yet, in Spain there have also been remarkable cases of coordination among economic actors at the regional level. As we have seen, there are structural imbalances in economic conditions; however, in the ground Spanish firms have developed distinctive initiatives to compete more effectively and exploit niche areas in R&D. This chapter analyses some of these initiatives that have promoted coordination at the regional level. They have been the result of the response of economic actors to a common set of negative (or positive) externalities, and have led to innovative strategies and institutional changes that have promoted coordination. These regional initiatives show that despite similar political institutions and social structures, the economic actors have a range of resources and policy tools to address competitive challenges.

These innovative strategies have been possible in the context of the quasi-federal structure of the Spanish state that originated in the 1978 Constitution. The literature on federalism has noted how attempts by central governments to implement reforms create new opportunities (and constraints) for actors at the regional level (see McDermott 2005, p. 34). Like in Italy (Locke 1995), regional governments in Spain have played an "enhancing" role for the "third Spain" of small and interconnected business. Indeed, the development of separate regions in Spain has led to the diversification of industry and the development of regional strategies to attract investment. The Basque Country is an example of this approach.

In this chapter I seek to explore ways in which subnational factors promote the ability of socioeconomic actors to develop public-private institutions. I seek to address the following questions: First, what types of factors contributed to the institutional innovations that emerged in Spanish regions? Second, why were public and private actors able to build these new institutions? I argue that coordination at the regional level has been promoted by regional governments, who have played a crucial role. They have been triggered by new competitive challenges and fostered by polices that promote the solution of collective-action problems.

This chapter examines processes of institutional change in one Spanish region: the Basque Country, which has been particularly successful at forging new sustainable institutions and interfirm networks where the need for cooperation and the development of capabilities to respond to collective-action problems were lacking. Spanish regions have important differences with regard to their economic structure, political and socioeconomic organizations, institutions, legal regimes, and sectoral regulations. The examination of this case helps capture the diversity of political and economic models within Spain, the variance in the ways the regional politics interact with the national ones, and the conditions under which institutional cooperation emerges at the subnational level (McDermott 2005; Snyder 2001).

In the Basque Country the process of institutional change was shaped by the capacities of the local governments, the existing social structure, and political strategies and incentives that led the economic actors to reshape their strategies. This chapter shows that the development of institutional coordination at the regional level is a collective-action problem conditioned by political, economic, and social factors. In response to new economic and competitive challenges the Basque regional government and the economic actors have developed innovative capacities that have promoted further coordination. They have built a constellation of private-public institutions that have helped firms address collective-action problems. This was a remarkable development given the deep historical antagonisms among political and socioeconomic actors. Hence, this chapter challenges the determinism of local, social, political, and economic structures for institutional change.

The examination of these cases will show that institutional change is also dependent on different political approaches to reform in times of crisis. In the Basque Country the economic and sectoral crises led to political initiatives based on empowering economic and social actors so they could build new institutions that fostered coordination. These institutions have worked to address the collective-action problems of fragmented and small-sized enterprises with few skills, limited access to capital and resources, as well as an insufficient R&D and knowledge base.

In response to deteriorating economic conditions and new competitive challenges, the regional government engaged local socioeconomic actors in the development of new institutional initiatives to build coordination capacities that would allow them to solve problems collectively. It became the leading instigator at efforts to build new ties among local companies, and to develop new associations and institutions to improve the collective capacity of local enterprises to address common challenges. The regional government took great efforts to encourage local firms to organize themselves to address these collective-action challenges, providing incentives and resources to small producers.

In order to understand the role played by the Basque governments, it is necessary to account for the process of decentralization that followed the establishment of democracy in Spain. One of the main outcomes of this process was the emergency or powerful and autonomous regional governments, with the resources to influence economic policies and business' behaviors within their regions. The first section of this chapter explains this process.

The Process of Regional Decentralization

The administrative map of Spain is now very different from what it was 30 years ago. Since Francisco Franco's death 32 years ago, Spain has gone from being one of Europe's most centralized countries to one of its most decentralized. From a unitary state with some fifty provinces, the country currently has 17 autonomous communities, each with it own executive government and parliament. The establishment of this quasi-federal structure was a remarkable given the long history of tensions between the central government and the periphery which has been a source of constant conflict and had been one of the reasons that led to the Civil War of the 1930s.

The establishment of the autonomous regions was one of the most contentious issues during the constitutional debate that followed the death of General Franco. One of the first steps in this process was the restoration, in September of 1977, of the Catalan historic regional government, the *Generalitat*.

The leaders of the parties who drafted the Constitution sought a balance between a centralized system that would guarantee the unity of the nation (the preference of the right) and a federal one (the preference of the left). In the end the 1978 Constitution enshrined a compromise establishing (Art. 2.1) the "indissoluble unity of the Spanish Nation," while guaranteeing "the right of autonomy of the nationalities and regions of which it is composed." It recognizes 17 autonomous communities and establishes a distinction between "nationalities" (the Basque Country, Catalonia, and Galicia) and "regions" (all the other), which affected the procedure for attaining autonomy and the powers of the new regional governments. The specific organization of this new structure was further developed in Section VIII of the Constitution, which also outlined the territorial basis for the establishment of autonomous regions and the three routes to autonomy (Newton 1997, pp. 118–123). The new Constitution thus launched a process to pass decision-making authority to the new autonomous regions.

As a result of this territorial reorganization, the 17 autonomous regions (*Comunidades Autónomas*, CCAA) gained different degrees of statutory, legislative, and financial autonomy. They have regional constitutions that frame their relationship with the central government. They were also endowed with their own legislatures with the right to draft, approve, and implement laws. Finally, they also gained control over financial resources. While the central government retained overall responsibility for taxation (with the exception of the Basque Country and Navarre), regional governments manage growing financial resources that originate from the central government, the European Union, and regional sources (such as a taxes on property, charges, and surcharges).

From an institutional standpoint the new autonomous regions all have a parliament (or regional assembly), an executive council, a president, and a high court of justice. The members of the regional assembly are elected directly by universal suffrage. This assembly largely mirrors the national Congress, and its powers are laid out in the statute of autonomy. The president of the autonomous community is the symbolic head of the region, and is also the president of the regional executive in charge of the administration of the region and policy implementation. Finally, the high court of justice is part of a nation-wide structure of justice (see Newton 1997, pp. 130–136).

The powers of the autonomous regions (*competencias*) were contingent, according to the Constitution, on the route by which autonomy was achieved. Article 149 lists the "exclusive powers of the state," including foreign affairs, defense, customs, and international affairs; and Article 148 lists areas that can be assumed by regions who choose the slow-route to autonomy, such as planning, public works, cultural affairs, health and hygiene, or environmental protection (see Gunther, Montero, Botella 2004, pp. 297–298). In reality, over the last 30 years there has been a growing process of devolution of powers from the central government to the autonomous ones, and all the regions have been gaining control over more and more areas, as reflected by the growth of regional administrations that employ nearly three times the staff of the central government. By the later 1990s the range of variation in *competencias* among the different regions had narrowed considerably, and areas such as education and health services were transferred to the CCAA by 2002. By 1998 the budgets of the CCAA reached over 10 percent of the country's GDP and their expenditures increased as a percentage of total government spending, reaching over 30 percent. The government has also increased the portion of the income tax that goes directly to the CCAA, which reached 30 percent following the Popular Party's victory in the 1996 election.

While the other 15 regions rely largely on the state for their financial resources, the Basque Country (and Navarre) was able to keep its historical rights (*fueros*). A special economic agreement (*concierto económico*) for the Basque Country grants the region the power to collect and levy all taxes except customs duties and the taxes on petroleum products and tobacco. From the income that they generate, they pay an annual quota (*cupo*) to the central government for the services that it provides, which is negotiated every five years. The overall tax level cannot be lower than that of the state level (Newton 1997, p. 130; Gunther, Montero, and Botella 2004, p. 299).

This process of decentralization is almost unparalleled as it has led to a profound transformation of the political, economic, administrative, and institutional organization of the country. CCAA can enact laws that have the same force as Spanish laws, and their executive governments are not subordinate to the central one. Most of them have their own TV networks, some of them their own police force, and they all control key policy areas such as education and health care. While there are problems with the system (i.e., disputes over decisions concerning transfers of specific programs, economic inequalities among regions, or demands for increasing joint responsibility for fiscal matters), and the future evolution of this structure is still unresolved, the process decentralization is considered largely a success and one of the main achievements of the 1978 Constitution because it has helped ameliorate one of the thorniest issues in Spanish history: the traditional tensions between the center and the periphery (see Gunther, Montero, and Botella 2004).

The process of devolution accelerated with the victory of the Socialist party in the general 2004 election. The Socialist-led government has encouraged regions to draft new regional constitutions granting them greater autonomy and giving them more powers. As a result some regions (such as Catalonia, Valencia, and Andalusia) have approved new charters, while others are in the process of redrafting them.

However, this acceleration of the devolution process has also been controversial, as there are growing concerns about the rupture of the Spanish internal market and the growing level of interventionism of the regional governments, which is affecting investment and efficiency. According to the OECD Spanish retail regulations are the third more rigid among its member states (only behind Greece and Belgium), thus undermining the competitiveness of this sector. The business associations and leaders have been particularly vocal expressing their concerns and calling on the national government to take steps to unify economic legislation. Gerardo Díaz Ferran, president of the CEOE, has argued that "the proliferation of regional legislation means that, in some cases, companies have to abide by 17 different regulatory frameworks in their domestic market . . . posing obstacles and higher costs for private enterprise." Even the governor of the Bank of Spain has warned that "we need to reflect and take the strong and positive aspects of decentralization and avoid those phenomena that hold risks for the efficiency of the economy."[1]

The autonomous governments have played a very active role in the economy of their regions and have been instrumental in developing coordination mechanisms among the social actors at the regional level. For instance, as is examined later, technological parks emerged in Spain through the impetus of the autonomous communities, which sought to develop spaces for business excellence and to host innovating companies, closely linked with the research and development of local universities.[2]

Since the focus of this chapter is to examine processes of institutional change in one Spanish region, the Basque Country, I now describe its main features.

The Basque Country

The Basque Country is a CCAA located in Northern Spain that straddles the French-Spanish border along the western Pyrenees, with just 20.864 sq. km and 2.9 million people. It has a rich and deep-rooted historical tradition of self-governments that preceded the *Reconquista*, which led to the unification of Spain in 1492. At the same time, the region's cultural and linguistic pluralism has been a source of strong nationalism. The first Basque statute of autonomy was approved in 1936 in the midst of the Civil War, and in the 1978 Constitution and subsequent statute of autonomy (which was signed by the Basque Assembly in Guernica the same day that the new constitution went into effect: December 29, 1978), it achieved an extraordinary level of autonomy, which includes nearly complete financial independence.

The per capita GDP of the Basque Country has grown from 89.6 percent in 1990 to 125.6 percent in 2005. The tertiary sector absorbs 64.59 percent of the active population and makes up 60.80 percent of Basque GDP. Yet, the Basque Country is one of the most industrialized regions of Spain: industry and construction represent 38.18 percent of GDP (compared with the average for EU countries of 26.41 percent). The most important industry is the capital goods industry, which accounts for approximately 5 percent of Basque GDP, 11.6 percent of industrial GDP (50 percent of the total sector in Spain). It includes large companies that design, manufacture and assemble mechanical and electro-electronic products, such as *ABB, Babcock Borsig S.A., Bombardier, General Electric, Construcciones y Auxiliar de Ferrocarril (CAF), Adtranz, Tubacex,* and *Tubos Reunidos.* These companies work the iron and steel industry, the power generation and distribution industry, chemical and petrochemical works, telecommunications, urban and intercity transport systems, water treatments and supply, urban and industrial waste treatment, and environmental impact and civil engineering. Furthermore, the heavy industry is supplemented by small- and medium-sized companies working in other sectors such as aerospace, telecommunications, energy, environment, machine tools, automotive, chemical, shipbuilding, paper, rubber and plastic, glass, metal articles, furniture, and engineering industries.[3]

The Basque country is a case in which local firms have been able to develop successful strategies to compete and flourish in international markets. The region has been able to overcome the crisis of the 1980s and early 1990s, which had devastating consequences for its economy. In 1980 GDP growth was negative and the main industries of the region were crippled. The shipyards, steel (i.e., Altos Hornos the Vizcaya), machine tools and capital goods industries, were all collapsing after years of neglect and intensifying competition from lower costs producers. The rebuilding of their industry became a central goal for the newly established regional governments. The first technology park in Spain, the *Parque Tecnológico de Bizkaia* in Zamudio, was founded in 1985. This chapter claims that a key reason for this success has been that public institutions and private organizations have joined forces on the way to develop new cooperative institutions and socioeconomic policies to promote competitiveness.

The Basque Country: Coordination from the Top

The Development of Industrial Clusters[4]

In response to the economic crisis of the late 1970s and early 1980s, which almost led to the collapse of its industrial sector, the new Basque government led by the *lendakari* (the president of the Basque government) Carlos Garaikoetxea, decided to take drastic actions in order to restore public confidence. One of the first decisions was to create in 1981 the *Sociedad para la Promoción y Reconversión Industrial* (the Agency for the Promotion of Industry, SPRI) within the Department of Industry Commerce and Tourism. The aim of the new company is

> to provide back-up and services to Basque industry. SPRI is the parent of a group of companies which provide a response to the requirements of a business project from the first idea to actual implementation of the project. SPRI also uses certain instruments which allow our small and medium-sized enterprises access to information technology, outward movements on overseas projects, location within business environments which are suited to the specific needs of each sector, and the use of venture capital funds to finance innovative and strategic projects.[5]

In the midst of the crisis and with escalating social conflict and unrest at the plant level, the first task of the new institution was to assist in the management of private companies. From this role it grew to promote the internationalization of Basque's businesses and their exports. Over the years SPRI continued expanding and focused on four strategic areas: Innovation, Globalization, Industrial Development and the Information Society, and it developed specific programs and activities to advance its goals in these areas. In addition, it developed new companies to further implement its goals: SPRILUR, which provides suitable and industrial facilities, the Technology Parks, one in Bizkaia, another in Gipuzkoa, and a third in Álava, providing state-of-the-art environments for companies which require these features; Sociedad De Capital Riesgo, which administers funds as minority and temporary stockholdings in business projects; and lastly the Business Innovation Centers, which smoothen the process of creation and development of company projects until these have reached maturity.

The second main initiative from the Basque Government was the development by the regional secretary of labor of the Department for Promotion and Economic Development in 1983 to supplement SPRI's activities. This department was charged with the mission to expand research and development (quite underdeveloped at the time), and to this end it opened several technology centers, a design center, and a robotics technology center. Furthermore, the Basque Government also focused on the improvement and development of infrastructure to support businesses and attract investment. For instance it created the *Ente Vasco de la Energia* (Basque Energy Board, EVE), which provides technical assistance to energy companies and invested on energy sources such as natural gas. Finally, the local secretary of education developed the *Technology Research Network*, which was charged with the establishment and management of new technological research centers to further the cooperation of local companies and universities on technology projects (Porter 2005, pp. 7–8).

In 1986 the Basque Government, under the leadership of a new *lendakari*, José Antonio Ardanza, launched a *Plan the Relanzamiento Excepcional* (the Exceptional Relaunch Program) to promote the development of SMEs, stepped up its investment on physical infrastructure and energy resources to facilitate businesses' operations and further attract investment to the region (which has been hindered by the ongoing conflict with the Basque terrorist Group, *Esukadi Ta Askatasuma*–ETA), and launched the program "Euskadi Europa 1993," which included a physical infrastructure investment and social programs in health and education aimed at preparing the region for the Europeans Single Market.

By the mid-1980s when the economy was emerging from the depths of the crisis, the Basque government (and in particular its health and labor secretary, Jon Azua) shifted focus and instead of propping up and restructuring troubled companies, it started advocating a long-term strategy based on the development of manufacturing clusters. Yet, this strategy was delayed when the 1987 Basque Parliamentary elections led to the formation of a coalition between the Basque Nationalist Party (PNV) and the Socialist Party (PSOE) and Azua left the government to become CEO of the Bilbao Stock Exchange. From this position he retained a group of advisors to evaluate the state of the Basque economy, and they identified nine clusters[6] based on established sectors and also new possible opportunities: Machine Tools, Automotives, Steel, Port and Logistics, Paper, Financial Services, Fisheries, Tourism, and Agroindustry. While there seemed to be support for this approach, the government did little to advance this program (the only exception was the Financial Sector cluster, which was developed under Azua's leadership) (Porter 2005, pp. 8–9).

It was only the crisis of the early 1990s, which led to the collapse of the European Monetary System, and three consecutive devaluations of the Spanish peseta, that created a new sense of urgency and propped the Basque government to act. The crisis caused a dramatic surge of unemployment (it reached over 20 percent by 1993) and a new industrial crisis. Azua was named new secretary of industry and from this position he was able to advance his previous agenda. His department identified critical shortcomings in the Basque economy: limited skills in areas such as strategy, marketing, and international competition; little emphasis on R&D; lack of competition; and dependency on government intervention. The Basque Government was interested in exploring all options to address these issues, and they invited the competitiveness scholar Michael Porter to visit the Basque Country. During his visit Dr. Porter stressed that in the microeconomics of competitiveness, everything mattered, and also that successful implementation of a plan would largely hinge on the understanding of the complex interrelationships between agents. He emphasized that a new approach based on clusters, would require a reshaping of the functions of the private sector, government, associations and institutions. Yet, policy makers understood that this approach could be a very useful industrial policy instrument, which made it very attractive.[7]

As a result of his visit and Porter's recommendations the Basque Government decided to move full speed with the strategy to develop manufacturing clusters. They developed a practical action plan: "Cluster Initiatives," which was "an organized effort to increase the growth and competitiveness of clusters within a region, involving companies, Government and/or the research community." This was a proactive attempt at institutional change. The policy makers understood that "mature cluster initiatives usually result in stable structures, called Institutions for Collaboration, or Cluster Associations in the Basque case."[8] Once they decided to proceed this way they determined the group of priority clusters and over the following years they developed the different Cluster Associations.[9]

The Basque Government also capitalized on existing opportunities (such as the restructuring of the steel sector, which led to a shift from basic steel production to the development of mini-mills; or the decision by McDonnell Douglas to establish a major new supplier, which led to the establishment of a public-private planning group[10]) to learn about companies and the process to build clusters. The government developed a new program called the "Las Tres Rs: Rescate, Restructuración y Reorientación Laboral" (the Three R's: Rescue, Restructuring, and Labor Reorientation) to help companies compete internationally, and worked closely with local companies from the identified clusters. The efforts to develop these clusters were overseen by the secretary of industry and the SPRI. While many companies were skeptical (and many of them from identified clusters refused to join), the government was able to convince them of the benefits. The enticement of government support was a powerful incentive (Porter 2005, pp. 10–11).

This strategy was underpinned by the Basque Government's strategic decision to work with the principal economic and institutional stakeholders to sponsor initiatives to improve the competitive position of Basque firms. These included two industrial policy plans (1991–95 and 1996–99), an Industrial Technology Plan (1993–96), and a Science and Technology Plan (1997–2000). A key component of these initiatives was the objective to promote cooperation among firms as a mean to compete in international markets through the development of cluster initiatives; as well as the attempt to increase the commitment of human and financial resources by Basque companies to R&D. As a result, starting at the beginning of the 1990s and as part of the implementation of the Basque Government's Competitiveness

Program, the main Basque industrial sectors developed sectoral organizations to promote technical and commercial collaboration among companies from the sector and with third parties. These clusters became industrial policy tools and instruments to foster cooperation among Basque companies. The first cluster to emerge was the Machine Tools (1992), which was quickly followed by the Appliances Cluster (1992) and the Automotives Cluster (1993). They were followed by nine others (see figure 6.1).

From an organizational standpoint the main goal was to achieve general coordination and to break down the formal borders between members and sectors. Hence each cluster association has a vertical head, reinforced with 12 SPRI staffers, and also a horizontal head, one on each strategic area. The horizontal heads are at the same time heads for horizontal standard policies. Their role is to link cluster policy and horizontal standard policy. Moreover, the civil servants of the Department of Industry and SPRI staff (with extensive experience and knowledge of each area) attend all the Boards of Directors meetings, and other committee meetings, but they do not vote. Their main role is to provide support and advice, but not to interfere or impose.[11]

AERONAUTICS: HEGAN—Aeronautics Cluster Association of the Basque Country (www.hegan.com)

AUTOMOTIVE: ACICAE—Cluster Association of Car Industries and Components of Euskadi (www.acicae.es)

AUDIOVISUAL: EIKEN—Audiovisual Cluster of Euskadi (www.eikencluster.com)

KNOWLEDGE: Cluster Association of Knowledge in Business Management (www.clusterconocimiento.com) (www.portaldelagestion.com)

ELECTRONIC HOUSEHOLD APPLIANCES: ACEDE—Cluster Association of Household Appliances of Euskadi (www.acede.es)

ELECTRONICS, IT, AND TELECOMMUNICATIONS: GAIA—Association of Electronics and Information Technologies of the Basque Country (www.gaia.es)

ENERGY: Energy Cluster Association (www.clusterenergia.com)

MARITIME INDUSTRY: BASQUE MARITIME FORUM. Association for the Promotion of the Basque Maritime Industry (www.foromaritimovasco.com)

MACHINE TOOLS: AFM—Spanish Association of Machine Tool Manufacturers (www.afm.es)

ENVIRONMENT: ACLIMA—Cluster Association of Environmental Industries (www.aclima.net)

PAPER: CLUSP AP—Paper Cluster Association of Euskadi (www.clusterpapel.com)

PORT: CPB—Port Cluster of Bilbao (www.uniportbilbao.es)

Figure 6.1   The 12 priority sectoral clusters in the Basque country

Source: Euskadi.net (http://www.lehendakaritza.ejgv.euskadi.net/r48–467/en/contenidos/informacion/cluster_sectoriales/en_cluster/clusters_s.html).

In addition, the government developed a new *Department of Industry and Clusters* to work closely with the companies to identify goals and needs and to develop plans to achieve their goals. The process was very much instigated by the government (and in particular by this Department) but the government still avoided excessive intervention and adopted a flexible strategy to let groups form naturally.[12] Yet, it still played a central role facilitating cluster meetings, providing funds for projects, and making cluster representatives focus on long-term goals.

The Basque Government and the companies were looking for increasing internationalization, technology development, quality and excellence in management, and improved logistics, and they accepted that these goals (and the strategic competitive strategic challenges facing Basque companies) could not be simple addressed by individual actions from individual companies. Hence they agreed that improving the competitiveness of Basque companies would require cooperation and coordination. In this regard, they felt that the clusters could play a central role as "net servers" with a catalytic function, because they would intensify the interactions and speed of communication among members of the cluster (see table 6.1). With the clusters they sought to "gather and spread strategic information; identify strategic challenges and potential synergies; evaluate the potential synergies, and finally identify and promote cooperation groups with common interests in order to generate cooperation projects."[13] Initially the program was funded with a modest amount: €2.3m per year for the whole program.

In order to improve the operations of these clusters and to create uniform structures, the Basque Government named a Board of Directors for each cluster, which brings together the CEOs of local companies. This Board oversees a general manager who is in charge of managing the cluster committees. In addition the Basque Government asked each cluster in 2000 to develop a process to capture date and information; identify areas of cooperation within clusters, evaluate potential synergies, and form groups to realize them (Porter 2005, p. 16).

This strategy was supplemented with a strong push toward the outside world, with the Basque Government giving incentives and subsidies to companies to establish links abroad and develop international units; as well as also opening representative offices and developing bilateral trade promotion agreements with other countries (Porter 2005, p. 14).

In addition to the clusters (see table 6.2), the Basque Government also developed technology parks. The first one was Bizkaia's Zamudio Technology Park which was inaugurated in 1985, and was followed by the Alava Technology Park (1992) and the San Sebastian Technology Park (1993). The parks are owned by the regional government with the participation of the local administration. These three parks were the first technology parks in Europe to be awarded ISO certification. They provide facilities for 230 companies with an annual turnover that exceeds 2 billion euros. Zamudio, for instance, hosts R&D operations of companies such as Rolls-Royce's Spanish partner ITP, Alcatel or Air Liquide, and it has been chosen by the EU as the headquarters

Table 6.1 The development and main actions of the 12 clusters

Cluster	Opening date	Identified barriers	Institutional development	Actions
Machine tools	1992	Overvalued currency, inflexible labor laws, lack of financial support.	Existing business association, AFM (and its technology committee INVEMA) led the efforts, and was joined by existing technological research and R&D Centers (IKERLAN and IDEKO).	Conducted strategic analysis; organized master degree courses in specialized machine tools; and designed ISO 9000 Total Quality programs for its members.
Automotive	1993	Lack of foreign language capabilities and export experience.	In 1993 new group created led by 12 companies (ACICAE) that joined forces with Department of Industry and Clusters to upgrade initiatives. Developed technology, quality, and human resources subcommittee. Expanded to 28 members in 1994.	Issued recommendations for the cluster; added German-language capabilities to strengthen relationship with German buyers; moved headquarters to Bilbao Technology Park; designed and engineered automotive parts; forged new alliances for supply and logistics; initiated Total Quality program to increase exports.
Household appliances	1992	Industry price war; over-employment.	Evolved from 1984 group convened to restructure sector. Formed by 10 companied, led by industry leader *Fagor*, which had a history of cooperation; it included home appliances manufacturers: suppliers of machinery, raw material, and components; as well as service providers; R&D education center; design services; and sales and distributions services. Signed agreement with Department of Industry and Clusters.	Identified issue areas and formed committees to address them, such as the Technology Committee, the Quality Committee, and the Commerce Committee. Developed plan to recycle 5–18 % of manufactured appliances; as well as quality-training targets for workers; new processes for plants to meet international standards; and a new R&D spending plan.

Ports and logistics	1994	Inadequate international marketing of port facilities; problems with customer service; insufficient contacts with Europe; need to develop new routes.	Companies working with customers since 1980s to improve services. Merge of two initiatives: one from Spanish government (started in 1993), and another from Basque Government working on strategic issues, to create Uniport in 1998. *Foro Industria Marítima* created in 2002.	Developed new shipping routes, and new connections to Europe; negotiated new Far Eastern lines. *Foro* worked to broaden the program and to include suppliers and value-added companies.
Electronics, computing, and telecommunications	1994	Need to promote the sector in the Basque Country; need to identify strategic priorities; lack of internationalization.	Institutionalized as GAIA composed by 170 companies with 8,000 workers. Department of Industry and Clusters was supportive but did not play active role.	Developed projects of common interest in areas of technology, competitiveness, internationalization, and basic services; identified strategic priorities; opened new Center of Excellence in Java Technologies; created registration and certification body for the use of electronic signatures; developed ISO 14001 standard certification methodology.
Environmental industries	1995	Need to introduce innovate, cleaner and more competitive technologies and practices.	Initiated by group representing 15 industries (IHOBE), with 65 private companies and 11 state-owned ones mostly in area of waste and sewage. Department of Industry and Clusters facilitated meetings.	Developed strategic plan to enhance competitiveness, and an inventory of sites with potential land contamination; created the first waste management plan in Spain, as well as a consumer program to recycle, and an industry program to minimize waste in production; worked with Basque technology centers to transfer new technologies to industry; established five research labs, including GAIKER

Continued

Table 6.1 Continued

Cluster	Opening date	Identified barriers	Institutional development	Actions
				specialized in environmental biotechnology; developed new instructional programs.
Knowledge in management	1996	Lack of management know-how in Basque companies; need to strengthen universities, research centers, and the local management consulting industry.	175 members including Basque business associations.	Hired a consultant to help define the cluster. Developed and disseminated case studies; organized forums to discuss strategic concepts; developed new research.
Energy	1996	Need to develop alternative sources of energy.	87 major companies from the energy sector signed agreement with the Department of Industry and Clusters.	EVE signed agreement with Iberdrola in 1996 to develop future scenarios for power Industry.
Aeronautics	1997	Lack of strong international presence, underdeveloped links with subcontractors; weak links with technology centers.	19 aeronautical companies and Department of Industry and Clusters.	Three large companies (ITP, Sener, and Gamesa) worked with Department of Industry and Clusters to develop strategic plan; ITP signed project with Rolls Royce and BMW on small aircraft engines; these 3 companies built relationship with over 100 subcontractors from the region and shared technological resources through the centers set up by Basque government (INASMET and LABEIN).

Industry	Year	Challenges	Members	Actions
Ship building industry	1997	Saturation of shipyards; need to improve levels of competitiveness.	ADIMDE, which represents some 400 businesses; *Foro Maritimo Basco.*	Developed strategic market niche in smaller vessels, including tugs, trawlers, fishing and freezer vessels; worked to stimulate and promote the Basque regional maritime industry.
Paper	1998	Lack of cooperation in the industry due to adversarial relationship with main company (Papelera Española); underdeveloped international markets.	Pulp and paper mills, suppliers of capital goods, engineering firms, and a training center.	Joined the Basque government's competitiveness program; developed agenda to develop international markets; R&D; developed cooperative projects in the areas of quality and management, internationalization, environment and technology.
Audiovisual	2004	Need to develop competitive capability of member firms in young and dynamic industry; need to promote competitiveness at the international level.	Forty-five member firms from the region's audiovisual and multimedia industry.	Identified five different strategic areas of action: new technologies, management quality, new markets, infrastructures, and contents.

Source: Porter (2005, pp. 11–13); and information from the clusters.

Table 6.2 Summary of the main features of the priority clusters

	Home appliances (ACEDE)	Machine tool (AFM)	Automotion (ACICAE)	Port of Bilbao	Telecommunications (GAIA)	Environment (ACLIMA)	Knowledge	Energy	Aeronautics (HEGAN)	Maritime industries	Paper
Creation	1992	1992	1993	1994	1994	1995	1996	1996	1997	1997	1998
No. members	13	68	49	138	160	64	160	76	24	116	19
Employment	9.200	4.602	15.560	4.300	8.000	2.888	—	25.000	4.732	14.000	2.059
Turnover M€	1.430	612	2.243	839	1.600	695	—	10.000	674	682	526
Exports: M€	646	390	1.337	—	540	132	—	2.200	—	532	240
% sales	45%	64%	60%	—	34%	19%	—	22%	—	78%	46%

Source: Juan Manuel Esteban, Opatija, April 19–21, 2007.

of the European Software Institute (ESI). They work on more than 1,500 research projects each year and spend in R&D more than 200 million euros a year (about 30 percent for the entire region).[14]

The Basque Government has also worked actively to promote innovation, technology, and science. To this end it developed SARATEK, a private, not-for-profit association involving 89 Basque science and technology agents working in R&D+I, with 10,000 research workers in all. The network includes 11 technological centers: TECNALIA, which is the largest private research corporation in Southern Europe, which brings together R&D businesses, IK4 (6 technological centers), as well as universities and private and public institutions working on development, innovation, and technology transfer.[15] It seeks to generate and develop scientific and technological knowledge, to improve business competitiveness. SARATEK works in many areas, including information and training, the promotion of cooperation and the creation of science- and technology-based businesses.[16]

Other government initiatives included the creation of *Ikerbasque*, the Basque Foundation for Science, which aims to help develop scientific research in the Basque Country by attracting researchers and helping them establish themselves; and the *Institute for Kompetitiveness and Development*, a privately managed, public service initiative linked to *Deusto University*, charged with the mission to provide support to the public administrations, social and economic agents, and all the universities in the Basque Country in the field of competitiveness.

A Model of Coordination[17]

As we have seen in the previous section, the Basque initiatives are a case of coordination from the top, with the Basque Government playing a crucial role. But it did not happen by accident. One of the keys was the timing: it all started with the collapse of the authoritarian regime at a time in which Basque companies wanted to expand but were facing one of the worst economic crises of the previous decades in sectors such as steel, shipbuilding, and paper in which the structure of costs was no longer competitive. This led to devastating job losses (around 250,000 jobs were destroyed at the time in a region with a population of 2 million people). This crisis, however, provided the impetus (and urgency) for change. The process of change was led by two main actors: on the one hand there were small- and medium enterprises, which needed to develop coordination mechanisms to address collective-action problems and on the other hand, the new democratic Basque Government, which was compelled to take immediate action to address the mounting crisis and unraveling social conflict. The priority was to develop a shock plan, and to address the mounting industrial crisis with a restructuring industrial plan. This plan planted the seeds of collaboration between the private and the public sector: the government was willing to provide funds for the restructuring of these companies but only in exchange of certain conditions, such as the development of technological innovations.

Once the process of industrial reconversion was completed in the mid-1980s, the Basque Government shifted gears and started focusing on the promotion of products and new industries, at a time in which unemployment, inflation, and interest rates were still quite high, and access to capital (and long term finance) was still significantly limited because of the existing quasi-oligopoly in the finance sector (Pérez 1997). The government played a very active role developing an industrial policy and involving economic and social actors in the development and implementation of these policies, including business associations, universities, training centers, trade unions, as well business schools. This helped set a tone of collaboration and a culture of consultation and participation.

The regional government also helped define the key priorities: technological and knowledge development, innovation, and training. In this regard, one of the first steps, as we have seen, was the development of the knowledge cluster in 1996, which was instrumental to developing supply and demand for the creation of new projects, and also to convince economic actors that in a context of increasing competition and higher costs, a model based on low costs was no longer viable and had to be replaced by a model based on technology and strong management capabilities.[18] To facilitate this transition the Basque Government focused on developing a new environment that would be very supportive of R&D efforts and new technologies.

Furthermore, the Basque Government was also instrumental in convincing Basque firms of the need to internationalize in order to force them to improve their competitiveness, reduce their quasi-complete dependence on the Spanish market; and also to diversify. This change, however, required a qualitative transformation not only in their production systems, but also in their management and organization. Yet, SMEs simply lacked the size to make this transition by themselves, and hence they had to find ways to develop mechanisms to coordinate with other firms and the Basque Government to resolve collective-action problems.

The lack of access to capital was one of the main instigators that led companies to start developing networks to raise funds and to promote exports.[19] At the same time, given the size and limited resources of the small- and medium enterprises, they were dependent on government intervention and support in multiple areas, such as capital and development of new technologies. The Basque Government responded to these demands from the private sector and started implementing new action programs, and developing technological centers. The funding of these initiatives was often split between the government and the private sector, but the government imposed specific conditions to the companies participating in these centers, which benefited from the new technologies. It was in this context that SPRI was created, with the initial focus to promote the creation of new enterprises. One of the first instruments to achieve this goal was the plan to work on the rationalization of the industrial landscape (*Industrialdea*) and the development of industrial centers (*polígonos industriales*). The government would lease land for 8–10 years to companies at the industrial center with a prearranged sale price, and the company would buy the property once it was already established and consolidated.

The government was also involved in funding initiatives. Companies faced two major barriers: lack of access to long-term capital and high financial costs (which were significantly higher than in the rest of Europe at that time). Originally, the reference was the venture capital model of the Anglo-Saxon countries. However, the private sector faced significant hurdles to raise capital: first venture capital firms did barely exist. Furthermore, the country lacked a culture of savings (and most of the savings went to Treasury Bonds). Finally, the secondary market was virtually inexistent, and public money was scarce because the central government still faced a significant public deficit. The central government passed a new law of *Sociedades de Garantia Reciproca* (Reciprocal Guarantee Societies) in 1978 and the Basque social actors took advantage of the new legislation. They created a management fund in charge of managing capital risk funds. Yet, it was still difficult to find investors and they had to turn to private stockholders (mostly companies) that invested in the fund to create new firms. In the end they created capital risk societies with different focus. For instance, the one focusing on new (and risky) technologies was mostly funded with public funds, while others with more moderate risks were funded with private funds. These initiatives were supported by fiscal incentives, which promoted the development of private societies. The government also played a role through the Basque savings and loans, which helped companies in crisis (during the crisis of the 1980s they bought participations in companies such as ACF). The savings and loans have provided a stable stockholder nucleus to these companies, which in turn have allowed them to focus on the long-term and to make investment decisions.

Once the seeds for cooperation were planted they started to flourish. For instance, in San Sebastian private firms joined in 1980 to develop ADEGI, the Gipuzkoa business association. This association emerged in response to the brutal crisis of the 1970s, which has led, as we have seen, to the dismantling of large companies, which in turn had devastating effects on the region's SMEs. They had two kinds of members: participating members (stockholders), and protective members (sponsors, commerce chambers, and the Basque Government). Private businesses have the majority of the capital.

One of the main objectives of the new association was to facilitate access to capital to participating member firms. To better fulfill this role the Basque businesses created ELKARGI, a reciprocal guarantee company. One of their first actions was to sign an agreement with the Basque Government to offer long-term funding to its members at subsidized interest rates, with ELKARGI providing bank guarantees (to lower the risk premium, and thus allow member firms to receive lower interest rates). It also provided participatory loans, in which ELKARGI participates in the evolution of the business. The initiative was revolutionary in Spain: the criteria to give loans was not only based on performance (such as venture capital), but on the economic expectations of a future benefit (i.e., firms have to be able to generate resources to have enough funds to return the loan).[20] ELKARGI has also promoted and funded innovation initiatives from participating member firms providing guarantees, and has facilitated the bureaucratic process.

Another area in which the Basque Government has played a central role was in professional training. While large companies had their own internal training systems, SMEs lacked the resources and knowledge. This became a central priority in a context marked by constant and rapid technological changes that required urgent upgrading and updating of skills. Hence the focus from all parties turned to enhancing the education system at all levels to improve human capital productivity.[21]

As a result, professional training has also been an important area of cooperation. As noted in chapter 2, the professional training system in Spain has traditionally been quite discredited and separated from the real needs of companies. In the Basque Country the economic and social actors have tried to address this shortcoming and have worked together to develop a well functioning professional training system. Once again the Basque Government played a central role. The economic crisis between 1985 and 1993, which caused a sharp increase in unemployment, created the urgent need to "recycle" those people and provide them with new qualifications to be able to find new jobs. Seventy percent of the demand at the time was for people with professional training skills.

To respond to this demand the government approved in October of 1997 the "Basque Plan of Professional Training," which included the development of an Integrated System of Qualifications and Professional Training. This plan involved three government departments: labor, industry, and education, as well as the social actors and the professional training centers, and it led to the establishment of the *Basque Council of Professional Training*. The plan was articulated around three main institutions. First, the *Basque Observatory of Professional Training*, which was put in charge of analyzing and researching in detail developments in the Basque labor market, and to predict patterns for the future. It is closely connected with the firms and collects data from the national office of employment (INEM), as well as from the press and other observatories.

The second institution was the *Basque Institute of Qualifications and Professional Training*. Based on the observatory's findings this institute is in charge of determining the qualifications in individual productive sectors and to develop the necessary training programs in a short period of time (usually no more than 3–6 months in order to satisfy urgent demands from firms). They have high competence standards that are determined with the participation of the representatives from nine key sectors for the Basque economy who work to prepare the necessary qualifications. The results of their work are then presented to syndical and business technicians who have to approve the technical specifications, which are then ratified by the *Basque Council of Professional Training*.

The last institution is the *Basque Agency for the Evaluation of Competences and Quality*, which is charged with the evaluation of the whole system and implements a process to recognize and make official the skills that have been learned by workers, which then become part of a registry of certifications of competences.

The program is articulated through agreements between the schools, companies and the Basque government, which provides funds and insurance, and the whole program is funded by companies and the Basque Government (partly with funds from the European social funds).[22] The system also provides businesses with funds for training and adaptation to new technologies.

CONFEBASK, the Basque Business Confederation (established in 1983 by the three regional business associations: ADEGI-Gipuzkoa, CEBEK-Bizkaia, and SEA-Alava) also played a central role in the initiative to improve the professional training system with two main objectives: to respond to the needs for specialized skills of the Basque companies, and also to improve the prestige of the professional training system and improve the employability of workers. To this end they worked with the Basque Government and took advantage of a legislative change in the national law regulating this field, which now allows students to do their internships in companies. In addition, business associations such as ADEGI have their own well-developed training programs.

Since the Basque Government started the program it has worked with over 12,000 students, which has improved significantly their employability (reaching rates of almost 100 percent in certain industrial sectors). The success of the program is also proved by the growth in registration rates of professional training programs (27,953 in the 2005–06 academic year) despite stagnant population rates. The Basque Government is now spending more in professional training (802.801 billion euros in 2005 or 39.7 percent of the total) than in higher education (252.237 billion euros, or 12.5 percent), and more people complete professional training programs (30 percent in 2004–05) than university programs (25.2 percent).[23]

The government has also established an assessment mechanism to poll the companies that employ the graduates from the program, in order to guarantee that students are learning what the companies need. Finally, while in the rest of Spain, as we have seen, there is a problem with the high levels of temporary work that results in high turnout rates, in the Basque country many firms have understood that if they have to invest in their workers it is in their best interest to keep them long term. Hence, firms such as ACF made strenuous efforts to keep the turnout to a minimum and the overall temporary rate is significantly lower (23.2 percent in 2005).[24]

The professional training system has also played a significant role in technology transfers because many of the schools have better and more modern equipment than the companies, which can now hire employees who can work with the latest technologies. Driven by the example of companies, the schools themselves, have made a push for quality, and many have achieved ISO quality certification, which has enhanced their prestige, and hence their ability to recruit students. It is a holistic approach with a very inclusive and responsive process that guarantees that the training programs respond to demands from the firms.[25]

Cooperation has not only flourished among businesses or between business and the regional government, but also with unions. And this despite the fact that in addition to the main confederations (CCOO and UGT), the Basque Country has a third union, ELA-STV, which has around 40 percent of representativeness (see Chapter 5), and almost 70 percent of the collective agreements could be signed without UGT and CCOO. This has been facilitated by a strong cooperative culture (the Basque Country has some of the most successful and larges cooperatives in the world like *Mondragon*[26]) and the institutionalization of cooperation mechanisms such as the creation of the tripartite *Basque Economic and Social Council*, which has played a central role at the macro level building bridges among the social actors and fostering a culture of consultation and consensus. But cooperation has extended to the micro level. Some companies (such as ACF) have gone as far as to selling stock to the unions at a subsidized price (they control 18 percent of the stock), and offering unions the possibility to participate in the managerial decisions (something similar to the German codetermination model).

In the area of industrial relations there has also been significant cooperation between unions, employers and the Basque Government, and this despite the relevance of national-level bargaining and the interference of political factors linked with the sovereignty dispute.[27] The social actors have been able to overcome historical conflicts and antagonisms, aggravated during the dictatorship when employers were largely associated with the regime. Unions now accept and do not question the role of the private sector and recognize that companies have to fulfill certain requirements in order to survive and compete.[28] The Basque Government has been very active in this field as well. The *Council of Labor Relations* of the Basque government, a bipartite institution (with 7 representatives from CONFESBAK and 7 from the unions—3 ELA, 2 CCOO, and 1 LAB/UGT), has played a critical role in areas such labor mediation and in refereeing in industrial collective conflicts, in which it pioneered an agreement in 1984.

The wage bargaining structure is regulated by national regulations. For most companies minimum salaries are negotiated at the sectoral level and they do not have the flexibility to lower them, or make substantive differences. CONFESBAK plays a central role in collective bargaining, although there are differences based on regions.[29] ELA supports a model based on provincial collective agreements that set minimum standards (including for salaries) and are then complemented by agreements at the firm level (which is the prevalent model in Guipuzkoa).[30] Basque employers, for their part, are trying (like in other parts of Spain) to extend the scope of collective bargaining to make it more comprehensive and include issues such as the management of human resources, or the organization of the firm and the deployment of human capital. They are also pushing for the decentralization of collective bargaining and to establish the firm as the bargaining unit, in order to better take into account the reality of specific firms and the increasing individualization of industrial relations. Unions, however, resist this push for decentralization because they are afraid it will hurt the principle of solidarity.[31] The social actors have been reasonably flexible to accommodate each other's demands and the institutional structure has facilitated agreements.[32] Overall, there is consensus that the system works relatively well: labor conflict is limited and the number of strikes has declined (i.e., the number of working days lost has decreased from 1,100 in 2000 to 603 in 2005), and there has been wage moderation (see later).[33]

Finally, the clusters and technology parks have also played a very constructive role in corporate governance and the rules governing intercompany relationships: that is, technology transfer, standard setting, and competitive policy. For instance, the process to register patents, which is considered quite bureaucratic (and individualistic) throughout Spain, has been facilitated by business associations such as ADEGI (the Gipuzkoa Business Association), and the technology centers are playing a central role in the transference of technology to firms throughout the region.

Outcomes and Performance

The institutional outcome of these initiatives has been notable. There are 10 applied technology centers, 13 R&D centers, 4 research laboratories, 2 public research organizations, and 3 technology parks (Porter 2005, p. 15). In addition to the increase in the number and quality of the projects launched by the clusters, other tangible results include the creation of several Export Consortiums; the development of technological projects "interclusters" (such as Electronics for Automotion, Automotion-Machine-Tool, or Energy-Environment), and finally there have been impressive results in Excellence in Management evaluated according to the EFQM model.

Other results are less tangible and difficult to measure, but they are still very important. For instance, the clusters helped foster trust among members, and cooperation among competitors. Furthermore, they helped to break down the traditional barriers between the public and the private sectors and helped reaffirm the principle that progress was contingent of public-private collaborations. Finally, they have helped to define a common strategic orientation and shared long-term objectives.[34]

The economic results have also been remarkable. The Basque Country has the highest disposable per capita in Spain (it grew from 74.37 percent of the EU average in 1980 to 100.2 by 2000, and 128.2 in 2006), and only 5 EU countries (Austria, Denmark, Holland, Ireland, and Luxembourg) have higher per capita GDP than the Basque Country. Unemployment has fallen to 3.4 percent in 2007, which has been supported by wage moderation (see table 6.3).

Table 6.3 Wage increases in the Basque country

	2002	2003	2004	2005
Sectoral agreement	4.17	4.25	3.86	4.50
Firm agreement	3.94	3.63	3.61	3.98
Total in all agreements	4.13	4.11	3.98	4.38

Source: Council of Labor Relations.

Moreover, the Basque GDP has been growing since the 1980s at a faster rate than that of Spain and the EU (see table 6.4).

Basque companies are also responding to the competitive challenge and have been investing in a model based in the generation of knowledge, innovation capacity, and the use of advanced technologies. The effort in R&D has also been very important. According to EUSTAT data in 2004, 769 million euros were spent in activities related to scientific research and technological development (1.44 percent compared with 1.07 percent in Spain). In 2005 total expenditure on R&D in the Basque Country reached 823 million euros, the equivalent to 1.43 percent of its GDP (in Spain it was 1.12 percent, still below average the EU levels—1.86 percent), and the Basque Country holds the third place in Spain, behind Madrid and Navarre, in terms of regional R&D effort. Business R&D investment accounted for 79.1 percent of total R&D expenditure in 2005 (79.1 percent in 2004) (17.2 percent by the academic world and the rest by other public institutions), as opposed to the average in Spain of 54.4 percent in 2005 and 64.3 percent in the EU. Business investment has also increased significantly (see table 6.5).[35]

This investment has translated into innovation. According to EUSTAT data, during the 2001–03 period 16.3 percent of the establishments were innovators, and this percentage reaches 31.9 percent if we only take into account establishments with more than nine employees. This is 2.2 percentage points higher than in Spain. Moreover, the only innovating sector is no

Table 6.4 GDP growth in the Basque country (1989–2005)

	1989	1990	1995	2000	2004	2005
Basque country	6.3	4.1	3.5	5.2	3.0	3.7
Spain	4.7	3.7	2.8	4.2	2.7	3.4
EU	3.4	2.9	2.4	3.5	1.9	1.5

Source: OECD, EUSTAT, and SPRI.

Table 6.5 Business investment (1998–2004)

	1998	2000	2004
EU 15	17.6	18.3	17.0
Basque Country	21.1	23.3	24.1
Spain	19.5	22.8	24.4
Italy	16.1	17.4	16.9
Germany	19.5	19.7	16.0
France	15.5	16.3	15.9
United Kingdom	16.3	15.7	14.6

Source: SPRI.

longer only the industrial one (22.3 percent of the industrial establishments and 36 percent of those with more than nine employees are innovators), but also the service sector, in which 17.7 percent of all the establishments and 34.2 percent of those with more than nine employees are also innovators. In the industrial sector the largest number of innovators is in the paper edition and graphic industry (47.5 percent of the establishments), chemical industry (43.3 percent), education (34.3 percent), and services to companies (30.8 percent). In terms of the type of innovations the most typical ones are process innovations (14.9 percent, versus 5.4 percent in product innovations). The total expenditures in technological innovations reached 2,010 million euros in 2004 (1,029 from the industry and 964 million for the service sector), which represents 3.8 percent of the GDP (1,836 million in 2003 or 3.9 percent). Most of these expenses have been in internal R&D (38.3 percent) and in the purchasing of machinery (39.6 percent).[36]

Furthermore, industrial production has also experienced extraordinary growth: between 2001 and 2004 the annual median growth has been 1.55 percent and the accumulated growth 6.2 percent (compared with 0.42 percent and 1.7 percent in Spain, and 0.25 percent and 1.0 percent in the EU15, respectively), and the importance of the Basque Country in the total production of Spain's principal sectors has also increased. This has been the result of the diversification of industrial production in the region, which has expanded from the traditional activities derived from metal (i.e., from the production of steel to machine tools) to now include sectors such as chemicals, petrochemical and refinery, industrial electronics, nanotechnology, robotics, and biotechnologies. Now Basque companies produce not only capital goods, but also consumer goods and other intermediate products (see table 6.6).[37]

Finally, Basque companies have been responding successfully to the competitive challenge of globalization and they have been increasing their

Table 6.6 The Basque country in the total production of Spain (2004)

Special steel	90%
Machine tool	80%
Forging/stamping	75%
Equipment goods	50%
Smelting	50%
Steel	40%
Electric appliances	40%
Professional electronics	40%
Automotive	30%
Aeronautical	22%
Electronics, computing, telecommunications	12%

Source: SPRI.

presence in other countries. The degree of economic opening of the Basque economy has increased (i.e., it was 123.25 percent in 2004 compared with 53.10 percent in Spain, 71.14 percent in Germany, or 55.2 percent in the United Kingdom), and the exporting tendency of the Basque economy (exports of goods and services over GDP) has grown to 30.65 percent, a figure well above other countries (26.64 percent in Italy, 25.97 percent in France, and 24.90 percent in Spain).[38]

Other Examples of Regional Coordination

It is important to highlight that the Basque Country is not the only Spanish region in which this type of cooperative initiatives have flourished.[39] While the Basque Country was a pioneer in the development of technology parks and clusters, other Spanish regions have followed (i.e., Madrid, Catalonia, Comunidad Valenciana, Castile and León, and Andalusia). Valencia, Madrid, and Catalonia have all studied high-tech clusters in Europe and the United States and are trying to emulate them. Catalonia, for instance, is trying to become a leading biomedical research center[40] and Madrid is becoming a logistic center for multinationals based in Southern Europe. Valencia has one of the fastest-growing ports in the Mediterranean (see table 6.7).[41]

Table 6.7   Examples of competitiveness projects in Spain

Cluster/project	Industry	Institution	Year
Leather tanning in Spain	Leather Tanning	Spanish Tanners Association	2004–05
Footwear, toys, furniture, home, textiles, nougat clusters in Valencia	Footwear, toys, furniture, home textiles, nougat	Generalitat de Valencia-Economía & CAM	2004–05
Mapping of tourism in Extremadura	Tourism	Junta de Extremadura	2004
Process engineering firms in Catalonia	Process engineering	Departamento de Trabajo e Industria de la Generalitat-CIDEM	2003
Biotechnology cluster in Catalonia	Biotechnology	Fundación Catalana para La Recerca	2003–04
Footwear industry in Aragón	Footwear	Instituto Aragonés de Fomento	2003
Toy Industry in Valencia	Toy industry	Asociación Española de Fabricantes de Juguetes and Generalitat Valenciana (DG Industry)	2003
Pharmaceutical industry in Catalonia	Pharmaceutical	Fundació Salut, Empresa i Economía (FUSEE)	2003

Continued

Table 6.7   Continued

Cluster/project	Industry	Institution	Year
Cluster mapping in Andalucia	Mapping	Instituto de Fomento de Andalucia, Andalucia Government	2002
Construction materials cluster in Lleida	Constructions materials	Departamento de Industria de la Generalitat	2002
Nougat cluster in Jijona	Nougat	Generalitat de Valencia-Economía & CAM	2002
Regional development in Repolles, Catalonia	Industry base transformation	Departamento de Trabajo e Industria de la Generalitat-CIDEM, Fundació Eduard Soler	2002
Aerospace cluster in Barcelona	Aerospace	Associació Barcelona Aeronaútica i de l'Espai (BAIE)	2001–02
Pharmaceutical cluster in Madrid	Pharmaceutical	Comunidad Autónoma de Madrid	2001
Marbles processing cluster in Alicante	Marble processing	Generalitat de Valencia-Economía & CAM	2001
Railway industry cluster in Barcelona	Railway industry	Departamento de Industria de la Generalitat	2001
Footwear clusters in Alicante-Elda, Elche, Villena	Footwear	Generalitat de Valencia-Economía & CAM	2000–01
Challenges of consumer electronics manufacturing in Catalonia	Consumer electronics	Dirección General de Industria del Departamento de Industria, Comercio y Turismo de la Generalitat	2000
Furniture cluster in Madrid	Furniture	Comunidad Autónoma de Madrid	2000
Furniture cluster in Valencia	Furniture	Generalitat de Valencia-Economía & CAM	2000
Fostering innovation in Catalonia	General	Dirección General de Industria del Departamento de Industria, Comercio y Turismo de la Generalitat	1999–2000
Furniture cluster in Mallorca	Furniture	Govern de Illes Balears	1999
Cheese cluster of Minorca	Cheese	Govern de Illes Balears	1999
Home textiles industry in Valencia	Home textiles	Generalitat de Valencia-Economía & CAM	1999
Ceramic tiles cluster in Castelló de la Plana	Ceramic tiles	Generalitat de Valencia-Economía & CAM	1998

Continued

Table 6.7 Continued

Cluster/project	Industry	Institution	Year
Plastic parts suppliers for the automotive industry in Barcelona	Automotive	Departamento de Trabajo e Industria-CIDEM-Generalitat de Catalunya	1998
Vision of the future for the audiovisual industry in Catalonia	Audiovisual	Centro de Telecomunicaciones de la Generalitat de Catalunya	1998
City development Análisis for Las Palmas de Gran Canaria	Urban Development	Ayuntamiento de las Palmas de Gran Canaria	1998
Tourism cluster in Lloret del Mar	Tourism	Ayuntamiento de Lloret del Mar	1998
Wine cluster in Calatayud Commercialization	Wine	Instituto Aragones de Fomento	1998
Moulds and dies suppliers cluster in Barcelona	Moulds and dies suppliers	Departamento de Trabajo e Industria-CIDEM-Generalitat de Catalunya, Hewlett packard, SONY, Mould Makers Association (ASCAMMM)	1997–98
Textile technology cluster in Catalonia	Textile technology	Departamento de Trabajo e Industria-CIDEM-Generalitat de Catalunya	1997
Telecommunications equipment cluster in Madrid	Telecom	Comunidad Autónoma de Madrid	1997
Packaging cluster in Navarra	Packaging	Navarra government-industry, commerce and tourism department	1997
Toy industry cluster in Valencia	Toy	Generalitat de Valencia-Economía & CAM	1997
Regional development in Solsona (Catalonia)	General	Departamento de Trabajo e Industria-CIDEM-Generalitat de Catalunya	1997
Competitiveness reinforcement plan for the companies in the industrial parks in Southern Madrid	General	Comunidad Autónoma de Madrid	1997
Identification of clusters in Castilla León	Mapping	Junta de Castilla León	1997
Olive oil cluster in Aragón	Olive oil	Instituto Aragones de Fomento-Aragón Government	1996
Tourism cluster in Bilbao	Tourism	Ayuntameinto de Bilbao	1996
Orientation of the design policy in Catalonia	Graphic design	Dirección General de Promoción Comercial del Departamento de Trabajo e Industria de la Generalitat-CIDEM	1996

Continued

Table 6.7 Continued

Cluster/project	Industry	Institution	Year
Digital entertainment cluster	Digital entertainment	Departamento de Trabajo e Industria de la Generalitat-CIDEM	1996
Ceramic cluster in Gerona	Ceramic	Departamento de Trabajo e Industria de la Generalitat-CIDEM	1996
Meat machinery cluster in Catalonia	Catalonia	Departamento de Trabajo e Industria de la Generalitat-CIDEM	1996
Tourism industry cluster in San Sebastián	Tourism	Ayuntamiento de San Sebastián	1995–96
Audiovisual cluster in Andalucia	Audiovisual	Junta de Andalucia	1995
Confectionary machinery Cluster in Estepa-Andalucia	Confectionary machinery	Junta de Andalucia	1995
Wood processing companies cluster in the Basque Country	Wood processing	Ayuntamiento de Bilbao	1995
Consumer electronics manufacturers in Vallés-Barcelona	Consumer electronics	Departamento de Trabajo e Industria de la Generalitat-CIDEM	1995
Industrial electronics manufacturers cluster in Vallés-Barcelona	Industrial electronics	Departamento de Trabajo e Industria de la Generalitat-CIDEM	1995
Motorcycle manufacturers cluster in Barcelona	Motorcycle	Departamento de Trabajo e Industria de la Generalitat-CIDEM	1995
Publishing cluster in Barcelona	Publishing	Departamento de Trabajo e Industria de la Generalitat-CIDEM	1994
Knitwear cluster in Marasme and Anoia	Knitwear	Departamento de Trabajo e Industria de la Generalitat-CIDEM	1994–95
Wooden toy cluster in Torelló (Barcelona)	Toy	Departamento de Trabajo e Industria de la Generalitat-CIDEM	1994
Meat processing cluster in Girona	Meat procesing	Departamento de Trabajo e Industria de la Generalitat-CIDEM	1994
Home furniture cluster in Montsia-Tarragona	Home furniture	Departamento de Trabajo e Industria de la Generalitat-CIDEM	1994
Clothing in Barcelona	Clothing	Departamento de Trabajo e Industria de la Generalitat-CIDEM	1994
Leather tanning industry	Leather tanning	Departamento de Trabajo e Industria de la Generalitat-CIDEM	1994
Tourism strategy for Galicia	Tourism	Xunta de Galicia	1993

Source: The Competitiveness Institute. (http://www.competitiveness.com/nps/corporate/com/en/company/List_of_projects.pdf).

Finally, as another instance of coordination, it is worth noting that by 2007 there were 25 technological parks in Spain, and 54 are waiting to move up to the "first division" affiliated to the *Asociación de Parques Científicos y Tecnológicos de España* (APTE) (they have to pass very stringent tests). In 30 years they have contributed to the development of almost 2,600 new innovating technology enterprises with almost 80,000 new jobs, of which 12,000 are devoted to research (see figures 6.2–6.6 for data on this technology parks[42]). These Technology Parks (PT) have become spaces of excellence that facilitate the transfer of knowledge and research to companies and the market, and provide their own funds to support the creation of new companies and training.

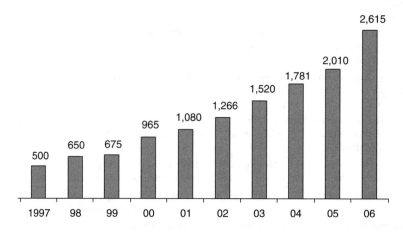

Figure 6.2   Evolution in the number companies in units

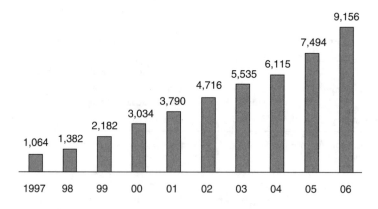

Figure 6.3   Evolution in production in million euros

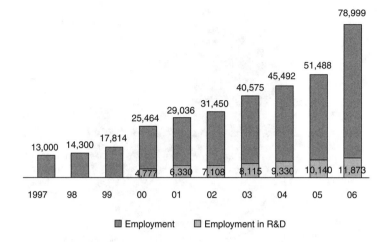

Figure 6.4   Evolution of employment in units

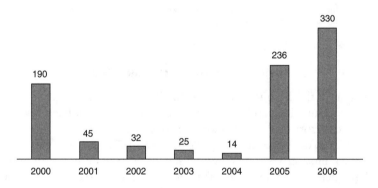

Figure 6.5   Evolution in the call for help for technology parks (aid given in million euros)

The central government has also played a key supporting role (despite the fact that Spain is still ranked 18 by the World Bank in R&D spending): in December of 2000 it approved a *Parquetazo*, an aid package of 3,000 million euros to support the PTs; the Ministry of Science and Education is playing a leading role supporting these initiatives and has given 411 million euros in soft credits at zero interest rates that can be repaid in 5 years to 309 projects supported by the PTs, and the presidency of the government has developed the program *Ingenio 2010* with the objective to increase public funding of R&D by 25 percent yearly to reach 2 percent of GDP by 2010 (it currently stands at 49 percent, compared to the 60 percent average of rich countries).[43] As a result of these efforts, Spain has become a leading country in the world in the development and promotion of these parks.

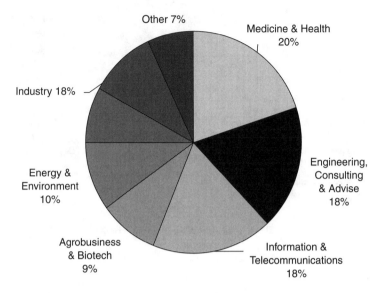

Figure 6.6   Infrastructure of RAD in Spanish parks (in percentage)
Source: "Un toque de pedigrí," in *El País*, Sunday, September 9, 2007.

Conclusion: Keys to the Basque's Success

The analysis of the Basque case shows that it is possible to create institutions to foster coordination, and this even in a region that has been ravaged by conflict and terrorism.[44] It illustrates the conditions under which it is feasible for countries to develop a sustainable path toward coordination (McDermott 2005, p. 8). First, crises and economic shocks provide moments of opportunity that open up the space for change and for new coalitions to emerge. Second, as we have seen in the case of the Basque Country institutional change is more likely to succeed when state policies and actions try to redress resource asymmetries and resolve existing problems in the provision of collective goods. Coordination is also more likely when associations are encompassing in membership, inclusive, and are established to address specific problems or challenges. Finally, government actions should be aimed at improving and facilitating collaboration among groups, sharing of resources, and the achievement of common goals.

These initiatives have been characterized by the following common threats. First, public-private network of organizations; second, public and private funding; third, pooling of resources to develop services to address common collective-action problems; and finally, the use of these institutions as deliberative bodies to identify new challenges and develop further areas of cooperation (see McDermott 2005).

The Basque model of coordination is a model of state-influenced "coordination form the top," which has been highly dependent on state intervention. However, while the Basque Government has played a central leadership role in the coordination efforts, it is important to stress that its main function has been to support and complement the actions of the private sector. The clusters were based on a real private-public partnership. It was clear that the role of the government was not to choke the efforts of the private sector, but mostly to define the mission and the objectives of the cluster. Indeed it leads but it does not impose. Cluster membership was open to all the organizations that were part of the "natural" clusters, and the success of these initiatives has been based on factors such as shared values and goals; the presence of a good facilitator (usually from SPRI or the Department of Industry, Trade and Tourism); regular meetings (almost daily) and interactions between civil servants and the heads of the Cluster Associations; and finally a high level of consensus on the decisions and actions.[45] In sum, the public sector has given independence to the private one, and has not become involved in the management of private firms.[46]

One of the key for the success of this model has been the independence from political interference. Civil society is strong, articulated, and well organized in the Basque Country, and, therefore, it is not easy for the public sector to influence or interfere. Firms and business leaders have bought into the model because they have valued the role that public institutions have played in fostering coordination among economic actors.[47] The strategic choices of the economic actors have been shaped by the local economic orders in which they were situated. Much like in Italy, in the Basque Country "economic actors embedded in local economic orders possessing dense but relatively egalitarian sociopolitical networks were able to share information, form alliances, build trust, and hence negotiate the process of industrial adjustment" (Locke 1995, p. 175).

And this happened at the time in which private firms needed the support from the Basque government to deal with the devastating consequences of the economic crisis of the 1970s–1980s and the new competitive challenges emanating from European integration and the emergence of new competitors from developing countries. Companies realized that they had to focus on exports and they needed a new regulatory and institutional frameworks that facilitated this transition.[48] Hence companies demanded a normative framework and the financial support, which made the development of these coordination institutions possible.

Another relevant factor to account for the success of this model has been the importance to move from the bottom up, and respond to demands from the firms (as opposed to trying to impose decision on the firms), and to grow little by little. An additional contributing factor has been the fact that key players were not only intimately connected, but also that there was a fluid transition between the public and the private sectors. Many of the leaders of many of the business association and commerce chambers had served in the public sector as well and vice versa; leaders of many companies had also served in the public sector and public servants had also transitioned to the private sector. This fluid movement from the private to the public sector (and vice versa) facilitated communication, cross-fertilization, and fostered a culture of dialogue in which the players were looking at the overall and long-term interests of the region, not just merely at their parochial ones. This fostered a culture in which regardless of where the initiative originated (whether it was in the private or public sector), there was a convergence of efforts. The small size of the Basque Country has facilitated all this. Finally, cooperative relations in the Basque Country have been fostered by the long *Foral* tradition of good administration, as well as a strong and entrenched cooperative culture (marked, as noted earlier, by the success of some of the largest cooperatives in the world such as Mondragon). This culture is quite unique to the Basque Country. Finally, it is important to note that there is not a homogenous and single model of cooperation throughout the Basque Country.[49] Indeed, coordination is more developed and has worked better in some regions than others.[50]

The model faces challenges. Recent data suggest that the new industrial model is showing signs of fatigue and slowdown. GDP has slowed down a bit since 2000. Part of it has been the general loss of competitiveness that Spain has experienced since it joined the Euro in 2002. Nationalism can also be a potential threat if it is used as a shield against outsiders: knowledge of the Basque language has become a requirement for some state-sector posts and it is making it difficult for scholars to work in a public university. Key companies such as the bank BBVA and Iberdrola have already moved to Madrid.[51]

Furthermore, the "flattening" of the world caused by the increasing loss of the importance of the concept of geography caused by shifting technological developments is a major source of concern. For instance, the Basque Country, which is an important supplier of automobile components, faces daunting prospects because of the turmoil in an industry beret of excess capacity, weak sales growth, as well as competition from new Asian producers. Analyses suggest that the number of tier-one auto-parts makers will halve to about 30 in the next decade. In the Basque Country alone there are nearly 300 tier-one and tier-two component makers, the heaviest concentration of production in Spain. Turnover from this cluster increased from 3 billion euros in 1993 to more than 9.5 billion in 2006, which makes it the single largest contributor to GDP in the region (16 percent of the total). These challenges are changing the sector's landscape and forcing companies to improve standards and develop more efficient production and delivery processes. Many have already shifted production to Eastern Europe, Asia, and Latin America. The cluster, which was built around cooperation in technology, raw materials, training and support services, is trying to respond to this challenge by developing an Automotive Intelligence Centre, the first in Europe. With this initiative they hope to be able to continue fostering investment in logistic, production systems, and machine innovation.[52] The Basque Government is still developing further initiatives to address new challenges.[53]

Indeed, the Basque Country shows the critical importance of geographical location and physical proximity, which generates important benefits and allows for effective responses to the challenges of globalization. The new ultra-competitive environment requires companies that are flexible to adapt to shifting circumstances and changes in demand. This environment will demand flexibility from companies and workers and also human capital with adequate skills. Yet, only cooperation mechanisms, along the lines of the ones that we have examined in this chapter, will allow the private and public sectors to educate people to succeed in this new system and optimize the use of new technologies. Therefore, places such as the Basque Country, with an industrial base of SMEs that uses medium-high technologies and have a high innovation capacity and an educated labor force are well positioned to compete, provided they constantly enhance their capacity to educate and train people, as well as their ability to innovate to develop processes and products with high value-added and high-technology capacity. They will also have to identify and focus on sectors of high demand. In the end, the key will be the management of knowledge in order to continue generating qualified human capital to attract investment and innovate.

Conclusion

Revisiting the Spanish Model of Capitalism

Introduction

This book pursued two main objectives. First, to review the political economy literature on institutions and to explain the ways in which they affect the behavior of economic actors in Spain. Second, since companies are the locus for wealth creation, it sought to examine how government actions, local contexts, and institutional settings could enhance their competitiveness and foster markets for ideas, capital, and people (Hall and Soskice 2001; Hamel and Prahalad 1996).

In addition, at a time in which there are significant competitive pressures across countries to deregulate and increase competitiveness it is also important to analyze the impact that different institutional settings have on business activities and also the possibility to build coordination capacity in countries that lack a propitious institutional framework. I have shown that institutional change is dependent on different political approaches to competitive pressures. Economic actors develop the institutions that they need, but it is necessary to explain how, why and when. Thus, this project has sought to address key questions such as: What kind of institutions favor enhanced competitiveness and promote entrepreneurship and innovation? How can firms exploit to their advantage the institutional setting in which they are operating? How are particular forms of coordination achieved and maintained? More specifically, are countries, such as Spain, moving in the direction of LMEs? How much institutional change is possible? Can employers (in non-CMEs or non-LMEs) develop mechanisms to coordinate? Can they create new forms of coordination? Are they unable to coordinate and develop complementarities?

While the VoC approach has theorized a great deal with regard to the different forms in which change occurs, it does not explain sufficiently why or how it occurs. This book seeks to address this shortcoming by exploring why (and how) change happened in Spain. It looks at the different varieties of coordination as changing systems, not as equilibrium systems. The book makes three important contributions to the Varieties of Capitalism literature (VoC) (see Hancké, Rhodes, and Thatcher 2007a, p. 4). First, by examining the politics, conflict, and power struggles among Spanish economic and social actors it brings the politics back onto center stage (Thelen 2004). The book looks at coordination as a political problem in which actors are constantly assessing and evaluating institutions, and views stability as a political outcome. It focuses not merely on the individual action of actors, but also on their collective actions as well. It examines political coalitions and political conflict, and it explains the process of change in Spain by ongoing political negotiations.

Second, by "bringing the state back in," it addresses the VoC literature's tendency to downplay state action and largely ignore its distinctive role in CMEs and LMEs (Schmidt 2006, pp. 9–11). This is a particular shortcoming given that the role of the state is still more important in Spain than in CMEs and LMEs. Indeed, coordination in Spain not only depends on the organizational capacities of actors, but also on state intervention, which also influences the shape and character of coalitions (Molina and Rhodes 2005). By deconstructing state actions and examining the degree and form of government actions and practices, the book considers state action in all its complexity (both at the national and regional levels).

Finally, by introducing an additional typology, *the State Influenced-Mixed-Market Economy* (SMME),[1] characterized by larger state influence over labor and business, a higher degree of fragmentation in the system, regional divisions, as well as different degrees of coordination across institutional areas, the book builds on the contributions of other scholars (Schmidt 2006; Molina and Rhodes 2007) and extends the VoC reductionist and static focus on a binary division of capitalism based on two ideal-type models (CMEs and LMEs). In Spain the institutional framework is fragmented and there is class conflict but economic actors and organizations have worked with the state to coordinate their actions. National pacts (both bipartite and tripartite) are examples or institutionalized coordination. This third category stresses the role of state influence and the logic of coordination of mixed economies, which tends to be from the top-down, and helps explain better the coordination process in the Spanish political economy and the process of institutional change.

This book has shown that the development of coordination capacities also depends on domestic social and institutional conditions. It has looked at the sociopolitical changes that lead to deliberative restructuring, including shifts in the balance of power between labor and capital in favor of the latter; technological change; increasing competition from low-cost countries; the erosion of the basis of the welfare state caused by the ageing of the population and increasing individualization of labor relations; and EMU, which has limited the governments' capacity to introduce macroeconomic stimulus.

At the same time, it has shed further light on political approaches to competitive pressures that tend to promote the interaction of the state and economic actors in new innovative ways that create further coordination capacities. It supports the view that economic and institutional change is also the product of policy choices (Locke 1995). In Spain globalization, European monetary integration, and increasing competition have led to political and distributional struggles, which in turn have generated impetuses for change and adjustment (Hancké, Rhodes, and Thatcher 2007a). The book shows that there are different trajectories of change. From a macroeconomic stand-point it has become more of an LME (a development that largely applies to all CMEs). Yet there is still a high degree of coordination in labor relations, finance, and corporate governance.

This book has also attempted to contribute to the debate of how institutions change and evolve over time (Pierson 2004; Thelen 2004). In Spain institutional evolution has been the result of the actions from actors with particular interests that have been influenced by "changes in the broader social environment and/or the character of the actors themselves" (Pierson 2004, p. 108) and by coalition shifts. It challenges traditional interpretations that view institutional change merely as a consequence of exogenous shocks (Olson 1982) and reaffirms the interpretation according to which institutional change is a dynamic and experimenting process that can develop as part of an incremental but cumulative transformative process (Streeck and Thelen 2005). A period of uncertainty and competitive challenges has provided pressures on the Spanish social actors to experiment within the existing institutions. They have added new elements that have altered the institutions' overall trajectory and shifted them toward new goals and functions. This is another instance of institutional adaptation in which institutions that were created for a set of purposes have been redirected to serve different goals (Thelen 2004, pp. 292–294). The analysis of the Spanish case confirms that change is incremental and involves political struggles, and also that institutional equilibrium is not static; on the contrary it is constantly negotiated and renegotiated. For instance, an institutional mechanism that originated with the goal to control wages has become an instrument of coordination aimed at changing the prevalent economic model based on low wages.

Indeed, the process of institutional change is influenced by both exogenous (such as EMU) and endogenous developments and sources of change, and it is largely driven by class-level coalitions that have formed at specific junctions and have pushed the system in certain directions in pursuit of their self-interest. Actors create the institutions that they need, and the direction of change is influenced by the interest of the actors. They support certain institutional arrangements for the benefits that they provide (e.g., social bargaining emerged as a mechanism to achieve wage moderation). The book also examined different mechanisms for institutional change including reforms from governments, reinterpretation of existing laws, development of new institutions to foster coordination (Economic and Social Council, clusters, and so on), or the informal behavior of employers.

The analysis of the Spanish case confirms the thesis that in the context of structural constraints that influence the range of options available to them, strategic actors with their own interests design institutions. It shows that countries are not stuck in a particular pattern of labor relations and practices, thus rejecting institutional deterministic approaches and illustrating that although institutions are path dependent, they still offer constraints and opportunities for change. Indeed, institutions were still the object of political contestation and in the industrial relations arena Spain is moving from "state capitalism" to "managed capitalism." Existing institutions affected the interests and strategic options available to the social actors and coalition shifts influenced institutional design.

This book rejects the convergence thesis. It argues that in a global economy countries adjust differently. CMEs, LMEs, and SMMEs will not stay the same, they will continue changing, but the direction of change will be different. In the end, the book shows that there is a significant amount of variation across and within countries, and that different systems have different efficient institutional arrangements. Even in places such as Spain, which do not meet the institutional preconditions, it is still possible to develop mechanisms to provide collective goods, which shows that there are different ways to produce these collective goods.

While national institutional arrangements and legal frameworks shape economic behavior, I agree with Locke (1995, p. 182) that even within these constraints "there still exists a range of possibilities open to economic actors." Hence it is important to look at complementarities at the micro level. The books has tried to shed light on the strategic choices pursued by the social actors within the existing industrial institutional setting, and it has also examined the way "sociopolitical networks" influence the strategic options open to these actors. As we have seen, there are also regional differences. By looking at subnational differences, like we did with the Basque Country, we find out that we get coordination where we least expect it. Finally, the analysis of the Basque Country also underscores the important role of ideas (Schmidt 2006), with the Basque Government supporting the general idea that coordination was essential for Basque firms to compete and hire experts (Michael Porter) to carry them out.

The Strategic Choices of Economic Actors

The book examined the ways in which endogenous and exogenous factors induce the social partners to review their positions and strategies vis-à-vis existing institutional arrangements. It stresses the need to complement neoinstitutional explanations with a new set of hypotheses concerning actors' behavior (see Regini 2000, p. 9). Institutions are the object of strategic action by economic actors, but actors are not defined by their institutions. They use them as resources to achieve their goals (Schmidt 2006). In the end, policy changes have to be examined through the analysis of political institutions and their impact on the strategies of the social actors. In Spain attempts to reform have largely been a top-down political-exchange process in which the social actors have resorted to social bargaining as an instrument to address conflicts and increase the governability of the system (Molina and Rhodes 2005, p. 23).

One of the key areas of coordination that we have examined has been the attempt to resolve the problems of collective bargaining in the 1990s, through social concertation. As we have seen, the collective bargaining structure in Spain has not moved toward decentralization and individualization. The political strategy of trade union organizations has been to support coordination and tripartite bargaining as a defensive strategy to retake the initiative, affirm their role as political actors, and influence policy outcomes. In addition, the resurgence of social bargaining has been fostered by the increasing autonomy of unions from political parties and a process of institutional learning motivated by the failure of previous confrontational strategies that convinced leaders of unions that such confrontational approach was detrimental to the interest of their constituencies and threatened the survival of their organizations (Royo 2002). Ultimately, in a new economic and political context, centralized concertation became an instrument for the unions (who tried to leave behind the grand tripartite pacts of the 1980s, with high short-term costs for them) to pursue specialized social dialogue to target specific areas of institutional reform, with the objective to halt decentralization attempts and consolidate arrangements beneficial to the workers (Molina and Rhodes 2005, p. 20).

For their part, employers' associations decided that while competitiveness and costs were contingent on the increasing flexibility of labor and production systems, they also depended on the governability of the national system; hence they needed to maintain some kind of centralized coordination to achieve this goal. Moreover, they finally realized that their long-term competitive success hinged on the ability of the national system in which they operate to provide the collective goods that they need to compete effectively—such as professional training, or wage coordination and wage moderation. Hence, they acknowledged that the crucial problem for their firms was the need to institutionalize further the production of collective goods (Regini 2000, p. 19). Consequently, employers have given priority to continuing social concertation and have supported cooperative strategies as instruments to further competitiveness. They understood that the most effective way to achieve wage moderation and to liberalize the labor market would be through the acquiescence of unions. Deregulation was never a real option for businesses given the unions' capacity to exercise effective veto power through intensifying industrial conflict. Indeed, employers recognize that confrontation had led to higher wages and the paralysis of the reform and liberalization processes in the second half of the 1980s and first half of the 1990s. Social bargaining, on the other hand, had resulted in wage moderation and offered a gradual and stable path toward reform and liberalization of the labor market (Royo 2002, pp. 176–177).

Indeed, the institutional structure of the Spanish economy combined with the competitive challenges faced by Spanish firms have made it more advantageous for them to support coordination. As we have seen, this strategic shift on the part of Spanish firms constitutes an institutional mechanism to support business competitiveness through coordination and social bargaining. Therefore, the strategic shift of Spanish firms in favor of coopera-tion is a refection of their attempt to reconcile the objective to control costs through more flexibility in hiring practices and in the deployment of their labor force, and the need for cooperative relations at the firm level in order to provide the necessary collective goods to remain competitive. The Spanish case thus confirms that "responses by the European economies differ accord-ing to the trade-off for their firms between deregulation and concertation, between more market and more adequate supply of collective goods" (Regini 2000, p. 19).

Like in France and Germany (Culpepper 2003) employers and unions have had to overcome uncertainty and mutual distrust to cooperate, and the government (both at the national and regional levels) has played a central role convincing them of the benefits of cooperation. Experience has shown them that confrontation in the 1980s and 1990s led to higher wages and the partial paralysis of the reform and liberalization processes; therefore, they have understood that the most effective way to increase competitiveness, liberalize the labor market, and achieve wage moderation is through the acquiescence of unions. Coordination, on the other hand, has resulted in wage moderation and has offered a gradual and stable path toward reform and liberalization of the labor market (Royo 2002, pp. 176–177).

At the same time, developments within the international economic environment and within the domestic structure have changed the balance of power among the social actors. The process of European integration has played a crucial role: the Spanish economy, as we have seen (chapters 1 and 2), has been affected by regulations emanating from the EU and has also benefited from funds from the EU. In Spain (as well as in the other member states) the process of economic integration is affecting unions, business, and governments and the country has responded differently to this impact. While other countries such as the Netherlands and Germany, are implementing liberal business-friendly regulation (Menz 2005), Spain has been moving toward further coordination. These changes have facilitated the emergence of new strategies among the social actors and have influenced their predispo-sition to negotiate and settle their differences through social bargaining. Indeed, these new challenges have provided the necessary impetus for change and compelled the social actors to redefine their interactions and strategies, and they have used social bargaining as an instrument to address some of these challenges.

While we have examined the case of the Basque Country, as we look at future research agendas it will be important to explore further the logic guiding the strategic decisions of company managers and union leaders at the micro level. As we have seen in the Basque Country, local actors are embed-ded in local economies that have different sociopolitical networks, which influence the resources and strategic options available to them in different ways. The local patterns of industrial politics are not a unique phenomena. On the contrary, what happened in the Basque Country is not exceptional, but rather indicative of a more general trend developing throughout Spain (and other countries as well) (Locke 1995). The proliferation of diverse subnational patterns of industrial politics is also creating new opportunities and challenges for the social actors. Unions and employers' associations in the Basque Country, for instance, are becoming more responsive to the local needs of companies, but this may present risks for the national labor and employers' movements, which are trying to maintain unity and coordination. Yet, in the context of international competition and technological change diversity will be an asset. The author is currently exploring these issues in the region of Valencia.

Spain as a State Influenced-Mixed-Market Economy (SMME)

As we have seen throughout the book, Spain lacked a tradition of social bargaining among democratic actors. In fact, it had no experience with the neocorporatist agreements that had been an integral part of the industrial relations setting in many other European nations. A comparison of these institutional factors across European countries suggests that Spain does not meet some of the institutional criteria advanced by the VoC and the neocorporatist literature for the success of coordination schemes (see chapter 3). Indeed, the institutional setting in Spain differs in several important respects from liberal and coordinated market economies common in other OECD countries.[2] However, like other European countries (such as France or Italy) Spain has transformed its economic management system over the last three decades through reforms that borrow from both models of capitalism, but the state and state actors continue to play an important role. Still Spain conforms to a large extend to a so-called "state capitalism" model (Schmidt 2002, pp. 141–146), in which the government is still a major institutional actor and leads business-labor relations.

Lacking the nonmarket coordination mechanisms that support the high-quality/value-added model of the CMEs, Spain is characterized in the literature as a country with limited strategic coordination on labor relations. Yet, as we have seen, this unpropitious institutional setting has not precluded the development of coordination among economic actors. Indeed, Spain has been able to overcome the relative absence of institutionalized coordination mechanisms between the social actors (rooted in the fragmentation of the economic systems, and the weak coordination capacities of employers and unions), and coordination among economic actors has flourished, as they have developed distinctive processes of tripartite bargaining to reform social policies, moderate wages, and reform the labor market.

The renewal of tripartite bargaining in Spain in the 1990s challenges the conventional wisdom that explains changes in industrial relation systems as a universal move on the parts of employers to deregulate labor relations and a movement along a continuum in which deregulation culminates in convergence toward an LME model. On the contrary, it shows that the trend has been toward greater coordination and centralization, not decentralization (i.e., the 1997 AINC), and toward strengthening the most representatives' unions against growing challenges. The social actors have supported the renewal of social pacts in the second half of the 1990s as a mechanism for securing labor cooperation and peace.

While some scholars (Schmidt 2002, p. 127) attribute the direction of reform in state capitalist countries toward greater coordination to "the relative levels of unionization and central organization of employers' associations and unions," and cross-national differences in outcomes to the differing capacity to resist these changes, in Spain the relative level of unionization and the organization of unions and employers' organizations has not changed significantly over the last decade and unions and employers are not much stronger than they were a decade ago. Moreover, contrary to Italy, the state has not always been a central actor in this process and the social actors have reasserted their autonomy.

Indeed, as noted in chapter 3, Spain (as well as France, Italy, and Portugal) forms a third type of economy characterized by state influence over business and labor, strong coordination in financial markets but not that much in the field of labor relations, a *State Influenced Mixed-Market Economy*, (SMMEs) (see Schmidt 2006; Molina and Rhodes 2005). Part of the historical reason for this development has been the high level of state intervention in economic policy making in these countries: the coordination of labor relations was a process led by the state, in charge of setting minimum wages, and with the ability to translate a wage increase in a firm to the entire sector. However, as states have become more and more reluctant to coordinate their labor relations in these countries, some of these economies are becoming less coordinated.

Yet the direction of change is not uniform. As we have seen throughout the book the direction of reform is Spain seems to be toward the CME model, as opposed to other countries such as France in which the dynamic of reform seems to be leading more toward the LME model (Schmidt 2006). The reason for this divergence is based on the importance of the principle of institutional complementarities (i.e., the notion that institutions supporting effective strategic—or market—coordination in one sphere of the political economy are usually complementary to institutions in other spheres) (see Hall and Gingerich 2004). While in France reforms in the corporate governance system are making takeovers more common (typical of the LMEs), in Spain there is still strong strategic coordination in financial markets (i.e., the role of networking and family financing) and hostile takeovers are rare (typical of the CMEs) (Schmidt 2006, p. 9).

Another reason for this divergence lies in the fact that while both countries have historically lacked the institutional complementarities that characterize CMEs, in France the movement toward an LME model has been possible because of the character of labor relations: unions are very weak, and, therefore, the government and business have been able to accommodate changes to the corporate governance system without strong resistance.[3] In other words, based on the principle of institutional complementarities, they can do this because of the system of industrial relations that they have (Schmidt

2006). In Spain, on the contrary, unions have been able to exercise effective veto power against government unilateral reforms (see Royo 2002, pp. 182–191), and employers have decided, for reasons that we have examined, that it is in their best interest to move toward further coordination. Yet, this divergence may still be temporary. In France employers and unions have just launched a historic negotiation (September 2007) on how to reform the labor market that will address thorny issues including hiring and firing, and unemployment benefits.[4] Like in Spain, unions facing questions about their legitimacy amid falling membership, and employers seeking to achieve more flexibility and lower costs to face international competition, have been forced to the negotiation table and have reached a historic agreement to reform the labor Market in January of 2008.[5]

Spain has also been relatively successful in addressing the fragmentation of reform coalitions. As we have seen, social bargaining has facilitated the process of exchange-based reform, widened the scope for collaboration and compromise, and contributed to reduce polarization. While structural fragmentation has led to the development of different logics of coordination and interaction among economic actors, the strong articulation of the business sector around an umbrella organization, the *Confederacion Española de Organizaciones Emresariales* (CEOE), which holds the monopoly of employers interest representation, and the strategic unity of action between the two leading confederations, (*Comisiones Obreras*, CCOO; and *Unión General de Trabajadores*, UGT) has allowed the social actors to articulate demands in effective ways in order to be able to deliver collective goods in the industrial relations realm.

The state has played a central role as a facilitator for coordination, but its role has increasingly changed over the last two decades as a result of combined processes of decentralization, liberalization, and deregulation, which have been deeper in Spain than in other European countries (such as Portugal, Italy, or France). In Spain the liberalization of social protection, labor markets, and financial markets has opened new spaces for economic actors to cooperate. The state continues creating the stable framework for the autonomous regulation of business operations and interactions, but it is acting less as a provider of resources, income, and collective goods than it used to, and more as a facilitator. The quasi-federal structure of the Spanish state has also played a facilitating role to compensate for the absence of coordination at the micro levels. As we have seen in the Basque Country, the regional governments have been able to play a crucial role pushing for coordination among the economic actors, and compensating the traditional weak coordinating capacities of small businesses, and their incapacity to provide collective goods.

Furthermore, the flexibility of the labor market, and in particular the extension of fixed-term temporary contracts and the dramatic increase in temporary contracts, has largely eliminated any incentives to invest in specific skills and has had a detrimental effect on productivity. This goes against the grain of any CME because it fosters a model based on labor-intensive, low-skill, low-technology intensity production. A continuation of this pattern would have reinforced the existing complementarities between the production and protection systems in the direction of LMEs. Yet, as we have seen, the social actors have finally realized the limitations of a model based on low-wages and prices, easy dismissals for temporary workers, and medium-low technology, and are working together to move away from such a competitive strategy. This major shortcoming, which threatens the sustainability of economic growth, has acted as a major incentive to propel the social actors to work together to overcome it. While the results remain to be seen, the coordination in Spanish financial markets, together with the further development of the Spanish welfare state, the increasing coordination in the collective bargaining and training systems, the role of autonomous governments, and continuing state intervention distance Spain from the LME model (Molina and Rhodes 2005, p. 17).

One of the main challenges for the so-called under-organized economies, such as Spain, is to build the coordinating capacity among the social actors that will allow them to respond to international pressures and solve the economic problems that result from increasing international competition and market integration (Hall and Soskice 2001). While changes in production regimes and occupational structure demand greater flexibility, increasing competition rewards institutional mechanisms that facilitate cooperation among the social actors and tilt the balance of wage-setting toward the tradable sector of the economy.

Paradoxically, the economic pressures that are eroding the coordination mechanisms of Coordinated Market Economies (CMEs) are offering incentives to the Spanish social actors to address new challenges through social pacts. Indeed, the experience of Spain suggests that market integration and international competition also create pressures that promote social bargaining. The main forces of change, such as monetary integration, financial liberalization, fiscal decentralization, technological changes, the transformation in the nature of business, relative inflexible labor markets, little labor mobility, inflationary pressures, and new demands on professional training systems, have pushed the social actors toward further coordination. In the end, structural pressures by employers for more flexibility to respond to changing market conditions, and a shift in the content of bargaining toward production issues have resulted in cooperative processes that have involved the collective management of industrial relations above the plant level.

In this light, the Spanish agreements conform to a mixed model of corporatism, so-called competitive corporatism, which is different in form from the traditional Social Democratic (SD) corporatism (Rhodes 1998), characterized by bargaining among weaker organizations, with governments acting as instigators of social pacts to reform labor legislation or social programs aimed at reducing labor costs and improving competitiveness (Rhodes 1998, p. 183; Hassel and Ebbinghaus 2000, p. 80). In this context, unions have to accept that the key to the future is to "protect the worker not the job."[6] The most successful countries in Europe, such as the United Kingdom or the Scandinavian countries, are the ones who have adopted policies that support that new paradigm, and in which people are willing to adjust.

In sum, the analysis of the Spanish case shows that countries are not stuck in a particular pattern of labor relations and practices. It rejects institutional deterministic approaches and illustrates that although institutions are path dependent, they still offer constraints and opportunities for change. In the industrial relations arena Spain is moving from "state capitalism" to "managed capitalism."

Future Prospects

What are the prospects for further sustainable coordination? It is still not clear whether current trends will persist in the future, whether they will consolidate the traditional dominant role of the state in industrial relations, or permit the social actors to take the initiative and assert their autonomy. The success (or failure) of these initiatives will determine the consolidation of this approach.[7]

Business coordination in Spain will be facilitated by the strong strategic coordination of financial markets that results from networking and family financing that makes hostile takeovers rare. While the Spanish takeover climate has changed with the passing of a new Takeover Code that came into effect on August 13, 2007, listed companies are still not obliged to dismantle their antitakeover armory, such as voting limits.[8] Moreover, as we have seen when analyzing the Basque Country, ties among government and business elites based on family links, and shared experiences (and often education and training), have created a closeness that will continue furthering coordination. Indeed, social connections and shared values are also critical variables to account for the development and sustainability of coordination in Spain.

With regard to social bargaining, which as we have examined throughout the book, has emerged as an important form to institutionalize the coordination capacity of the social actors; its return has had positive consequences for the Spanish economy and it has contributed to sustained rapid growth. At the same time, the preceding discussion suggests that the motivations that led the social actors to return to national social bargaining are more structural than simply the goal of participation in EMU and are likely to persist in the future. The social actors should have powerful incentives to continue this approach given the difficulties that the government and employers had in the past in controlling overall wage growth without the support from unions, coupled with the erosion that further fragmentation would have on the position of the main confederations. Furthermore, the examination of the role played by the Economic and Social Council (CES) suggests that a cooperative strategy based on social bargaining will last longer when the social actors have been able to develop a capacity for strategic learning.

At the same time, other developments favor the continuation of these processes. First, wage moderation is crucial to close the gap with the EU

richer countries, to exploit Europe-wide specialization, and to attract investment from its European partners. In addition, the abandonment of comprehensive macrobargaining strategies—which covered every issue and culminated
in macroagreements—in favor of a new strategy based on different bargaining
tables is more conducive to agreements. The Spanish social actors have
adopted a more flexible approach through the parallel negotiation of various
agreements, each of limited scope. This bargaining strategy is based on
package deals that include both labor market organization and flexibility,
as well as substantial social policy reforms. The new pacts seek to maintain
equilibrium between flexibility and solidarity, and between equity and efficiency. They are part of a political exchange: social benefits and employment
in exchange for flexibility and wage moderation. In countries such as Spain,
where unilateral reforms have not been effective and have encountered
significant resistance, governments are likely to continue using this strategy
in order to gain legitimacy for unpopular labor and social reforms and to
overcome the institutional veto by the social partners. The social partners, in
turn, are likely to accept this approach as long as they participate in the policy-
making process and receive compensation. Finally, an additional incentive is
the fact that social bargaining helps prevent a negative spillover from social
policy into wage bargaining (Hassel and Ebbinghaus 2000).

For Spain, with an industrial relations' settings deeply rooted in the law
and with significant state intervention, the challenge will be to build new
institutional mechanisms that will provide the instruments needed for
governments to adopt the adequate supply-side policies and contain inflation
while maintaining sound fiscal policies, and for the micro actors to have the
necessary internal and external flexibility and the lower costs to compete
effectively in a globalize market. Social bargaining is the adequate instrument
to achieve these goals. It provides the social actors with processes to achieve
a balance between efficiency and solidarity while overcoming veto points.

The sustainability of cooperation efforts in Spain will also hinge on the
resolution of a trade-off: a slower decision-making process versus the
likelihood of the successful implementation of its outcomes (Regini 2003,
p. 260). Even if the involvement of different economic actors slows down the
decision-making process, as long as it ensures the success in the implementation
of those decisions, the economic actors will have incentives to return to the
bargaining table and continue cooperating. In Spain with a long history of
relative failure of unilateral regulations, the economic actors will have powerful
incentives to continue cooperating.

European Monetary Union means further restrictions on domestic
economic policies because monetary union subjects macroeconomic policy in
the EMU area to a single monetary authority, the independent European
Central Bank. Although some scholars have already predicted the dismissal of
centralized concertation schemes, new analyses are proving the importance
that incomes policy will have in the context of the monetary union (Iversen
1999). Incomes policy, with its influence on labor relations and labor costs,
seems to continue to be an adequate instrument to enhance competitiveness

and contribute to the convergence objective pursued by the European economies. The benefits of centralized wage bargaining, however, hinge largely on the ability of union leaders to control overall wage growth in order to avoid monetary policy measures that will result in higher unemployment (Pérez 1998; Hall and Franzese 1998). EMU may result in the decentralization of the level of wage bargaining across the EU because overall, the most encompassing union organizations will be less inclusive, and, therefore, they may have fewer incentives to internalize the inflationary pressures of wage increases.[9] The risk will be that in the new EMU context, in which wage bargaining is relatively fragmented but there is s single monetary authority for the area, wage bargainers will be less responsive to threats from the ECB. Nevertheless, since unit labor costs will still remain a critical factor in improving competitiveness, there will be strong pressures on governments, employers, and unions to pursue social bargaining.

The Challenges for the Spanish Economy

As examined in chapter 2, despite all the significant progress accomplished during the past two decades, the Spanish economy confronts difficult challenges in the new millennium. In comparison with other European countries the Spanish economy is experiencing faster rates of growth. Yet, it has not reached the development levels, particularly in technology, of the richest European countries. Furthermore, the competitive position of the Spanish economy has deteriorated lately and this is a very worrisome development that must be addressed. Failure to do so may have dire consequences. Some observers have argued that Spain is about to experience a German-style economic stagnation or worse[10] while others are raising the possibility that Spain may have to leave the Euro.[11]

From an economic convergence standpoint, given the existing income and productivity differentials with the richer countries, Spain will have to continue raising its living standards to bring them closer to the current EU average. For this to happen, it is necessary for the Spanish economy to grow faster than the other rich European countries. This will require further liberalization of its labor structures (both internal and external), as well as increasing competition within its service markets and improving the utilization of their productive resources. Convergence will also demand institutional reforms in R&D policies, in education, improvement of civil infrastructures, as well as further innovation, an increase in business capabilities, more investment in information technology, and better and more efficient training systems. Moreover, Spain needs to find the right balance of labor flexibility and worker incentives to promote productivity. A successful convergence policy will also require a debate about the role of public investment and welfare programs. In Spain increases in public expenditures to develop the welfare states have sometimes caused imbalances in the national accounts. Yet it still spends significantly less in this area than its European neighbors (i.e., Spain spends 6.3 points less in welfare policies than the EMU average). Effective real convergence would demand not only effective strategies and policies, but also a strong commitment on the part of Spanish citizens to achieve this objective.

Moreover, the Spanish economy still has considerable ground to cover to improve its competitiveness. Since the country is part of EMU and any adjustment through a devaluation of its currency is no longer feasible, the only way for Spain to regain lost competitiveness is through a long period of wage moderation and increasing productivity. This will demand improvements in the working of markets and the elimination of distortions, as well as further liberalization of the economy particularly in the gas and electricity sectors and enhanced energy efficiency to diminish the country's continuing dependence on import energy, which contributes to inflation. Furthermore it will require the use of new technologies and increasing spending on research and development.

A competitiveness agenda will have to focus on productivity growth, which is even more important in Spain than nominal wage growth. To address this shortcoming will demand actions to improve policy across a wide front: higher investment in infrastructure, improvements in land-use planning, efforts to increase the quality of education, rigorous promotion of competition in all areas of the economy, tax simplification, and rationalization of existing regulations.[12] Furthermore such agenda will demand a shift from a low-cost, low-skill manufacturing base that relies on technical design and marketing skills from elsewhere, toward more capital-intensive industries that require greater skills in the labor force and rely on standard technology—for example, chemicals, vehicles, steel and metal manufacturers, as well as a change in the existing growth model (based on relatively low production costs) in order to build a new framework based on innovation, quality, value-added, and productivity. Small companies have to carve out market niches in the global market and develop the technical capacity for short production runs to be able to respond to shifting demand. They have to develop their own brands and distribution networks, and create their own customer bases. This will require the development of a technological know-how and marketing techniques.

The goal must be to increase productivity by increasing the capital intensity of production. Innovation and higher productivity will require the following four main conditions:

1. Investment in capital technology (i.e., information systems and telecommunications);
2. A new culture of entrepreneurship, innovation, and risk;
3. Human capital with strong skills and the flexibility to adapt to new technologies and processes, based on a model of continuous training; and
4. A flexible and adaptable industrial relations framework.

As this book goes to press (Fall 2007) the Spanish economy is showing signs of decelerating. Rising interest rates, inflation (motivated by the increase in the costs of oil and food), and the slowing of the real estate market have begun to cool down the economy. According to data from the National Statistics Institute, second quarter year-on-year GDP growth was 4 percent, down from the 4.1 percent recorded in the first quarter, and quarterly growth also dipped to 0.9 percent. The main laggard has been construction (which still represents about 18 percent of GDP), due to the softening of demand for new home and public works. Property-related shares collapsed in April 2007 and the market has been hit by the global subprime crisis. Inflation has reached 4.1 percent, and the differential with the EU average has increased to 1.1 points, the highest in years. At the same time, rising mortgage costs have softened consumer spending and the effects of the global financial crisis will impact consumption: the average mortgage payment has increased almost 100 euros in one year, which is already depressing consumption (particularly in sectors such as tourism). Housing investment will decrease in 2008 for the first time in the last decade, after six years in which it has been the most dynamic sector of the economy with growth rates over 5 percent, and it is expected that construction will continue decelerating reaching approximately 3.8 percent.

Yet, all this has been offset by the strength in capital investment and the growth in exports (4.8 percent in the second quarter). But the subprime financial crisis is bound to affect Europe (particularly Germany), which will hinder Spanish exports. While the economy is still expected to growth a robust 3.7 percent this year, the broader slowdown seems to indicate that the end of an economic cycle may be near. Most observers have already reduced the growth estimate for 2008 to 3 percent (about 3,300 million euros). Unemployment is also expected to increase but will remain around 8 percent in 2008, and the creation of employment is set to decline (from 3 percent to 2 percent), with particular impact on immigrants and workers with low skills.[13]

These negative factors are offset by the strength of the Spanish financial sector, which has been barely affected by the subprime crisis, and the limited impact of this crisis in Latin America, a key market for Spanish companies and investors. Inflation is also expected to fall to 2.7 percent by the end of the year, the lowest this decade, and the top Spanish companies that constitute the Ibex 35 are expected to have record benefits, with an average growth of 34 percent in 2007. The budgetary situation is still very positive: Spain had a budget surplus in 2005 and 2006 and is expected to have a similar surplus in 2007 (around 1.8 percent of GDP). By 2010 Spain will be the country with more kilometers in highways of Europe, and the efforts to increase the technological capitalization of the country with investments in research and development, and innovation, have begun to bear fruit. The productivity of the private sector has grown in four years from 0.3 percent to 1.1 percent. The construction sector is losing weight in the economy and it is expected that future growth may be more balanced in its composition: for the first time in years the industrial sector has grown faster than the construction sector in the first six months of 2007.[14] Still, nothing can be taken for granted yet: the industrial production has decelerated to 1.3 percent in the first half of 2007.

Do the Spanish people want to continue building houses or do they want to increase their salaries and develop a model based on value-added? There are other European countries that have developed knowledge-based economies with very strong results, and can serve as references (i.e., the Scandinavian countries). Yet these challenges do not hinge as much on Europe as they do on Spain itself. The wide scope of the reforms outlined earlier reflects the daunting challenge facing Spanish governments. They will face growing resistance from the people likely to be hit hardest by these reforms. However, the lack of political willingness to implement these reforms will hinder the convergence process and erode further the competitiveness of the Spanish economy. It will not be easy. Globalization is forcing economies to open up markets and embrace reforms, but the current stalemate in support for reforms in Europe, growing protectionism (manifested by the opposition of national governments to cross-border mergers and acquisitions in sectors such as energy), and increasing backlash against "Anglo-Saxon" free-market capitalism will make the reform process even more difficult.

This book has shown that the development of coordination mechanisms has been instrumental for Spanish firms at the national and regional level to address the challenges posed by globalization. Some of the most successful experiences have been the result of this approach. There are reasons for optimism. Between January and September of 2006, the number of companies established in the country reached 111,753, 8.49 percent more than that during the same period in 2005; and the percentage of companies that survived at least 42 months increased during the same period by 35.2 percent, reflecting the strength of the Spanish economy.[15]

Spain is also creating new state-of-the-art clusters on knowledge in areas such as clean energy. Led by companies such as Gamesa or Iberdrola, Spain has taken advantage of its natural conditions (it is Europe's second-most mountainous country, one of the least densely populated ones, and it has a favorable climate) to develop its clean energy industry. It has also benefited from being an early adopter of tariff premiums, which has offered producers an attractive return and a guarantee of stable income, thus encouraging investment. As a result Spain has become the world's second biggest producer of wind energy after Germany, and is a leading power in other renewable energies such as solar power and bio fuels. Thousands of high-wind turbines have been installed all over the country that produce 8,375 megawatts of power (27 percent of the country's electricity supply), and new private equity funds have emerged dedicated to renewable energy investments.[16]

The focus on R&D and the collaboration between public research bodies and the business community in new technology projects (which is largely viewed as one of the main causes for the country's poor productivity performance) has intensified as well. The Spanish economic actors have understood that it is essential to incorporate homegrown R&D and to develop and use new advanced technologies. Research groups throughout Spain are producing some of the most advanced technology in the country. For instance, the *Salvador Velayos Laboratory* of Madrid's Institute of Applied Magnetology (IMA), part of Universidad Complutense de Madrid, has become a leader in its field, signing R&D contracts and cooperation agreements with leading companies such as Iberdrola (energy), and Aena (air control operator). One of the main reasons for their success is that they turn basic research into successful application and develop practical solutions for the real problems facing companies.[17] These kinds of initiatives are key if Spain is to address its very weak productivity performance, which has led to increases in unit labor costs and diminished international competitiveness. Coordination in this area is essential given the small- and medium-size of Spanish companies, which lack the funds to invest and develop research.

As we have seen in the Basque Country, the focus has to be on developing market niches and technical capacity so firms can respond to shifting demands and deliver quickly. In the last few years there have been several instances of cooperation between employers and unions that have paid off. For instance in 2006 the automaker General Motors decided to manufacture one of its new cars (the Meriva) in the plant that the company has in Figueruelas (which was competing against the Polish Gliwice). The reasons for this decision were as follows: the higher productivity of the Figueruela workers, the agreement between GM and the unions to increase productivity in order to produce the car in 16 hours (against the current 21), and the support from the regional government of Aragón.[18]

In Valencia, the challenge of low-priced competition from China and other countries has inspired local footwear and clothing manufacturers to develop their own brands and distribution networks. For decades Valencia was a low-cost, low-skill manufacturing base of foreign groups, but as a result of competition they have closed and moved their operations to lower-cost countries (particularly China). In the last decade they have been making a bold leap into the fashion arena, developing their own customer bases, and carving out a niche in the global market. Through clusters and cooperation, they have developed their own technical expertise and marketing knowledge and they no longer rely on technical design and marketing skills from other places.[19]

Ford Europe has invested 420 million euros in the auto plant that they have in Almussafes since it opened in 1976 and it is committed to investing another 425 million euros in the next five years, despite a very attractive offer that they had from the Romanian government. This commitment has been the result of a recent agreement, which took three years to negotiate, between the company and UGT (which represents 80 percent of the workers in that plant), facilitated by incentives from the regional Government of Valencia. In exchange for the company's agreement to increase the plant's workload to 350,000 units between 2008 and 2012, the union has agreed to moderate its demands in future collective bargaining and reduce costs, to renounce any reduction in working hours, and to split workers' vacations so that they only take half of them during the summer months, and the rest at different times contingent of production needs. By introducing more flexibility into the production process this plant has become one of the most dynamic in Europe and has been able to produce four different models at the same time.[20]

The national government is also launching a program to give incentives to register patents for technological innovations as part of a new R&D plan for 2008–11 with the ultimate goal of increasing the number of patents registered to 150 per million of inhabitants by 2015 (from the current 14.3). This is part of the *Ingenio 2010* program launched in June 2005 that seeks to increase public spending in R&D and innovation by 25 percent a year until 2010 with the aim to reach the equivalent of 2 percent of GDP (from 1.3 percent) with the private sector contributing 55 percent of the total (from the current 46 percent).[21]

Finally, one of the main shortcomings that has hindered the development of new projects and companies, the lack of funding, has been addressed and funding for new companies and projects has become more widely available. In the last decade and a half private equity has also come a long way in Spain, as Spaniards have been setting up their own private equity operations to change liquidity into new sectors and taking advantage of tax breaks on reinvested capital gains and debt interest payments. New private equity funds have emerged and just in the last year (2006) they have raised about 500 million euros. And some of these new funding initiatives are collaborative efforts. For instance *Univest* has emerged as Spain's first university-based risk capital company. It has raised $18.5 million in 2006 for its start-ups, and it has invested 8 million euros in 14 advanced technology companies in sectors such as biotechnology and nano materials. Observers note that if this trend continues private equity may emerge as a competitor to the stock market as an instrument to fund new companies or new projects.[22]

Final Thoughts

These are just examples of particular initiatives. What is missing in Spain (and in Europe) is the integration of the different reforms agendas into a common logical framework that defines clear priorities, goals, and instruments in a coherent reform strategy.[23] In a global economy, countries have to nurture and reward individual imagination, and invest in people who have the ability to create and to take risks. As some authors have stressed in a "flat world the most important competition is between you and your imagination, because energetic, innovative and connected individuals can now act on their imagination farther, faster, deeper, and cheaper than ever before. Those countries and companies that empower their individuals to imagine and act quickly on their imagination are going to thrive."[24] The best ideas and the revolutionary ones are usually generated by young people. This is a particular challenge for a country such as Spain with a culture largely marked by hierarchies and fear of failure, in which the main ambition for generations of young Spaniards has been to pass a national exam and get a job for life. This mind-set has to change; younger generations need to be empowered to dream and use their imagination.[25] Spain also needs to tap further into the enormous potential of its female population: female participation in the workforce still stands (in 2007) at 62 percent (compared with more than 75 percent in Northern Europe), and female unemployment at 11.4 percent; this is almost double the rate for Spanish men. The country cannot afford this luxury.[26]

Furthermore, a new growth model will require a cultural shift. The temporary rate problem is merely a reflection of a wider cultural problem among employers who have been trying to maximize profits at the expense of employees. According to recent studies, Spanish companies are still largely attached to an obsolete culture characterized by authoritarianism, control, and lack of trust, which still needs to transition toward a model based on efficiency, objectives, flexibility, and autonomy. Spaniards are among the workers that work the longest hours (1,780 on average in 2006, 219 hours per year more than the EU 15 average): 15 percent of the workers devoted more than 50 hours a week to their profession (not counting extra time, lunches, or commuting); 50 percent more than 40 hours, and only 25 percent between 25 and 40 hours. Yet, productivity has only increased 0.9 percent in the last decade, and it is currently 16 points below the EU-15 average (25 percent lower than France, Italy, and Germany), and the country is ranked twenty-ninth by the *Davos Forum* competitiveness ranking.

A business model that focuses mostly on costs is no longer sustainable because it is undercut by lower costs from other countries, it is available to any company, and does not generate value added. At the same time, as we have seen, this model is also depressing wages for average workers who are losing purchasing capacity (while the salaries of top managers have grown to reach between 40 and 100 times those of the average workers), and it is generating increasing stress (it affects 32 percent of the active population), which provokes psychological and mental problems among workers. Burnout workers are not productive workers.[27] A model that satisfies neither workers nor employers is no longer sustainable. Companies need workers who are productive and who share the goals of their employers, and workers need the stability to commit and "invest" in their companies. A change toward a model based on stability, trust, and cooperation is thus necessary.[28] We need to believe in people and get the best out of them.

Finally, the country also needs to exorcise the demons of the dictatorship and the Civil War, because increasing factionalism and political polarization is making more difficult any common view of the national interest.[29] Spaniards deserve better from their leaders.

In the end, Spain has to become a country of innovators and the main role for the national and regional governments should be to promote a successful entrepreneurial economy, facilitate the establishment of firms, reward entrepreneurial activity, and provide incentives for innovation and growth.[30] It is also important to accept the limitations of state intervention. Public policy can help but, as we have seen in the Basque Country, models of excellence tend to arise from coordination strategies and cooperation. Efforts should focus in further empowering individuals and firms, and fostering processes of accommodation and coordination from the bottom-up. The success of the Spanish economy will hinge on its ability to balance the legacies of the past with the reforms needed to meet the challenges of the new century.

Notes

Introduction

1. Yet this productivity growth was uneven among the EU countries: while Germany and Greece experienced increases of 2.7 percent, the United Kingdom of 2 percent, and France of 1.2 percent, productivity only increased by 0.7 percent in Spain and by 0.2 percent in Italy. See, "Europa eleva la productividad y se acerca a la de Estados Unidos," in *El País*, Thursday, November 22, 2007.
2. Martin Wolf, "European Corporatism Needs to Embrace Market Led Change," in *Financial Times*, January 24, 2007.
3. Edmund Phelps, "Macroeconomics for a Modern Economy," Oslo: December 8, 2006. Published by the *American Economic Review* 97/3 (June 2007), pp. 543–561.
4. Mica Panic, "Child Poverty Exposes the Anglo-American Model," in *Financial Times*, April 2, 2007; and "Does Europe Need Neoliberal Reforms?" in *The Cambridge Journal of Economics*, January 2007.
5. See Christopher Shea, "Vive la Welfare State!" in *Boston Sunday Globe*, January 29, 2006, p. E5.
6. Andre Sapir, "Globalisation and the Reform of European Social Models," September 2005, www.bruegel.org. Other scholars, such as Richard Layard, have argued that painting a stark contrast between models misses the point, because the real distinction is "between countries that have had effective active labor policies and those that have not." According to Layard the picture of the United Kingdom producing high levels of inequality is no longer accurate: since the mid-1990s this trend has been halted, and the United Kingdom currently has some of the fastest growth in health spending in the world. See "EU Set for Clash on 'Anglo-Saxon' versus 'Social' Welfare Models," in *Financial Times*, October 25, 2005, p. 2.
7. Interview with Professor Vicente Salas, Madrid, May 14, 2003.
8. This typology borrows from Schmidt's *State Influenced Market Economies* (SMEs) (2006); and Hancké, Rhodes, and Thatcher's *Mixed Market Economies* (MMEs) (2007). Other European countries that have been included in this category are France, Portugal, Italy and Greece.
9. For an analysis of the role of the state sustaining varieties of coordination in other European countries see Martin and Thelen (2007).
10. For an examination of the role that state policy plays in political-economic coalitions see Iversen (1999), Chapter 4.

11. See David Coates's book review of Hall and Soskice (2001) in *American Political Science Review* 96/3 (2001), pp. 661–662.

12. "Zapatero Accentuates Positives in Economy, but Spain Has Other Problems," in *Financial Times*, April 16, 2007, p. 4; and "Spanish Economy at Its Best for 29 years, Says Zapatero," in *Financial Times*, April 18, 2007, p. 3.

13. "El paro se sitúa en el 7.95% y alcanza su nivel más bajo desde 1978," in *El País*, Friday, July 27, 2007.

14. "La economía española se hace fuerte," in *El País*, March 25, 2007 and "La economía repuntó al 3.9% en 2006 tras el mayor avance de la productividad en nueve años," in *El País*, February 22, 2007.

15. "Spain's Bold Investors to Offset 'Gentle Slowdown,'" in *Financial Times*, February 22, 2007.

16. From "Modernised Nation Faces Uncharted Territory," in *Financial Times: Special Report*, Thursday, June 21, 2007, p. 1.

17. Emilio Ontiveros, "Redimensionamiento Transfronterizo," in *El País*, July 15, 2007.

18. "Siesta's Over for Spain's Economy," in *Los Angeles Times*, April 7, 2007.

19. Deloitte's "Barometro de Empresas," from "Un año de grandes resultados," in *El País*, Sunday January 14, 2006.

20. "Spanish Bulls," in *Financial Times*, Tuesday, February 20, 2007.

21. According to the *Financial Times*, 17 percent of those polled selected Spain as the country where they would prefer to work ahead of the United Kingdom (15 percent) and France (11 percent). See "España vuelve a ser diferente," in *El País*, February 19, 2007, and *Financial Times*, February 19, 2007.

22. Calativa provides a detailed analysis of the immigration experience in Spain and exposes the tensions associated with this development. She also highlights the shortcomings of governments' actions in regard to integration, and the impact of lack of integration on exclusion, criminalization, and radicalization.

23. "Tolerant Spain Is Booming as It Absorbs Flood of Foreign Workers," in *Financial Times*, Tuesday, February 20, 2007, p. 3.

24. "Spanish Bulls," in *Financial Times*, Tuesday, February 20, 2007. Yet, 59 percent thought that there were "too many foreigners" in the country.

25. "Immigrants Boost British and Spanish Economies," in *Financial Times*, Tuesday, February 20, 2007, p. 3.

26. "El paro baja hasta el 8.3% en 2006, la mejor tasa desde 1979," in *El País*, January 26, 2007.

27. Guillermo de la Dehesa, "La Próxima Recesión," in *El País*, January 21, 2007.

28. "La Economía española creció en la última década gracias a la aportación de los inmigrantes," in *El País*, Monday, August 28, 2006.

29. See Martin Wolf, "Pain Will Follow Years of Economic Gain," in *Financial Times*, March 29, 2007.

30. "Fears of Recession as Spain Basks in Economic Bonanza," in *Financial Times*, Thursday, June 8, 2006.

31. "Los expertos piden cambios en la política de I+D," in *El País*, Monday, December 18, 2006.

32. Angel Laborda, "El comercio en 2006," in *El País*, Sunday, March 11, 2007, p. 20.

33. Wolfgang Munchau, "Spain, Ireland and Threats to the Property Boom," in *Financial Times*, Monday, March 19, 2007; "Spain Shudders as Ill Winds Batter US Mortgages," in *Financial Times*, Wednesday, March 21, 2007.

34. "Spanish Muscle Abroad Contrast with Weakling Status among Investors," in *Financial Times*, December 11, 2006.
35. "La Comisión Europea advierte a España de los riesgos de su baja competitividad," in *El País*, February 4, 2007.
36. "Zapatero Accentuates Positives in Economy, but Spain Has Other Problems," in *Financial Times*, April 16, 2007, p. 4.
37. As defined by the International Monetary Fund, 1999. See Kesselman (2007).
38. See Martin Wolf, "The New Capitalism: How Unfettered Finance Is Reshaping the Global Economy," in *Financial Times*, June 19, 2007, p. 11.
39. Ibid.
40. Martin Wolf, "Employment Policies Can Ensure a Fair Share of the Feast," in *Financial Times*, March 11, 2007, p. 11.
41. According to an FT/Harris poll the number of Britons, French, and Spaniards who believe that globalization is having a negative effect outweighs those with a more positive outlook by three to one. This feeling is rooted in the perception that the gap between rich and poor in their countries is widening. See "Poll Reveals Backlash in Wealthy Countries against Globalization," "Globalisation Generates Dark Thoughts," and "A Difficult Sales Job," in *Financial Times*, July 23, 2007.
42. Lawrence Summers, "Harness Market Forces to Share Prosperity," in *Financial Times*, Monday, June 25, 2007. p. 18.
43. Martin Wolf, "The New Capitalism: How Unfettered Finance Is Reshaping the Global Economy," p. 11.
44. Martin Wolf, "Employment Policies Can Ensure a Fair Share of the Feast," in *Financial Times*, March 11, 2007, p. 11. He also points out that "imports of intermediate manufactured and service inputs accounted for only about 5% of gross output and 10% of total intermediate inputs in the high-income countries in 2003."
45. Wolf, "The New Capitalism: How Unfettered Finance Is Reshaping the Global Economy," p. 11.
46. Robert Lawrence, "Slow Real Wage Growth and the US Income Inequality: Is Trade to Blame?" in http://ksghome.harvard.edu/~rlawrence/lawrence%20for%20brandeis.pdf. From Clive Crook, "Why Middle America Needs Free Trade," *in Financial Times*, June 28, 2007, p. 9.
47. "Los salarios pierden frente al capital," in *El País*, Sunday, July 8, 2007, p. 73.
48. "OECD Counters Globalisation Fear," in *Financial Times*, June 20, 2007, p. 2.
49. From: http://www.oecd.org/dataoecd/26/35/38795690.pdf.
50. See "Prisoners of Markets," in *The Economist*, December 6, 1997.
51. Martin Wolf, "The New Capitalism: How Unfettered Finance Is Reshaping the Global Economy," p. 11.
52. http://www.oecd.org/document/12/0,3343,en_2649_201185_38792716_1_1_1_1,00.html.
53. Dani Rodrik, "The Cheerleaders' Threat to Global Trade," in *Financial Times*, March 27, 2007.
54. Interviews took place in Spain in 1996–97, 2000–01, and 2003–05. For an extensive comparative study of social concertation in Spain, from which this book draws, see Royo (2002).
55. This section draws from a lecture that Peter Hall gave at the *Real Colegio Complutense at Harvard University* on August 1, 2005.

56. John Zysman, book review of Torben Iversen's *Capitalism, Democracy and Welfare*, and Pontusson's *Inequality and Prosperity*, in *Perspectives on Politics* (Cambridge University Press: American Political Science Association), 5/1 (March 2007), pp. 215–216.

1 European Integration and the Modernization of Spain

1. This chapter borrows from: Sebastián Royo, "The Euro and Economic Reforms: The Case of Spain," in Joaquín Roy and Pedro Gomis-Porqueras, eds., *The Euro and the Dollar* (Aldershot, UK: Ashgate Publishing, 2007); Sebastián Royo, *Portugal, Espanha e a Integração Europeia: Um Balanço* (Lisbon: Instituto de Ciencias Sociais da Universidade de Lisboa, June 2005); Sebastián Royo, "The Challenges of EU Integration: Iberian Lessons for Eastern Europe," in Joaquín Roy and Roberto Domínguez, eds., *Towards the Completion of Europe: Analysis and Perspectives of the New European Union Enlargement* (Miami: Jean Monnet EU Chair, University of Miami, 2006); Sebastián Royo, "The 2004 Enlargement: Iberian Lessons for Post-Communist Europe," *South European Society & Politics*, Summer/Autumn 2003 (Vol. 8, No. 1–2); and Sebastián Royo and Paul C. Manuel, "Some Lessons from the Fifteenth Anniversary of the Accession of Portugal and Spain to the European Union," *South European Society & Politics* Summer/Autumn 2003 (Vol. 8, No. 1–2).

2. References to the European Economic Community (EEC) or the European Union (EU) can be misleading if the historical period covered extends past the last two decades. This chapter addresses themes in the EEC prior to the introduction of the EU label in the Maastricht Treaty of 1991. The terms "the European Community" (EC) or "the European Union" (EU) are used indistinctly to refer to the European integration process and institutions throughout the chapter. Similarly, "Europe" is here always used to refer to the countries that are members of the EU, either before or after the Maastricht Treaty. In the section "Spanish Lessons," when I focus on the ongoing enlargement process, I refer to the EU.

3. The Spanish Socialist Party, PSOE, under its leader Felipe González has led the opposition to integration in NATO. When they won the general election the following October, Mr. González used the threat of exiting the Alliance as a tool to speed the negotiations with the EC. The Socialist government linked the permanence in NATO with the country's accession to the Community and "threatened" the U.S. and the EC members with a referendum about the country permanence in NATO that he had promised during the electoral campaign. In the end Mr. González himself supported Spain's permanence in the Alliance during this referendum, and Spain achieved its objective of joining the Community. Nevertheless, this shows that political considerations, again, were critical during the negotiation process. See Gómez Fuentes (1986, 41–42).

4. Julian Marias, *José Ortega y Gassett: Circumstance and Vocation* (Norman: RO, 1970), p. 166.

5. The democratization literature has theorized about how external influences may affect democratization processes and has generated a range of concepts. Pridham (2002, 183) outlines the following ones: "Diffusion, contagion, consent, penetration, demonstration effect, emulation, reaction, control (or, externally monitored installation of democracies), incorporation, obviously interdependence, and finally conditionality."

6. Supporters of decentralization and the regionalist parties viewed the process of European integration as a model of decentralization, and saw EC integration as an instrument to ensure the decentralization of the Spanish political system. See Alvarez-Miranda (1996) and Magone (2002, 229).

7. From "Not Quite Kissing Cousins," in *The Economist*, May 5, 1990, v. 315, n. 7653, p. 21.

8. For example, EC vehicles imported to Spain paid a custom duty of 27 percent to 30.4 percent plus a compensatory tax of 13 percent.

9. The framework for section on trade draws from Hine (1989).

10. Imports of manufactured goods in 1986 were equivalent to 11.0 percent of Spain's GDP. On the other hand, the relatively closed nature of the Spanish industry was also reflected in the amount of industrial exports, which was only 10.9 percent of GDP. In the EC the averages were 14.4 percent and 27.7 percent of GDP, respectively. See Hine (1989, p. 7).

11. For instance, since the late 1950s, Spain had been moving away from industries based on low-technology, low-capital requirement, and unskilled labor such as textiles, leather, shipbuilding, and food, toward more capital-intensive industries that required more labor skills such as chemicals or vehicles. See Hine (1989, pp. 9–12).

12. Joaquín Estefanía, "La mayor operación de solidaridad histórica," in *El País*, March 21, 2006.

13. José A. Herce, "La Política de Cohesión," in *El País* November 15, 2006, p. 4—Negocios.

14. I would like to thank Jeffrey Kopstein, Ramón de Miguel, Kalypso Nicolaidis, George Ross, and Francisco Seixas da Costa for their valuable comments during the last roundtable of the conference *From Isolation to Europe: 15 Years of Spanish and Portuguese Membership in the European Union*. Minda de Gunzburg Center for European Studies, Harvard University, November 2–3, 2001. Their comments inform this chapter. A shorter version of this section ["Spanish Lessons"] (pp. 51–57) has been published as "Lessons from the Integration of Spain and Portugal to the European Union," in *PS: Political Science and Politics*. <http://www.apsanet.org/section_223.cfm?> *American Political Science Association*. Vol. XL, No. 3, October 2007 (pp. 689–692). Courtesy of Cambridge University Press and PS.

15. Some observers have noted that these new members may learn even more from Greece than from Portugal or Spain. In Greece, e.g., the government was reluctant to cede control of vital economic sectors; it was behind in consumer protection, environmental and competition policies, and corruption was a systemic problem. In addition, Greece had weak civil institutions, which slowed the convergence process. For years Greece squandered the opportunities of EU membership through poor fiscal management, corruption, political cronyism, justice mismanagement, and misadministration and mismanagement of domestic and European funds. While fiscal discipline has been achieved, the change of attitudes and values is still a pending issue. See "Is Poland the new Greece? Why Warsaw's Entry into the European Union May Be Rough," in *Financial Times*, Monday, December 9, 2002, p. 11.

16. While there is significant controversy over the definition of real convergence, most scholars agree that per capita GDP is a valid reference to measure the living standards of a country.

17. See "UK Leads Way on Opening Borders to New Workers," in *Financial Times*, Friday, December 13, 2002, p. 2; "Fears of Big Move West May Be Unfounded," in *Financial Times*, Tuesday, December 2, 2002, p. 4.
18. See "EU Novices Hope to Roar Like Irish 'Celtic Tigers' Rather than Star in Greek Tragedy," in *Financial Times*, Thursday, April 22, 2004, p. 3; "Coming Together: A Small Step for Europe's Economy but a Giant Leap for the Continent," in *Financial Times*, Monday, April 26, 2004, p. 11.
19. Static effects refer to trade creation and diversion, while dynamic effects refer to foreign direct investment.
20. See "The EU 'Is Losing Battle on Competitiveness,'" in *Financial Times*, Monday, January 13, 2003, p. 3. Spain has lost 3 positions (and is listed at number 20) in the Globalization Index published by *Foreign Policy*, January/February 2003 (No. 134): 60. In addition, the *World Economic Forum* has placed Spain among the least competitive countries in the EU (with only Greece behind) in its *Report on Global Competitiveness*. This report examines economic conditions in 80 countries focusing on 2 main indexes: MICI (Microeconomic Competitiveness Index), which measures the quality of business development, and the GCI (Growth Competitiveness Index), which examines growth prospects in 5–8 years based on macroeconomic stability. Spain is listed 29 in the latest Globalization Index, which measures economic integration, personal contact, technological connectivity, and political commitment, published by the journal *Foreign Policy* (November/December 2007 issue).

2 The Challenge of Economic Reforms

1. A previous draft of this chapter was presented as "The Euro and Economic Reforms: The Case of Spain" at the *Conference on the Euro and the Dollar*, organized by the University of Miami. I would like to thank Professor Joaquín Roy for his generous support, and all the participants in the conference for their valuable comments. This chapter is a revised, extended and updated version of my chapter: "The Euro and Economic Reforms: The case of Spain." Published in Joaquín Roy and Pedro Gomis-Porqueras, editors. *The Euro and the Dollar in a Globalized Economy*. (Aldershot, UK: Ashgate Publishing, 2007). Courtesy of Ashgate Publishing
2. From "Dos décadas de impulso a la economía," in *El País*, January 2, 2006.
3. Guillermo de la Dehesa, "La Próxima Recesión," in El *País*, January 21, 2007.
4. Emilio Ontiveros as quoted in "Fears of Recession as Spain Basks in Economic Bonanza," in *Financial Times*, Thursday, June 8, 2006.
5. "Solbes urge a reorientar el patrón de crecimiento porque no 'es sostenible,'" in *El País*, Tuesday, June 6, 2006.
6. From "La Convergencia Real a Paso Lento," in *El País*, Monday, February 14, 2000.
7. See Oficina Económica del Presidente, *Convergencia y Empleo: Programa Nacional de Reformas de España*, Madrid: OEP, October 2005.
8. "El gobierno prevé que España alcance en 2010 el nivel medio de renta de la UE," in *El País*, December 27, 2006.
9. Daniel Gros, "Will EMU Survive 2010?" Centre for European Policy Studies, January 2005, www.ceps.be.
10. Oficina Económica del Presidente, *Convergencia y Empleo: Programa Nacional de Reformas de España*, Madrid: OEP, October 2005, pp. 27–28.

11. Martin Wolf, "Pain Will Follow Years of Economic Gain," in *Financial Times*, March 28, 2007.

12. Ibid.

13. Angel Laborda, "La inflación se nos va," in *El País*, November 18, 2007.

14. "Almunia Says Inflation Dampens Spain's Potential Growth Level," in *El País*, *English Edition with International herald Tribune*, Saturday, February 18, 2006; and Angel Laborda, "La inflación se nos va," in *El País*, November 18, 2007.

15. "El paro se sitúa en el 7.95% y alcanza su nivel más bajo desde 1978," in *El País*, Friday, July 27, 2007.

16. "La tasa de empleo en España supera por primera vez la media de la OCDE," in *El País*, June 19, 2007.

17. "Spain Plans to Ban Sex Discrimination at Work," in *Financial Times*, March 4–5 2006, p. 2. In response to this challenge the Socialist government has supported a new law that will oblige companies with more than 250 workers to introduce "equality plans" to eliminate discrimination against women in pay, benefits, and promotion.

18. Despite the efforts from the trade unions, fixed-term employment has remained persistently high, and it is increasing in the public sector where it represented over 20 percent of all employment in 2003. One of the reasons is the high rate of turnover experienced by temporary workers (in abuse of the law): in 1994 each temporary worker had signed an average of two contracts per year, but in recent years the figure was three. Half of the temporary contracts have a duration of less than a month. See EIRO (2003).

19. "La Tasa de Temporalidad española duplica la media comunitaria y es la más alta de la UE," in *El País*, Thursday, December 28, 2006.

20. This development is also partly a consequence of the productive structure of the country, very dependent on seasonal activities such as tourism, agriculture, and construction. See "España tiene más eventuales que Italia, Reino Unido, Bélgica y Suecia juntos," in *El País*, August 10, 2005.

21. "El 65% de los españoles de entre 15 y 24 años tienen un trabajo temporal y precario," in *El País*, September, 2009.

22. See Jesús Benegas Nuñez "Innovación, Productividad y Empleo," in *El País*, July 10, 2005.

23. "'Garbage Jobs' Stifle Spanish Innovation," in *Financial Times*, October 21, 2005, p. 3.

24. Although employers' associations frequently express their antagonism toward trade unions, criticize an environment that they consider hostile to them, and demand greater labor market flexibility, in private, during the course of the interviews that I conducted with their leaders they recognized the need for greater cooperation and stressed the benefits of concertation. One of the leaders of the CEOE, Jiménez Aguilar, has recognized that the increasing segmentation of the labor market between permanent and temporary workers "hinders workers' professional training, their motivation, and in sum the competitiveness of the firm and the quality of its products."

25. In Valencia, e.g., many companies that used to produce textiles or shoes have seen their low-cost competitive advantage eroded as a result of competition from Asia and have been forced to close their plants and import products from China. They are now focusing on design and distribution, activities that require little labor.

26. IESE, *Euroíndice Laboral* (Adecco). December 12, 2006. From "Bruselas considera insostenible la deuda exterior de España," *in El País*, December 19, 2006.

27. "España es el cuarto país de la OCDE en el que es más difícil abrir un negocio," in *El País*, Monday, September 11, 2006; and "Spanish Muscle Abroad Contrasts with Weakening Status among Investors," in *Financial Times*, December 11, 2006.

28. The surge of immigration, which resulted in a sharp increase in the participation rate, has led to a decrease in average remuneration per worker (about 3.7 percent between 2002 and 2004).

29. "Diez años con el mismo sueldo," in *El País*, Tuesday, November 27, 2007.

30. Paul de Grauwe, "Germany's Pay Policy Points to a Eurozone Design Flan," in *Financial Times*, Friday, May 5, 2006.

31. "La productividad de España equivale al 75% de la estadounidense," in *El País*, Thursday, July 20, 2006.

32. "Los expertos piden cambios en la política de I+D," in *El País*, Monday, December 18, 2006.

33. "Europa eleva la productividad y se acerca a la de Estados Unidos," in *El País*. Thursday, November 22, 2007; and "Diez años con el mismo sueldo," in *El País*, Tuesday, November 27, 2007.

34. "Almunia Says Inflation Dampens Spain's Potential Growth Level," in *El País, English Edition with International Herald Tribune*, Saturday, February 18, 2006. See Martin Wolf, "Britain Must Get to Grips with Lackluster Productivity Growth," in *Financial Times*, November 8, 2005.

35. After this enlargement the EU is rich and homogeneous, with a population of 376 million, a GDP of US$8.660 billion, and a GDP per head of US$23,550. The richest EU country is Luxembourg, with a per capita GDP of US$27,470 and its poorest Greece with US$16,860. In contrast, the new member states have a combined population of almost 75 million (Poland accounts for 39 million) and their GDP per head is at an average of only US$10,550. See Martin Wolf, "Europe Risks Destruction to Widen Peace and Prosperity," in *Financial Times*, December 11, 2002, p. 15.

36. "Sólo dos comunidades de las 11 actuales podrán recibir fondos europeos en 2007," in *El País*, January 24, 2003.

37. "Siete comunidades autónomas tienen un PIB por habitante mayor que la media europea," in *El País*, Wednesday, December 28, 2005.

38. Joaquín Estefanía. "La deslocalización como alarma social," in *El País*, Monday, May 22, 2006.

39. For a discussion on the effects of enlargement in Spain see José Ignacio Torreblanca, "Por fin, la ampliación: la Unión Europea tras el Consejo de Copenhague," mimeo, *Real Instituto Elcano de Estudios Internacionales y Estratégicos*, September 21, 2002.

40. "Fernández Ordóñez califica de 'ridícula' la formación secundaria," in *El País*, June 26, 2007.

41. "La OCDE señala el alto número de repetidores como 'punto débil' de la educación en España," in *El País*, Tuesday, September 12, 2006.

42. If we take into account only the student population (not the total one) the percentage is 72 percent, 10 points lower than the OECD average, and 15 points lower than the EU. Spain is ranked 23 among 26 countries, only ahead of Mexico and Turkey, and at the same level as New Zealand. The worst

performance is in the professional training system, in which only 36 percent of the students complete their degrees (versus 44 percent in high school). These results are published at a time in which Spain is debating a new educational reform. The government has drafted a controversial proposal that would allow students who fail four courses to move onto the following level and not repeat the level. See OECD (2007b). Also, "La educación se atasca en secundaria," in *El País*, Tuesday, September 18, 2007.

43. OECD (2007b). Also, "El título universitario se devalúa," in *El País*, Tuesday, September 18, 2007.

44. Aghion, Philippe, Mathias Dewatripont, Caroline Hoxby, Andreu Mas-Colell, and André Sapir, "Why Reform Europe's Universities?" in *Bruegelpolicybrief*, www.bruegel.org.

45. "La educación se atasca en secundaria," in *El País*, Tuesday, September 18, 2007; "El título universitario se devalúa," in *El País*, Tuesday, September 18, 2007.

46. "Garbage Jobs Stifle Spanish Innovation," in *Financial Times*, October 21, 2005, p. 3.

47. "Un Informe del Banco Mundial denuncia el exceso de papeleo para abrir un negocio en España," in *El País*, October 1, 2007.

48. "Europa pierde la carrera en I+D," in *El País*, Sunday, October 12, 2006. Japan invested in R&D the equivalent of 3.13 percent of its GDP in 2004; the United States 2.68 percent, and the EU25 1.81 percent in 2003 (the last year with available data).

49. "La inversión en I+D de España está lejos del nivel de la UE según Cotec," in *El País*, June 15, 2006.

50. "España pierde terreno en innovación y baja al puesto 16 de la Unión Europea," in *El País*, Friday, January 13, 2006, p. 45.

51. "En el furgón de cola tecnológico," in *El País*, May 14, 2007.

3 Patterns of Labor Market Coordination in Spain

1. Peter Hall has argued that as states become more reluctant to coordinate labor relations in countries such as Spain, they will become less coordinated. Lecture at the *Real Colegio Complutense at Harvard University* on August 1, 2005.

2. Defined as a mode of policy formation.

3. The first part of this historical section about concertation in Spain borrows from Sebastián Royo, "The Collapse of Social Concertation and the Failure of Socialist Economic Policies in Spain," *South European Society & Politics* 6/1 (Summer 2001), pp. 29–33. Also Sebastián Royo, *A New Century of Corporatism? Corporatism in Southern Europe: Spain and Portugal in Comparative Perspective* (Westport: Praeger, 2002).

4. For an analysis of the reasons behind the collapse of social concertation in Spain see Royo (2000).

5. On December of 2001, UGT, CCOO, and the CEOE signed an Interconfederal agreement that established the recommendations for collective bargaining in 2002, including wage increases. Although it did not explicitly state a numeric wage increase ceiling, this pact defined the parameters that should guide subsequent wage negotiations (i.e., the government inflation forecast for 2002 and productivity).

6. Lecture by José María Fidalgo, Madrid, Club Siglo XX, January 30, 2006.
7. Union leaders labeled this agreement as "a clear example of social consensus in Spain"; see "All Sides Hail Spain's Job Pact," *Financial Times*, April 10, 1997, p. 3. Unions agreed to this reduction in return for a promise by employers to convert temporary contracts into indefinite ones. The result of this reform after two years was the creation of 2 million new indefinite contracts. However, one of the major objectives of the reform, which was to reduce the level of temporality (at 32.5 percent the highest in Western Europe) has not been achieved.
8. "Diez años con el mismo sueldo," in *El País*, Tuesday November 27, 2007; and "El salario medio sube un 3.8%, por encima de la inflación," in *El País*, September 21, 2007.
9. See M. Wolf, "The Gain in Spain," *Financial Times*, Wednesday, July 7, 1999, p. 10. See also IMF, *Public Information Notice 99/65* (June 1999).
10. See "Gobierno y agentes sociales cierran la reforma laboral tras más de un año de negociaciones," in *El País*, May 4, 2006.
11. See "La conversión de contratos temporales a fijos se triplica," in *El País*, Friday, September 1, 2006; and "Diez años con el mismo sueldo," in *El País*, Tuesday November 27, 2007.
12. Most union members belong to the trade unions listed. However, there are some other organizations such as a number of regional trade unions, and the Independent Trade Union Confederation of Public Servants *(Confederación Sindical Independiente de Funcionarios*, CSIF)—for which no membership information is available. The data are self-reported by unions.
13. Rhodes (1998) has defined this new form of corporatism as "competitive corporatism."
14. The general strike of 2002 in Spain organized by the unions in response to a unilateral labor reform by the government illustrates this point. The success of this strike led to government to back off, modify the reform, and satisfy most of the unions' demands. Despite this confrontation, unions and employers reached new agreements (including a collective bargaining one to set wage increases for 2003) in subsequent months.

4   Business and the Politics of Coordination

1. This chapter is a revised, extended and updated version of my article: "Varieties of Capitalism in Spain: Business and the Politics of Coordination." Published in the *European Journal of Industrial Relations* <outbind:// 127/%20http://ejd.sagepub.com/> Vol. 13, No. 1, Spring 2007. Courtesy of SAGE Publications. Inc. and EJIR.
2. From Royo (2002), Chapter 4; Royo (1996, pp. 128–130).
3. The CEPYME is the most significant one and still maintains its own structure and statutes within the CEOE. The other two, the *Confederación de la Pequeña y Mediana Empresa* (COPYME) and the *Unión de la Pequeña y Mediana Empresa* (UNYPIME), also represent small- and medium-sized firms.
4. In the CEOE Congress of 1982, 314 delegates came from the sectoral structure, 183 from the territorial, and 83 from the CEPYME. The larger groups of representatives came from metal (46 representatives), construction (39), and the chemical sector (18). The most important territorial organizations are the Basque and the Catalonian (represented by the *Fomento Nacional del Trabajo*—FNT—one of the oldest business organizations in Spain, dating

from 1771). The weight of the Catalonian organization was proven by the fact that its president, Carlos Ferrer Salat, was elected as the first president of the CEOE. The CEOE is dominated by larger firms who contribute the most to the organization and have the larger number of votes. The banking sector is particularly influential. See Führer (1996, 229–231). Later on, with the delegation by the state of powers to the autonomous regions, the CEOE intensified a process of decentralization. See Pardo Avellaneda and Fernández Castro (1995, p. 162).

5. What was paradoxical, given this approach, was the response of businesses to unions' wage demands. During the first years of the transition, there was a dramatic explosion in wages. For the first time in years, wages increased above productivity. Business acquiescence, however, cannot be interpreted as a tolerant position toward unions. On the contrary, businesses were concerned about the shaky political context and accepted unions' demands to avoid further confrontations, which would worsen the already poisoned political climate. They preferred to increase prices than face the wrath of workers. The consequence was a sharp increase in inflation. See Pérez Díaz (1984, p. 40).

6. F. Moreno, F. Jimeno, E. de la Lama, and J. Iranzo confirmed these points during interviews with the author in December 1996. The author interviewed Fernando Moreno again in May 13, 2003.

7. Overtime work is still a significant component or working time among Spanish workers and firms: in 2003, 70 percent of the collective bargain agreements included clauses on overtime. More than 35 percent of these pacts established monetary compensation for overtime, and 45 percent of them compensated more for overtime hours than for regular ones. See CES (2004, p. 346).

8. During an interview with Fernando Moreno, secretary of industrial relations of the CEOE, in May of 2003, he stressed that some employers prefer unilateral reforms from the government because they perceive that they may be faster and deeper. He indicated, e.g., that in 1997 *Fomento del Trabajo Nacional*, the CEOE's territorial organization in Catalonia, was critical of the 1997 agreement. They would have preferred an imposed solution from the government that would have introduced a new contract with lower and fixed dismissals costs. He also stressed that although the CEOE supported the articulation of collective bargaining and resisted the PP's attempts to reform unilaterally the existing system, many of their affiliates were pushing for decentralization and wanted the government to impose the reform.

9. See "The EU 'Is Losing Battle on Competitiveness,'" in *Financial Times*, Monday, January 13, 2003, p. 3.

10. Investors looking for low-cost economies are investing in Asia and Central Europe, and Spain have been unable to develop its innovation capacity sufficiently to be able to attract a more sophisticated kind of investment/projects. The entering FDI is mostly to companies that are already based in Spain to fund their projects (with a significant portion going to the real estate sector), but there is little new capital coming in. See "La Inversión Extranjera en España Cae a Menos de la Mitad desde el Año 2000," in *El País*, Monday, March 14, 2005, p. 71.

11. "Dos empresas textiles cierran y dejan sin trabajo a 100 personas," in *El País*, May 6, 2007.

12. See Jesús Benegas Nuñez, "Innovación, Productividad y Empleo," in *El País*, July 10, 2005.

13. As noted previously, despite intense efforts from Spanish trade unions the temporary rate has remained very high in the country, particularly in the public sector, where it has been growing steadily in the last decade. This development has been largely caused by the high rate of turnover among workers with temporary contracts: on average they sign approximately three contracts per year. See EIRO (2003).

14. The productive structure of Spain, which is very dependent on seasonal activities, has contributed to exacerbate this pattern. See "España tiene más eventuales que Italia, Reino Unido, Bélgica y Suecia juntos," in *El País*, August 10, 2005.

15. "Garbage Jobs Stifle Spanish Innovation," in *Financial Times*, October 21, 2005, p. 3.

16. During the course of the interviews that I conducted with leaders of the employer's association they recognized the need for greater cooperation and stressed the benefits of concertation.

17. "El 65% de los españoles de entre 15 y 24 años tienen un trabajo temporal y precario," in *El País*, September 5, 2009.

18. "Sólo el 40% de los universitarios tiene un trabajo acorde con su nivel de estudios," in *El País*, Monday, September 19, 2005.

19. See OECD (2007b).

20. "El CES augura un futuro precario si no mejora la calidad de empleo," in *El País*, July 5, 2007.

21. "Una juventud capeando el temporal," in *El País*, Sunday, June 3, 2007, p. 73.

22. "Sólo el 40% de los universitarios tiene un trabajo acorde con su nivel de estudios," in *El País*, Monday, September 19, 2005.

23. In Valencia, textile and shoe companies are now focusing on design and distribution, activities that require little labor.

24. Interview with Fernando Moreno, secretary of labor relations of the CEOE, in May 2003. See also "El CES denuncia 'descontrol y lagunas' en las estadísticas sobre el despido en España," in *El Mundo*, Wednesday, August 31, 2007, p. 28.

25. "El CES denuncia 'descontrol y lagunas' en las estadísticas sobre el despido en España," in *El Mundo*, Wednesday, August 31, 2007, p. 28.

26. "Zapatero pide a las 'pymes' que reduzcan la temporalidad laboral," in *El País*, Thursday, May 18, 2006; "Gobierno y agentes sociales cierran la reforma laboral tras más de un año de negociaciones," in *El País*, Thursday, May 4, 2006.

27. See Antonio Ferrer Sais, "Mejores empleos, mejores salarios," in *El País*, Saturday, July 14, 2007. In 2006, workers whose wages have been negotiated in collective agreements have recovered purchasing capacity, with an average increase of 3.21 percent (inflation went up by 2.7 percent). "Los trabajadores con convenio colectivo recuperaron capacidad adquisitiva en 2006," in *El País*, January 4, 2007.

28. Interviews with Eduardo Garcia Elosua, leader of CCOO in the Basque Country (May 8, 2003), and Fernando Moreno, director of labor relations of the CEOE (May 13, 2003).

29. The entrance of all these people with low salaries into the labor market is what has pushed down the average salary. The increase in the number of part-time workers has also contributed to this development. See Angel Laborda, "Salarios," in *El País*, Sunday, July 1, 2007.

30. "El salario medio ha bajado un 4% en 10 años pese al fuerte crecimiento económico," in *El País*, June 21, 2007.
31. "España es el cuarto país de la OCDE en el que es más difícil abrir un negocio," in *El País*, Monday, September 11, 2006; and "Spanish Muscle Abroad Contrast with Weakling Status among Investors," in *Financial Times*, December 11, 2006.
32. "El reto de la pequeña empresa," in *El País*, Sunday, October 12, 2006.
33. Ibid.
34. It was also the result of the frustration of the social actors with the 1994 labor reform. See "Patronal y sindicatos negocian medidas para crear empleo estable porque la reforma laboral no funciona," in *El País*, Friday, May 10, 1996.
35. The agreement sought to promote permanent employment by tightening the use of fixed-term contracts and shifting financial incentives. It introduced a new indefinite contract for new hires and temporary workers with lower redundancy costs (from the existing 45 days and 42 months, to a maximum of 33 days and 24 months) and reduced social contributions to incentive-indefinite contracts over temporary ones. In order to fulfill these objectives, the government passed legislation in June 1997, granting a two-year payroll tax cut of 40–60 percent for the new open-ended contracts, and revoking all financial incentives for temporary contracts, except for handicapped people. The accord also clarified when employers were justified in dismissing workers. The new agreement reformed Article 52-C of the Workers' Statute to facilitate its implementation by labor courts. The new rule allows dismissals related to firms' competitive position or changes in demand.
36. "La reforma laboral cumple su primer año con un aumento de la contratación indefinida," in *El País*, July 1, 2007. Progress is still inconsistent: the percentage of companies in which at least 90 percent of their workers have indefinite contracts has descended from 63.7 percent in 2005 to 43.8 percent in 2006; see Deloitte's "Barometro de Empresas," from: "Un año de grandes resultados," in *El País*, Sunday, January 14, 2006.
37. "¿Satisfecho con su trabajo? El 45% de los españoles no lo esta," in *El País*, June 26, 2007.
38. "Más de la mitad de los universitarios acepta empleos por debajo de su formación," in *El País*, June 12, 2006.
39. "Las empresas que concilian son más productivas," in *El País*, March 4, 2007.
40. "Suspenso en economía del conocimiento," in *El País*, March 25, 2007.
41. "España pierde terreno en innovación y baja al puesto 16 de la Unión Europea," Friday, January 13, 2006, p. 45.
42. Interview with Maurici Lucena, general director of the Center for Industrial Technology Development, "Hay un problema de escasez inversora en investigación," in *El País*, April 15, 2007.
43. This was confirmed during interviews with Antonio Gutierrez in December 1996, José María Fidalgo on May 2001, and Antonio Ferrer on May 2001.
44. This development contradicts other analyses that have argued that wage moderation and employment are reinforced by central bank independence in countries with intermediate levels of centralization in wage bargaining (Iversen 1999). In Spain wage bargainers have not been particularly responsive to threats from fiscal or monetary authorities. See Hall and Franzese (1998) and Pérez (1998).

45. During my interview with the leaders of the CEOE in 1996 and 2003, they emphasized their preference for centralized bargaining. See Royo (2000), Chapter 4. For a clear picture of the PP strategies. See also interviews with José María Aznar, the Conservative prime minister, in "Government Takes a Siesta," in *Financial Times*, Monday, August 3, 1998, p. 13 and "Ode to the Common Man with a Nation at His Feet," in *Financial Times*, Weekend, September 12–13, 1998, p. iii.

46. The problem was aggravated by the failed attempt to force employers in the exposed sectors of the economy to resist higher wage demands and set wage standards. In Spain, however, in the context of a fragmented and decentralized bargaining structure, the reliance on a tight monetary policy in the late 1980s "downgraded the role of the exposed sector in the wage bargaining round and allowed wage bargainers in sheltered sectors (mainly in the service and construction sectors) to set wage standards" (Pérez 1998, p. 17).

47. After the collapse of concertation in 1987, some mechanisms of cooperation continued to operate: the government announces every year an inflation forecast and asks unions to adjust wage increases to that forecast. The union confederations and the employers issue bargaining guidelines for their members. This process, however, was different from the one that takes place in Germany where industry-level actors, led by IGMetall, bargain first with employers, and set a pattern for others.

48. The failure of these policies helps account for the employers' interest in a return to national social bargaining. Some employers had favored a decentralization of bargaining toward the firm level. This was precisely the objective of the 1994 labor reform implemented by the government with the opposition from unions. Despite this reform employers in the tradable sectors exposed to competition found that wage restraint was not possible in a context of a fragmented and decentralized wage setting in which the sheltered sectors set wage standards (see Pérez 1998, p. 19). This led the national business confederation, CEOE, to seek agreements with unions to limit the fragmentation of collective bargaining (Royo 2000, 2002).

49. Regini (1999, pp. 21–23) compares the Italian and German cases. Germany derives its competitive advantage from the capacity "of its institutional context to efficiently provide firms with collective goods like labor force cooperation, coordination of wage dynamics, and highly skilled human resources." Yet there is strong emphasis in Germany today to make its economy more flexible, even at the risk of weakening those collective goods. In Italy they have the opposite problem—weak collective goods and high versatility and rapid adjustment to changing markets. What is interesting about both countries, according to Regini, is that German and Italian employers' associations are not currently seeking to reinforce their competitive advantages by enhancing the existing institutional structure on which they are based.

50. The leaders of the employers' association emphasized these arguments when I interviewed them in 2000, 2001, and 2005. They stressed the need to upgrade the capital stock and productivity of their labor force, particularly in the context of the expansion of the EU, which will make it virtually impossible for Iberian firms to compete effectively against firms from new entrant countries based merely on costs. The need to add value has become one of the most pressing needs for Spanish firms.

51. Analyzing the agreements of 1997 to reform the Spanish labor market, the leader of the Spanish employers' association, the CEOE, J. M. Cuevas, has recognized

that some employers wanted to let the government adopt a unilateral reform because they considered that such a reform would be deeper than a negotiated one. Mr. Cuevas, however, has stressed that these employers forget that such reforms have been adopted in other countries by governments with absolute majorities in Parliament, and that they had not been accepted socially, which diminished their efficacy and resulted in social protests and confrontations. It is for this reason that he concludes that it is very important to try to build consensus and involve all the social actors in order to increase credibility, trust, and the social acceptance of the negotiated reforms. See Cuevas (1997).

52. This argument is adapted from the one developed for the Italian case by Regini (2000, p. 19).

53. While, in public, employers demand greater labor market flexibility, in private during the course of the interviews that I conducted with employer associations' leaders they recognize the need for greater cooperation and the benefits of social bargaining.

54. I am currently working on research projects analyzing these cases.

55. While the government had been one of the leading actors in the first period of social bargaining, in the 1990s and 2000s it played more of a supportive role. In industrial relations issues, the social partners have asserted their autonomy and rejected an interventionist approach. The government enacted the legislation to implement the agreements, but the bulk of the bargaining and the trade-offs have taken place between the unions and employers.

56. Social concertation is a historically rooted process and in the 1990s it has been aided by previous positive experiences during the transition and first years of democracy. However, the context, the actors, and the goals, are quite different. This new phase of social bargaining is a response to a new set of economic and political challenges.

5   Unions and Economic Adjustment

1. This chapter is a revised, extended and updated version of my article: "Beyond Confrontation: The resurgence of social bargaining in Spain." Published in *Comparative Political Studies* <http://cps.sagepub.com/>; Vol. 40, No. 8, October 2006. Courtesy of SAGE Publications, Inc. and CPS.

2. For a much more detailed analysis of the resurgence of social bargaining in Spain, from which this chapter borrows, see Royo (2002).

3. This section borrows from Royo (2003), Chapter 4.

4. This section borrows from Royo (2003, pp. 140–144).

5. The government also issued two decrees clarifying the rules of industrial relations. One of the decrees regulated collective bargaining and the right to strike, and the other one established worker representation through work councils and the rules for the first democratic elections to the work councils.

6. As I have indicated elsewhere (Royo 2000, p. 115), in work council elections in workplaces with more than 50 workers, voters have to choose between lists, not candidates, and each list includes only candidates from the same union. This system gives great power to the union, which is the one that nominates the candidates. While groups of workers registered to unions do not need to collect any signatures, independents do need to obtain a certain number of signatures from their coworkers in order to become candidates. This system makes it very difficult for independent workers to run in these elections. The consequence of this system, however, has been that there are a significant

number of council members elected on union lists who are not union members. See Escobar (1995, pp. 168–169) and Bouza (1989).

7. Under this system both work councils and trade union sections have rights to negotiate collective agreements at the firm level and to organize strikes. Personnel delegates are appointed in firms that have between 6 and 50 employees, whereas larger firms have work councils. Work councils have the power to monitor the implementation of collective agreements and labor legislation. They also have information rights in areas such as employment, production, health, safety, and turnover. Trade union sections, for their part, have the right to organize meetings, collect membership fees, and distribute information within the firm. See Escobar (1995) and Van der Meer (2000, pp. 578–579).

8. According to this law the most representative unions would be granted bargaining rights at the firm and national level, as well as participation in certain tripartite institutions for social security, health, employment, and the Economic and Social Council.

9. The consolidation of the labor movement was reinforced in 1977 when some of the USO leaders, led by its secretary general, José María Zufiaur, defected from the USO and joined the UGT. This development definitely strengthened the position of UGT. The CNT failed to recover the support that it had before the Civil War and was later divided into two unions. Only the ELA-STV, with strong links with the Basque Nationalist Party, PNV, reorganized in the Basque Country and eventually became the strongest union in that region.

10. Other unions include USO (*Unión Sindical Obrera*, the Syndical Union of Workers), with a social-Christian orientation, which played a role during a Franco regime but was weakened as a result of an internal split in 1979 when a significant group of members abandoned it to join UGT; ELA-STV (*Euzko Langillen Alkartasuna-Solidaridad de Trabajadores Vascos*, the Solidarity of Basque Workers); LAB (*Langille Abertzale Batzordeak*), the Basque nationalist unions, which have a majority in the Basque country; and CIG (*Confederación Intersindical Gallega*), which is strong in Galicia. In the public sector there are also a number of independent unions that organize specific groups of professionals.

11. Some scholars have applied to Spanish unions the theory of the median voter (i.e., Downs 1957 and Nordhaus 1989) to explain union concentration. See Malo (2001).

12. The syndical elections do not take place in a single day. On the contrary, each company and workplace establishes a calendar for voting. Most of the elections take place between September 15 of one year and December 31 of the following year, in multiples of four starting in 1994 (1994–95, 1998–99, 2002–03, 2006–07, 2010–11, and so on). From Wikepedia.es.

13. The federations are responsible for industrial relations issues in each sector—i.e., collective bargaining, decisions about strikes, resolution of conflicts, problems specific to the sector, prevention of accidents, legal support and other assistance to members, organization of the elections to works councils at firm levels, membership, fund raising, training, and union representation at lower levels. Federations thus have critical responsibilities within the unions. The confederations, for their part, are responsible for negotiations with the government, institutional representation of the union as a whole, coordination,

union representation, social and political activities, and support to branches. The confederations, however, given the centralist tendencies of unions and the number of representatives that they send to congresses (50 percent), still play preponderant roles, and the executive committees of the unions have extraordinary powers. They sign their own wage agreements, have their own strike funds, can veto wage agreements signed by affiliates, participate in demand formulation and wage bargaining for lower levels, and have veto powers over strikes. Moreover, federations are subordinated to the strategies and union policies defined by the confederations—which operate at the level that outlines unions' strategies and conducts negotiations with the government and the business associations. The executive committees also define the strategies regarding wage policies and wage demands. The power of the executive committees has been shown through their capacity to implement the agreements that were signed with the CEOE and the government. In the 1980s in order to overcome the fragmentation of their organizations, union leaders embarked in a process that resulted in further centralization. They encouraged mergers, centralized administrative and managerial responsibilities, and streamlined the organization at the regional level. Centralization was reinforced by the fact that federations are totally dependent on the confederations for their economic support (see Führer 1996, pp. 164–167; Royo 2000, pp. 125–128).

14. See interview with José María Fidalgo, secretary general of CCOO, in *El País*, Monday, February 12, 2001.

15. According to Van der Meer (2000, pp. 587–588) this turnaround in absolute membership can also be linked to the search for job protection from groups of workers (particularly in larger industrial firms) at a time of high unemployment and restructuring. He also emphasizes that unions have become better organized and more professionalized in workplaces, and have started to provide services to members (e.g., tax advice and organized holidays), a process that has facilitated recruitment efforts. He stresses the fact that unions have been able to bargain wage increases above the inflation rate, and that the rate of unionization has increased partly because employment has not grown and union membership has expanded.

16. This section borrows from Royo (2002, pp. 173–217).

17. Overtime work is still a significant component or working time among Spanish workers and firms. See CES (2004, p. 346).

18. The number of part-time workers has remained stable in Spain at around 8 percent. In comparison the average in the EU is 18 percent. Only a fifth of those who work part-time in Spain (81.5 percent of them women) would not rather have a full-time job. The reason for this has to do with the fact the jobs involved are mostly poorly paid, have little social recognition, and require low qualifications. Seventy percent of these jobs are in services and most of them temporary. Home service (maids) is the sector in which this kind of employment is the most popular with 49 percent of the employed working part-time. See EIRO (2003) and CES (2004, pp. 218–220).

19. Despite the efforts from the trade unions, fixed-term employment has remained persistently high. See EIRO (2003).

20. Richards and Polavieja show that labor market precariousness reduces union involvement because it seriously impedes collective action, and it produces sentiments and attitudes of apathy toward unions. They conclude that temporary

workers neither identify with nor feel represented by the unions. In addition, they report that temporary workers are less likely to have access to wage-related benefits, earn lower wages (approximately 10 percent less than permanent workers), and are not entitled to as many welfare benefits. They suffer harsher working conditions, are more likely to suffer accidents, and have fewer possibilities for promotion and for the acquisition of skills.

21. See interview with Cándido Méndez, Secretary General of UGT, in *El País*, "La reforma laboral no ha producido ningún efecto positivo," Friday, October 27, 1995, p. 58. See also "Los sindicatos proponen hoy a la patronal CEOE el reparto del empleo y medidas contra la precariedad laboral," in *El País*, Thursday, May 9, 1996.

22. It was also the result of the frustration of the social actors with the 1994 labor reform. See "Patronal y sindicatos negocian medidas para crear empleo estable porque la reforma laboral no funciona," in *El País*, Friday, May 10, 1996.

23. As noted in chapter 2 one of the leaders of the CEOE, Jiménez Aguilar, has recognized that labor segmentation "hinders workers' professional training, their motivation, and in sum the competitiveness of the firm and the quality of its products."

24. Interview with José María Fidalgo and Cándido Mendez, leaders of CCOO and UGT respectively, in *El País*, "Más I+D para frenar la precariedad," Sunday, April 30, 2006.

25. During an interview with Antonio Moreno, secretary of industrial relations of the CEOE, in May of 2003, he stressed that some employers prefer unilateral reforms from the government.

26. See quotes in Espina (1999, p. 394) with interview with Antonio Gutiérrez in *ABC* April 27, 1997 and with Cándido Méndez *in La Vanguardia* on November 1, 1996.

27. Some scholars have argued that voters behaved like rational actors and recognized that general strikes were not the appropriate venue for adopting and changing important political decisions (see Espina 1999, pp. 380–383; Boix 1998). This development demonstrates the structural separation between the political and industrial relations systems.

28. See interview with José María Fidalgo in *El País*, Sunday, April 22, 2001. He restated this point during an interview with author in May 2001.

29. Interview with the author on May 7, 2001.

30. Ibid.

31. His interpretation of the situation was that moderation had led UGT to electoral victories, while confrontation had led CCOO to the erosion of its electoral support among workers. Interview with author December 1996.

32. See "CCOO desplaza a UGT como primera fuerza sindical y crece el apoyo a los nacionalistas," *El Mundo*, Saturday, December 9, 1995, p. 33.

33. For an analysis of the impact of these electoral results on UGT's strategies, see the interview with Cándido Méndez, secretary general of UGT, in *El País*, "La reforma laboral no ha producido ningun efecto positive," Friday, October 27, 1995, p. 58.

34. See interview with Antonio Gutiérrez, former secretary general of CCOO, in *El Mundo*, "Mantener a los críticos en la cúpula crearia confusion," Sunday, January 14, 1996, pp. 33–34. Both Antonio Gutierrez and José María Fidalgo confirmed in interviews with the author that the opposition to the social concertation process was one of the key cleavages in this internal

conflict. The victory of their positions facilitated the implementation of this strategy.

35. This strategic shift was confirmed during the interviews that I conducted with the leaders of the unions, including Antonio Gutiérrez, in December of 1996.

36. This was in contrast to the situation at the regional level. In Catalonia the 40 percent minority had negotiated responsibilities in the management bodies.

37. The agreement included the possibility to increase the number of years of employment that would be used to calculate pensions, therefore opening the door to the possible reduction of pensions. UGT adamantly refused to consider this possibility.

38. This was confirmed my interviews with Antonio Gutierrez 1996, José María Fidalgo in May 2001, and Antonio Ferrer in May 2001.

39. This was confirmed my interviews with Antonio Gutierrez 1996, José María Fidalgo on May 2001, and Antonio Ferrer on May 2001.

40. Espina (1999) views this development as the capstone of an "institutional learning process."

41. Cándido Méndez, the secretary general of UGT, in answer to a question about *Izquierda Unida*, stated in 1995 that "our strategies cannot be conditioned by any political positions no matter how respectable they are" in *El País*, "La reforma laboral no ha producido ningun efecto positive," Friday, October 27, 1995, p. 58.

42. According to the European Industrial Relations Observatory On-line (EIRO) "crude" union density figures in Spain stand between 10 and 19 percent, the lowest in the EU with Estonia, Latvia, and Poland.

6 Linking the Macro and the Micro: The Politics of Coordination and Institutional Reform at the Regional Level—The Basque Country

1. "Does Devolution of Power Cost Too Much?" in *Wall Street Journal Europe*, August 3, 2007, p. 1. The article highlights the concerns of Spanish businesses in heavily regulated sectors. In the retail sector, e.g., opening hours, sales periods, and other issues concerning businesses are dictated by more than 7,000 national and regional norms. Regions, e.g., can dictate which Sundays they will allow stores to open, and when retailers can hold sales which, according to businesses, hinder the development of coordinated marketing campaigns and translates into higher costs for companies. Some regions, heavily influenced by the clout of small-shop owners, have even banned the opening of new large retailers (such as the Balearic Islands). In the Chemistry sector, the cost of pollution-control regulation in Catalonia is ten times as high as in Aragon.

2. "Un toque de pedigrí," in *El País*, Sunday, September 9, 2007.

3. See Euskady.net: http://www.lehendakaritza.ejgv.euskadi.net/r48–7914/en/.

4. This section draws from the Harvard Business School case study from Michael Porter "The Basque Country: Strategy for Economic Development" (Cambridge: Harvard Business School, March 11, 2005).

5. From SPRI's website: http://www.spri.es/aSW/web/eng/spri/who/index.jsp.

6. According to the *World Economic Forum* (http://www.weforum.org/en/index.htm), "Clusters are geographically-centered groups of related firms and

industries operating in an environment characterized by a high degree of specialization, intense competition and a critical mass of highly educated employees from which to extract competitive advantages . . . This permits the generation of a series of operative synergies that constitute sources from which to extract competitive advantages."

7. Presentation by Juan Manuel Esteban, coordinator of Cluster Policy, Department of Industry, Trade and Tourism, Basque Government. Opatija, April 19–21, 2007 (juan-esteban@ej-gv.es).
8. Ibid.
9. Ibid.
10. The investment from McDonnell Douglas did not materialize but the work of this group planted the seeds for future collaborations.
11. Presentation by Juan Manuel Esteban, April 19–21, 2007.
12. One member of the Automotive Cluster acknowledged that "without the government we wouldn't have existed. The government encouraged us to think about our long term vision when we may have been swept up in the day business or running our companies" (Porter 2005, p. 12).
13. Presentation by Juan Manuel Esteban, April 19–21, 2007.
14. See "Economy in the Ascendancy," in *FDI: Foreign Direct Investment,* April 2004.
15. SPRI: http://www.usa.spri.net/aUS/web/en/spri/index.jsp.
16. SARATEK brings together "a whole range of bodies, including basic research centres, centres of excellence, the four universities operating in the Basque Autonomous Community, technology centres, international technology development and transfer centres, sector-based research centres, health R&D units and centres, business R&D units, laboratory and certification units, public research bodies, innovation intermediaries and the regional technology parks and business innovation centres," from http://www.lehendakaritza.ejgv.euskadi.net/r48–2286/en/contenidos/informacion/inves_saretek/en_3201/saretek_i.html.
17. For this section of the book I traveled to the Basque Country in 2003 and interviewed the leaders of the main business associations, chambers of commerce, regional government, unions, and business firms participating in the clusters.
18. Interview with Andrés Arizcorreta former president of the Knowledge Cluster, May 7, 2003.
19. Interview with Jesús Alberdi, leader of ELKAR, May 7, 2003. All the employers and representatives of business associations that I interviewed in the Basque Country for this project were quite critical of the role of the traditional Spanish banks and their lack of support to businesses. Spanish banks have been accused of being too traditional and reluctant to assume risks, a problem compounded by the lack of savings and risk culture in the country. The traditional industrial banks (such as Banesto of Central) have been changing (most have been absorbed by other Spanish banks), and now their focus is mostly on international operations and on the financial business. Savings and loans, on the contrary, have played a more active industrial role.
20. This is one of the main services that ELKARGI has been providing to member companies through its *Sociedad de Garantia.* The goal was that companies would not have to pay premiums if they do not make money. This program has grown over the years and they currently work with over 8,200 companies managing more that 70 million of capital and providing around 200 million

euros of guarantees per year. The participatory loans are long term (10 years) and with a combination of fixed and variable interest rates that are adjusted and applied to the firm based on whether or not it has profits. These interests are below the Euribor. Since 1994 it is a financial entity regulated by the Bank of Spain and subject to credit regulations (Interview with Alberdi 2003). The problem of high cost and limited access to capital was significantly reduced when Spain joined the Euro and also with the emergence of capital risk firms.

21. Interview with Felix Iraola, leader of the Chamber of Commerce, San Sebastián, May 8, 2003. He stressed that he misses a greater participation from the Basque universities in this process.

22. The Social Security system returns half of the contributions so that the administration, employers, and unions administer the professional training program. In Spain the Forcen administers it. There have been problems with the model (including corruption scandals) because in order to get funds employers and unions developed programs, which in some cases are not needed—it is a supply-based model. In the Basque Country the system responds better to demands from employers.

23. Data from *Memoria Socioeconómica Comunidad Autónoma del País Vasco 2005* (Bilbao: Consejo Económico y Social, 2006), p. 260.

24. Interview with Andrés Arizcorreta manager of ACF, May 7, 2003.

25. Interview with Jorge Arevalo, vice counselor for Professional Training of the Basque Government, May 9, 2003. He recognized, however, that cooperation with the universities is still insufficient.

26. Mondragón is the largest cooperative in the world as well as the largest business group in the Basque Country and the seventh largest in Spain. It was founded in 1956 by a Catholic priest (José María Arizmendiarrieta), and it is composed by 264 companies that operate in three main sectors: finance, industry, and distribution. It has operations all over the world.

27. The ELA union was founded in 1911 as part of the nationalistic movement in the Basque Country, with Catholic roots, which separated it with the class struggle that marked the actions of the class-based unions in Spain. After the transition there was a generational change. Historically the union has had a subordinated relationship within the Basque Nationalist Party (PNV), but after the transition the unions established its own independence (including the incompatibility of position in both organizations). Most of ELA supporters are PNV supporters but they also receive support from socialists and conservative workers. The union supports an autonomous Basque framework of labor relations separated from the Spanish one, but the Workers' Statue that emanated from the transition established a centralized model. The level of unionization in the Basque Country is still quite low (23–25 percent), but a little higher than the Spanish average: ELA has about 40 percent of support, LAB 16 percent, CCOO about 19 percent, and UGT 15 percent. Interview with José Miguel Unamue, from ELA, May 9, 2003.

28. Interview with Martin Auzutendi, counselor of labor relations of the Basque government, May 9, 2003.

29. The unions and CONFESBAK have signed six general agreements that covered the Basque Country. In Gipuzkoa they usually negotiate the provincial agreement first and then it is applied at the firm level (the social actors can agree not to apply the provincial agreement to a firm, and in some cases the provincial salary pact can even be substituted by a firm-level agreement),

whereas in Bizkaia there are provincial agreements but also firm-based ones (and the large firms have their own agreements and are not affected by the sectoral one), and in Alava the firm agreements tend to prevail over the provincial ones. One of the consequences of these distinctive models is differences in salaries (in Guipuzkoa salaries tend to be higher and the working week shorter). These differences are rooted in the history and economic structure of each province: in Gipuzkoa, e.g., there is a predominance of SMEs working in the metal industry, whereas in Bizkaia there are very large companies, and in Alava many companies come from other territories (Interview with Rubia from CONFESBAK, May 2003, and with Martin Auzutendi, counselor of Labor Relations of the Basque Government, May 9, 2003.).

30. Interview with José Miguel Unamue, from ELA, May 9, 2003. He argued that the existing bargaining model works. Ninety-seven percent of Basque workers are covered by collective agreements (mostly sectoral ones). He expressed concerns, however, about the hardening positions of the new ELA leaders, which was making it more difficult to reach agreements with the business associations. He contended that the future of industrial relations in the Basque Country will be intimately linked with the future of the Basque Country and the transfer of competences. They are not satisfied with the existing framework.

31. Interview with Eduardo García Elosua, leader of CCOO in the Basque Country (May 8, 2003). In this interview he expressed concerns about the potential politization of the collective bargaining process by ELA-STV, which could use it as a pressure instrument in the fight over the independence of the Basque Country. Martin Auzutendi, counselor of Labor Relations of the Basque Government, also stressed this risk and mentioned the increasing radicalization and confrontational stance of ELA.

32. For instance, in some companies, such as Michelin, the unions and the firms have reached agreements which include the total number of hours that workers have to work during the year, but then there is flexibility to distribute those hours throughout the year based on demand and production considerations.

33. Interview with Martin Auzutendi, counselor of Labor Relations of the Basque government, May 9, 2003. He acknowledged, however, that there are factors that hinder the development of a more structured and efficient system such as the different levels of support that each union has on each of the three Basque provinces, the fact that each province has its own business association, which has its own individual priorities and strategies, and the different bargaining structure on each province.

34. Presentation by Juan Manuel Esteban, April 19–21, 2007.

35. Data from *Memoria Socioeconómica Comunidad Autónoma del País Vasco 2005* (Bilbao: Consejo Económico y Social, 2006), p. 120.

36. Ibid., pp. 120–126.

37. SPRI: http://www.usa.spri.net/aUS/web/en/spri/index.jsp.

38. Ibid.

39. "Ready to Take a Larger Role on the European Stage," in *Financial Times*, Wednesday, October 26, 2005, p. 3 of "Special Report: Investing in Spain."

40. They are also developing business parks. One of the most heralded is the San Cugat business park, a multipurpose facility with R&D at its core. Like in the Basque Country, these initiatives were prompted by the closure of

manufacturing production lines throughout the region, which resulted in industrial conflict. For instance, Hewlett Packard decided to shift its Spain-based production of desktop and large-format printers to Singapore. However, the company took advantage of the new San Cugat Park to develop a state-of-the-art global business center (one of four in the world), retrained half of the redundant workers to work in its calls centers and the assembly of prototype printers in the design center. The company currently provides more than 2,000 jobs and has a 400-strong research team responsible for product innovation in a global market worth $3 billion a year. Since HP's decision, other multinationals such as Winterthur, Pfizer, and Sharp have chosen the park as the base for European call administration centers, logistic platforms, and R&D facilities. The park benefits from the region's quality of life and it draws from some of the best business European schools based in Barcelona (such as IESE and Esade). In fact, one of the leading Spanish business schools, Esade, is planning to open a new campus and a "creative center" to foster links between academia and business. The goal is to make the park a university of ideas. See "Redundant Manufacturing Base Rises from the Ashes," in *Financial Times*, Thursday, June 21, 2007, p. 2 of "Special Report: Spain."

41. The author is currently working in a project exploring coordination initiatives in Valencia.
42. Data from: "Un toque de pedigrí," in *El País*, Sunday, September 9, 2007.
43. "Un toque de pedigrí," in *El País*, Sunday, September 9, 2007.
44. Since the 1970s, more than 800 people have been killed by ETA, and employers have been targets of extortion and abduction (e.g., the leader of ADEGI was assassinated, and when the author interviewed the current leadership of the business group they all had bodyguards). As a result some companies have shifted their operations to other parts of Spain and Europe, and the conflict is also draining the region from some of its best talent. The impact of this instability on FDI is hard to quantify but the overall impact has been estimated at about 10 percentage points of growth over the last 10 years. See "Peace Dividend in Prospect," in *Financial Times*, Wednesday, October 25, 2006, p. 6 of "Special Report: Investing in Spain."
45. Presentation by Juan Manuel Esteban, April 19–21, 2007.
46. Interview with Joss Rubia from COFESBANK, May 8, 2003.
47. Interview with Andrés Arizcorreta, director of the rolling stock producing company ACF, which employs over 20,000 people and has operations all over the world (including in the United States: they work with the subway system in Washington DC and Sacramento) on May 7, 2003. As noted earlier, he had been president of the knowledge cluster.
48. Interview with Felix Iraola, leader of the Chamber of Commerce, San Sebastián, May 8, 2003.
49. Interview with Felix Iraola, leader of the Chamber of Commerce, San Sebastián, May 8, 2003.
50. Most of the people that I interviewed agreed that it has worked better in Guipuzkoa than in Bizkaia. Differences have to do with the economic structure (smaller companies in Gipuzkoa than Bizkaia); historical patterns; or the fact that the administrative institutions are relatively young (only 30 years) and some have achieved a greater degree of optimization and efficiency than others.
51. This was a concern that was expressed by most businessmen during the interviews that I conducted in 2003. See also "Peace Dividend in Prospect,"

in *Financial Times*, Wednesday, October 25, 2006, p. 6 of "Special Report: Investing in Spain."

52. See "Automotive Companies in Drive to Become Cluster of Excellence," in *Financial Times*, Wednesday, October 25, 2006, p. 6 of "Special Report: Investing in Spain."

53. As of 2007 The Department of Transport has created the Transport and Logistics Cluster and the Department of Industry, Trade and Tourism is currently consolidating a biocluster (BIOBASK 2O1O), studying the option of establishing a Tourism Cluster, and examining the possibility of clustering some metal-mechanical associations. See presentation from Juan Manuel Esteban, April 19–21, 2007.

Conclusion

1. This typology borrows from Schmidt's *State Influenced Market Economies* (SMEs) (2006); and Molina and Rhodes's *Mixed Market Economies* (MMEs) (2005). Other countries that have been included in this category are France, Portugal, Italy, and Greece (also Korea and Taiwan).

2. Spain is still viewed as a model of inflexibility in labor relations. Recently an article on British Airways labor problems stated that "BA is seen as the hotbed for Spanish practices: the demarcation lines and inflexible working conditions that use to bedevil the Fleet Street newspaper business in London," in "Captains of Turbulence," *Financial Times*, August 13–14, 2005, p. 7.

3. Peter Hall, Presentation at the *Real Colegio Complutense-Harvard University*, Cambridge, MA, August 6, 2005.

4. Yet, French employers are still pushing for cooperation with the unions. President Sarkozy has called for a "new social contract," and has started a process to negotiate with the social actors the reform of the labor market, the pension system (which currently gives large privileges to public sector workers), the health system, and the unemployment insurance. See "Sarkozy propone 'un nuevo contrato social,'" in *El País*, Wednesday, September 19, 2007. In a recent article about economic reforms, Laurent Parisot, president of the business association *Medef*, stated that "consensus must lead the way." See also "Sarkozy Can Bring Us 'la strategic revolution,'" in *Financial Times*, August 30, 2007, p. 7.

5. See "French Labour Talks Start," in *Financial Times*, September 8–9, 2007. Amaury Eloy, founder of a French digital printing company, states in the article that an agreement is critical to address unemployment and slow economic growth. He claims that a key objective should be to reduce wage costs and social charges, which he claims are higher than in other countries: "In Spain my costs would represent just 33% of my turnover and I could hire 20 more staff." He points out that at an identical Iberian company called Work Centre, "they have created 300 jobs, [while] we have only 80, and their profitability is 15 points higher than ours. The only difference is the weight of the social charges." "French Industry Hails 'Revolutionary' Pact," in *Financial Times*, January 22, 2008, p. 3.

6. Anthony Giddens, "Coronar todas las cumbres," in *El País*, Sunday, December 3, 2006, p. 17.

7. This section borrows from Royo (2003, pp. 247–253).

8. The new rules are modeled on a European Union Directive of 2004. The new code introduces important modifications, and it responds to the recent

tortuous battle for control of the energy producer Endesa by the German Eon, which was outmaneuvered by Enel and Acciona. It includes rules that allow an initial bidder to make a revised offer to shareholders if its offer comes to less than 2 percent below that of a competitor. Companies are also allowed to buy up to 30 percent of a target's shares in the open market after announcing an offer, but they cannot make a last-minute pitch to shareholders after the period of contesting bids has expired. The new legislation empowers minority shareholders by putting an end to "partial takeovers" under which Spain's large financial, industrial, and family groups were able to gradually build minority control of one another with little regard for minority shareholders. Investors are now forced to extend an offer to all shareholders once it controls equity carrying 30 percent of the votes, or more than half of the board. Finally, the new Code includes a clause under which a buyer can force recalcitrant shareholders to sell once it controls 90 percent of the equity. From "Spanish Takeover Climate Changes," in *Financial Times*, Monday, August 13, 2007, p. 15.

9. "Towards a Euro Wage?" by the U.K. research institute, Industrial Relations Services, suggests that the Euro will push bargaining systems both ways, toward centralization and decentralization, depending on the regions, economic sectors, and firms. See *Financial Times*, October 13, 1998, p. 3. Sirkka Hamalainen from the European Central Bank's executive board stated in a speech in London that labor flexibility has improved and wage settlements have become more moderate since the Euro's introduction. She stated that "there is evidence of a very significant change in labor market behavior in the euro area countries, particularly in the filed of wage negotiations . . . discipline has greatly improved in that field, with wage demands apparently assuming a permanently lower level of inflation and adjusting faster to cyclical conditions that was the case prior to the introduction of the euro." See "ECB Hails Euro Effects on Labour Markets," in *Financial Times*, Tuesday, February 26, 2002, p. 4.

10. Daniel Gros, "Will EMU Survive 2010?" Centre for European Policy Studies, January 2005, www.ceps.be.

11. See Wolfgang Munchau "Spain Has More Reason to Quit the Euro than Italy," in *Financial Times*, Monday, February 20, 2006; and "Monetary Union Is Not for the Poor," in *Financial Times*, Monday, January 30, 2006.

12. See Martin Wolf, "Britain Must Get to Grips with Lackluster Productivity Growth," in *Financial Times*, November 8, 2005.

13. "Spanish Economy Cools on Property Slowdown," in *Financial Times*, August 30, 20007, p. 4; "La economía española se enfriará en 2008," and "El mercado laboral pierde fuelle," in *El País*, September 9, 2007.

14. Interview with José Luís Rodríguez Zapatero, in *El País*, September 8, 2007.

15. "Malestar en la empresa," in *El País*, September 2, 2007.

16. See "Revolutions turn nation into green leader," in *Financial Times*, Thursday, June 21, 2007, p. 4 of "Special Report: Spain."

17. As many observers point out, the main challenge is not so much the lack of capital to carry out research, but instead how to turn research concepts into viable commercial technologies. See "Conceptual Seeds Need Nurturing," in *Financial Times*, Thursday, June 21, 2007, p. 6 of "Special Report: Spain."

18. See Emilio Ontiveros, "Exitosa relocalización," in *El País*, Monday, February 27, 2006.

19. The author is currently working on a research project examining the Valencia experience.
20. "Ford reinventa Almussafes," in *El País*, September 2, 2007.
21. The program has identified five priority areas: energy and climate change, biotechnology, information and communication technologies, health care, and nanotechnology. See, "Conceptual Seeds Need Nurturing," in *Financial Times*, Thursday, June 21, 2007, p. 6 of "Special Report: Spain."
22. See "Buy-Out Groups Signal Convergence and Charm Business," in *Financial Times*, Thursday, June 21, 2007, p. 6 of "Special Report: Spain."
23. See Debrun and Pisany-Ferry (2006). Also Wolfgang Munchau, "The Dutch Are Leading a Popular Rebellion," in *Financial Times*, Monday, November 27, 2006.
24. Thomas Friedman, "Israel Discovers Oil," in *The New York Times*, June 10, 2007.
25. It will also be critical to produce more researchers to generate new ideas and produce patents (there were approximately 100,000 in 2004 and it is estimated that we would need another 50,000 by 2010) "Europa pierde la carrera en I+D," in *El País*, Sunday, October 12, 2006.
26. Spain has the longest working hours in Europe, and office hours often stretch past 8 p.m. Therefore, many women drop out of the workforce after they have children, or take up part-time jobs in the service sector. The Socialist government has passed a new gender equality law that seeks to eliminate the relics of discrimination in the country, and promote the role of women in the private sector, politics, and public service. This law mandates equal pay for equal work and requires companies to become more "family friendly," and of those with more than 250 employees to develop "equality plans" to recruit, train, and promote women; and to "seek a balanced representation of men and women" at boardroom level (they have 8 years to achieve this). This last request has been quite controversial: currently 63 percent of listed companies have no women in their boards, and only 6 percent have appointed female directors. The government plans to reward companies that fulfill these requirements by giving them preference in public tender contracts, and by giving them an "equality seal" to showcase those that follow these policies. It also established 13 days of paternity leave. See, "Spanish Court Heralds Era of Sex Equality," in *Financial Times*, September 12, 2007.
27. According to recent data, depression affects between 15 and 30 percent of the Spanish workers and it costs companies over 750 million euros in labor absences/leaves; and 35 percent of the workers suffer insomnia, loss of appetite, emotional exhaustion, lack of concentration, and moments of emotional anxiety when they return from vacation (the so-called post-vacation syndrome). See "Malestar en la empresa," in *El País*, September 2, 2007.
28. See "Malestar en la empresa," in *El País*, September 2, 2007.
29. See David Gardner, "Spain Must Exorcise the Demons of the Francoist Era," in *Financial Times*, August 24, 2007, p. 11.
30. For a possible articulation on how to move forward such a strategy see Baumol, Litan, and Schramm (2007).

Bibliography

Albert, Michael. *Capitalism against Capitalism*. London: Whurr, 1992.

Alesina, Alberto and Giavazzi Francesco. *The Future of Europe: Reform or Decline*. Cambridge, MA and London, England: The MIT Press, 2006.

Alston, Lee J., Thrain Eggertsson, and Douglass C. North. *Empirical Studies in Institutional Change*. New York: Cambridge University Press, 1996.

Alvarez-Miranda, Berta. *El Sur de Europa y la Adhesion a la Comunidad. Los Debates Politicos*. Madrid: CIS, 1996.

Amable, Bruno. *The Diversity of Modern Capitalism*. Oxford: Oxford University Press, 2003.

Aoki, M. *Toward a Comparative Institutional Analysis*. Cambridge: MIT Press, 2001.

Barreto, José and Reinhard Naumann. "Portugal: Industrial Relations under Democracy." In A. Ferrer and R. Hyman, eds., *Changing Industrial Relations in Europe. Portugal*. Cambridge: Blackwell, 1998, pp. 395–425.

Bates, Robert. 1988. "Contra Contractarianism: Some Reflections on the New Institutionalism." *Politics and Society* 16 (2): 387–401.

———. *Open-Economy Politics*. Princeton: Princeton University Press, 1997.

Baumol, William J., Robert E. Litan, and Carl J. Schramm. *Good Capitalism, Bad Capitalism and the Economics of Growth and Prosperity*. New Haven and London: Yale University Press, 2007.

Becker, Uwe. "Dutch Corporatist Capitalism Moving into Liberal Direction: How to Theorize?" Paper presented at the Annual Meetings of the American Political Science Association, Philadelphia, PA, August 31–September 3, 2006.

———. "Open Systemness and Contested Reference Frames: A Framework for Understanding Change in the Varieties of Capitalism." Paper presented at the Minda de Gunzburg Center for European Studies, Harvard University, February 6, 2006a.

Bentolila, Samuel and Juan J. Dolado. 1994. "Labour Flexibility and Wages: Lessons from Spain." *Economic Policy* 9 (18): 55–99.

Bentolila, Samuel, J. Segura, and L. Toharia. 1991. "La Contratación Temporal en España." *Moneda y Crédito* (193): 225–265.

Berger, Suzanne, Ed. *Organizing Interests in Western Europe*. Cambridge: Cambridge University Press, 1981.

———. *How We Compete*. New York: Doubleday, 2006.

Berger, Suzanne and Ronald Philip Dore. *National Diversity and Global Capitalism*. Ithaca, NY: Cornell University Press, 1996.

Berman, Sheri. *The Primacy of Politics: Social Democracy and the Making of Europe's Twentieth Century*. New York: Cambridge University Press, 2006.

Bermeo, Nancy. *Unemployment in the New Europe*. New York: Cambridge University Press, 2002.

Bhagwati, Jagdish. "The Demands to Reduce Domestic Diversity among Trading Nations." In Bhagwati and Robert Hudec. *Fair Trade and Harmonization*. Cambridge: MIT Press, 1996, pp. 9–40.

———. *In Defense of Globalization*. New York: Oxford University Press, 2004.

Blanchard, Olivier J., J. Andrés, C. Bean, E. Malinvaud, A. Revenga, D. Snower, G. Saint-Paul, R. Solow, D. Taguas, and L. Toharia. *Spanish Unemployment. Is There a Solution?* Madrid and London: Consejo Superior de Cámaras de Comercio, Industria, y Navegación/Center for Economic Policy Research, 1995.

Blasi, Joseph, Maya Kroumovoa, and Douglas Kruse. *Kremlin Capitalism: Privatizing Russian Economy*. Ithaca: Cornell University Press, 1997.

Blyth, Mark. 2003. "Same as It Never Was: Temporality and Typology in the Varieties of Capitalism." *Comparative European Politics* 1 (2): 215–225.

Boix, Carles. *Political Parties, Growth and Equality. Conservative and Social Democratic Strategies in the World Economy*. New York: Cambridge University Press, 1998.

Botella, Joan, Richard Gunther, and Josè Ramón Montero. *Democracy in Modern Spain*. New Haven and London: Yale University Press, 2004.

Bouza, Fermín, ed., 1989. *Perfil, Actitudes y Demandas del Delegado y Afiliado a UGT*. Madrid: Fundación Largo Caballero.

Bover, Olympia, Pilar García Perea, and Pedro Portugal. 1997. "A Comparative Study of the Portuguese and Spanish Labour Markets." Servicio de Estudios. *Documento de Trabajo # 9807*. Madrid: Banco de España.

Bover, Olympia, Samuel Bentolila, and Manuel Arellano. 2000. "The Distribution of Earnings in Spain during the 1980s. The Effect of Skill, Unemployment, and Union Power." Servicio de Estudios. *Documento de Trabajo # 0015*. Madrid: Banco de España.

Bowman, John. *Capitalist Collective Action*. New York: Cambridge University Press, 1989.

Boyer, Robert. *The Regulation School: A Critical Introduction*. New York: Columbia University Press, 1990.

Broz, J. Lawrence. 1999. "Origins of the Federal Reserve System." *International Organization* 53 (1) (Winter): 39–70.

Bruno, Michael and Jeffrey Sachs. *The Economic of Worldwide Stagflation*. Cambridge: Harvard University Press, 1985.

Burgess, Katrina. *Parties and Unions in the New Global Economy*. University of Pittsburgh: Pittsburgh Press, 2004.

Burki, Shahid and Guillermo Perry. *Beyond the Washington Consensus*. Washington, DC: World Bank, 1998.

Cable, Vincent. 1995. "The Diminished Nation-State: A Study in the Loss of Economic Power." *Daedalus* 124 (2) (Spring): 23–54.

Cabrero Moran, Enrique. 1997. *La Democracia Interna de los Sindicatos*. Madrid, CES.

Callaghan, Helen. "The Domestic Politics of EU Legislation: British, French and German Attitudes towards Takeover Regulation, 1985–2003." Paper presented to the Conference of Europeanists, March 2004.

Calmfors, Lars and John Driffill. 1988. "Bargaining Structure, Corporatism, and Economic Performance." *Economic Policy* 3: 13–61.

Calvert, Randall. "Rational Actors, Equilibrium and Institutions." In Jack Knight and Iai Sened, eds., *Explaining Social Institutions*. Ann Arbor: University of Michigan Press, 1995, pp. 57–94.

———. *The Rational Choice Theory of Institutions: Cooperation, Coordination and Communication*. In Jeffrey S. Banks and Eric A. Hanuschek, eds., *Modern Political Economy*. New York: Cambridge University Press, 1995, pp. 216–268.

Calavita, Kitty. *Immigrants at the Margins: Law, Race, and Exclusion in Southern Europe*. Cambridge University Press: Cambridge, 2005.

Cameron, David. *Social Democracy, Corporatism, Labor Quiescence and the Representation of Economic Interest in Advanced Capitalist Society*. In John H. Goldthorpe, ed., *Order and Conflict in Contemporary Capitalism*. New York: Oxford University Press, 1984, pp. 143–178.

———. "Creating Supranational Authority in Monetary and Exchange Rate Policy. The Sources and Effects of EMU." In Wayne Sandholtz and Alec Stone Sweet, eds., *European Integration and Supranational Governance*. New York: Oxford University Press, 1998, pp. 188–216.

———. "The Challenges of EU Accession." Paper presented at the annual meeting of the *American Political Science Association*, Boston, September 2002.

Camisón, César and Javier Molina. 1998. "Evaluación de la proximidad de una colectividad de organizaciones al modelo ideal de distrito industrial y desempeño empresarial: una aplicación a los casos de los distritos de la industria cerámica de Italia y España." *Revista de Estudios Regionales* (50): 15–37.

Camisón, César, María Luisa Flor, and María Josè Oltra. *Enfoques, problemas y mètodos de investigación en Economía y Dirección de Empresas*. Castellón: Fundació Universitat Empresa, 2003.

Camp, Roderic. *Entrepreneurs and Politics in Twentieth-Century Mexico*. New York: Oxford University Press, 1989.

Campbell, John A. *Institutional Change and Globalization*. Princeton: Princeton University Press, 2004.

Campbell, John. A., John A. Hall, and Ove K. Pedersen. *The State of Denmark*. Montreal: McGill University Press, 2006.

Campos, José and Hilton Root. *The Key to the Asian Miracle*. Washington, DC: Brookings Institution, 1996.

CCOO. *Documentos Aprobados en el Séptimo Congreso*. Madrid: Confederación Sindical de Comisiones Obreras, 2000.

CES. *Memoria sobre la Situación Socioeconómica y Laboral de España*. Madrid: CES, Various years.

CIS. *Opiniones y Actitudes de los Españoles Ante el Proceso de Integración Europea*. Madrid: CIS, 1999.

Coates, David, Ed. *Varieties of Capitalism, Varieties of Approaches*. Houndmills: Palgrave Macmillan, 2005.

Collier, Ruth and David Collier. *Shaping the Political Arena*. Princeton: Princeton University Press, 1991.

Corkill, David and Joseph Harrison. *Spain: A Modern European Economy*. Ashgate: Great Britain, 2004.

Costa Pinto, António and Nuno Severiano Teixeira. "From Africa to Europe: Portugal and European Integration." In António Costa Pinto and Nuno Severiano Teixeira, eds., *Southern Europe and the Making of the European Union*. New York: Columbia University Press, 2002.

Costa Pinto, Antonio and Nuno Severiano Teixeira, Eds. *Southern Europe and the Making of the European Union*. New York: Columbia University Press, 2002.

Clift, Ben and Jonathan Perraton. *Where Are National Capitalisms Now?* London: Palgrave Macmillan, 2004.

Crouch, Colin. *Capitalist Diversity and Change*. New York: Oxford University Press, 2005.

Crouch, Colin and Wolfgang Streeck, Eds. *Political Economy of Modern Capitalism. Mapping Convergence and Diversity*. Newbury Park, CA: Sage Publications, 1997.

———. *Capitalist Diversity and Change*. New York: Oxford University Press, 2005.

———. *Complementarity and Fit in the Study of Comparative Capitalism*. In G. Morgan, R. Whitley, and E. Moen, eds., *Changing Capitalism? Internationalization, Institutional Change and Systems of Economic Organizations*. New York: Oxford University Press, 2006.

Cuevas, José María. 1997. "Economía, Trabajo y Sociedad. El Análisis de las Organizaciones Empresariales." Paper presented during the *Jornadas sobre el Dialogo Social*. Cursos de Verano de la Universidad Complutense. El Escorial, July 9. Mimeo.

———. 1999. "Visión Institucional del Mercado de Trabajo." In *Revista del Instituto de Estudios Económicos. El Mercado de Trabajo en España I. Realidades y Posibilidades*, Nos. 1 and 2, 1999.

Culpepper, Pepper D. *Creating Cooperation: How States Develop Human Capital in Europe*. Ithaca: Cornell University Press, 2003.

Culpepper, Pepper, Peter A. Hall, and Bruno Palier, Eds. *Changing France: The Politics that Markets Make*. London: Palgrave Macmillan, 2006.

Curtis, Gerald. "Big Business and Political Influence." In Ezra Vogel, ed., *Modern Japanese Organization and Decision-Making*. Berkeley: University of California Press, 1975.

D'Mello, Bernard. "Reebok and the Global Footwear Sweatshop." In Jim Yong Kim., ed., *Dying for Growth: Global Inequality and the Health of the Poor*. Monroe, ME: Common Courage Press, 2000.

Debrun, Xavier and Jean Pisany-Ferry. 2006. "Economic Reforms in the Euro Area: Is There a Common Agenda?" *Bruegel Policy Contribution* (5) (November).

De Vicuña, Josè Luis Larrea Jimènez. *El Desafío de La Innovación*. Barcelona: Editorial UOC, 2006.

Diniz, Eli, Ed. *Empresários e Modernização Económica*. Florianópolis: UFSC, 1993.

Djelic, Marie-Laure and Sigrid Quack. *Globalization and Institutions: Redefining the Rules of the Economic Game*. Cheltenham: Edward Elgar, 2003.

Dobbin, Frank. "Cultural Models of Organization: The Social Construction of Rational Organizing Principles." In Diana Crane, ed., *The Sociology of Culture*. Oxford: Blackwell, 1994, pp. 117–191.

Dollar, David and Aart Kray. 2002. "Spreading the Wealth." *Foreign Affairs* 81 (1) (January/February): 120–133.

Dore, Ronald. 2003. "Varièta e dinamiche del capitalismo." *Stato e Mercato* 69 (December): 363–383.

Downs, Anthony. *An Economic Theory of Democracy*. New York: Harper Collins, 1957.

Edleman, Marc, Patrick Heller, Richard Sandbrook, and Judith Teichman. *Social Democracy in the Global Periphery: Origins, Challenges, Prospects*. Cambridge University Press: Cambridge, 2007.

Edwards, Sebastian. *Crisis and Reform in Latin America*. New York: Oxford University Press, 1995.

Eichengreen, Barry. *The European Economy since 1945*. New Jersey: Princeton University Press, 2007.

EIRO. 2003. *Trade Union Membership Online*, http://www.eiro.eurofound.eu.int/ 2004/03/update/tn0403105u.html.

Encarnación, Omar G. *The Myth of Civil Society*. New York: Palgrave, 2003.

Escobar, Modesto. "Spain. Works Councils or Unions?" In J. Rogers and W. Streeck, eds., *Work Councils*. Chicago: Chicago University Press, 1995.

Espina, Alvaro. "El 'Guadiana' de la Concertación Neocorporatista en España. De la Huelga General de 1988 a los Acuerdos de 1997." In Faustino Miguélez and Carlos Prieto, eds., *Las Relaciones de Empleo en España*. Madrid: Siglo XXI, 1999, pp. 375–398.

Esping-Anderson, Gosta. *Social Foundations of Postindustrial Economies*. New York: Oxford University Press, 1999.

Estache, Antonio and David Martimort. "Transaction Costs Politics, Regulatory Institutions and Regulatory Outcomes." Paper presented at the Conference on "Regulation Post-Privatization." Buenos Aires, May 21 and 22, 1998.

Estefanía, Joaquín. *La Larga Marcha: Medio Siglo De Política (Económica) Entre La Historia Y La Memoria*. Barcelona: Ediciones Península, 2007.

Estevez-Abe, Margarita. "Welfare Capitalism in Post-War Japan." Harvard University, Working Paper, Government Department, 1999.

Etchemendy, Sebastián. 2004. "Revamping the Weak, Protecting the Strong, and Managing Privatization: Governing Globalization in the Spanish Takeoff." *Comparative Political Studies* 37(6) (August): 623–651.

Evans, Ana. "Preemptive Modernisation and the Politics of Sectoral Defense: Adjustment to Globalisation in the Portuguese Pharmacy Sector." Unpublished manuscript, 2005.

Evans, Peter. *Dependent Development*. Princeton: Princeton University Press, 1979.

Fairbanks, Michael, Stace Lindsay, and Michael E. Porter. *Plowing the Sea: Nurturing the Hidden Sources of Growth in the Developing World*. Cambridge: Harvard Business School Press, 1997.

Fernández Guerrero, Agustin González Ismael, and Celestino Suárez Burguet. "Spanish External Trade and EEC Preferences." In George N. Yannopoulos, ed., *European Integration and the Iberian Economies*. New York: St. Martin's Press, 1989.

Fernández Méndez De Andes, Fernando, Ed. *La Internacionalización de la Empresa Española: Aprendizaje y Experiencia*. Madrid: Universidad Nebrija, 2006.

Fields, Karl. "Creating Cooperation and Determining the Distance." In Sylvia Maxfield and Ben Ross Schneider, eds., *Business and the State in Developing Countries*. Ithaca: Cornell University Press, 1997.

Fishman, Robert. *Working Class Organization and the Return of Democracy in Spain*. London: Cornell University Press, 1990.

———. "Shaping, not Making, Democracy: The European Union and Spain's Post-Franco Political Transformation." Paper presented at the conference *From Isolation to Integration: 15 Years of Portuguese and Spanish Membership in Europe*, Minda de Gunzburg Center for European Studies at Harvard University, November 2–3, 2001.

———. *Democracy's Voices*. Ithaca: Cornell University Press, 2004.

Fishman, Robert and Anthony Messina, Eds. *The Year of The Euro*. Indiana: University of Notre Dame Press: Indiana, 2006.

Fraile, Lydia. "Tightrope. Spanish Unions and Labor Market Segmentation." In Andrew Martin and George Ross, eds., *The Brave New World of European Labor*. New York: Berghahn Books, 1999.

Franzese Jr., Robert J. *Macroeconomic Policies of Developed Democracies*. New York: Cambridge University Press, 2002.

Frieden, Jeffry A. 1991. "Invested Interests: The Politics of National Economic Policies in a World of Global Finance." *International Organization* 45: 425–451.

———. *Debt, Development, and Democracy.* Princeton: Princeton University Press, 1991.

———. *Global Capitalism, Its Fall and Rise in the Twentieth Century.* New York: W.W. Norton and Company, 2006.

Frieden, Jeffry and Ronald Rogowski. "The Impact of the International Economy on National Policies: An Analytical Overview." In Robert O. Keohane and Helen V. Milner, eds., *Internationalization and Domestic Politics.* New York: Cambridge University Press, 1996, pp. 108–136.

Friedman, Thomas. *The Lexus and the Olive Tree: Understanding Globalization.* New York: Farrar, Straus and Giroux, 2000.

———. *The World is Flat: A Brief History of the Twenty-First Century.* New York: Farrar, Straus and Giroux, 2006.

Führer, Ilse Marie. *Los Sindicatos en España.* Madrid: CES, 1996.

Garrett, Geoffrey. *Partisan Politics in the Global Economy.* New York: Cambridge University Press, 1998.

Garrett, Geoffrey and Peter Lange. 1995. "Internationalization, Institutions, and Political Change." *International Organization* 49: 627–655.

Geddes, Barbara. *Politician's Dilemma.* Berkeley: University of California Press, 1994.

Gerschenkron, Alexander. *Economic Backwardness in Historical Perspective: A Book of Essays.* Cambridge: Belknap Press of Harvard University Press, 1962.

Gibson, Edward L. 1997. "The Populist Road to Market Reform: Policy and Electoral Coalitions in Mexico and Argentina." *World Politics* 49 (April): 339–370.

Gillespie, Richard. 1990. "The Break–Up of the 'Socialist Family.' Party–Union Relations in Spain 1982–1989." *West European Politics* 16 (1) (January): 47–62.

Giner, S. and E. Sevilla. "Spain from Corporatism to Corporatism." In A. Williams, ed., *Southern Europe Transformed.* London: Harper & Row, 1984.

Goldthorpe, John A., Ed. *Order and Conflict in Contemporary Capitalism.* New York: Oxford University Press, 1984.

Gómez Fuentes, Ángel. *Asi Cambiara España: La Batalla del Mercado Común.* Madrid: Plaza & Janes, 1986.

González, Felipe. "Diferentes Perspectivas y Alternativas." In *España y el Mercado Común: Políticas y Alternativas.* Madrid: Instituto Nacional de Industria, 1980.

Goodin, Robert. 2003. "Choose Your Capitalism?" *Comparative European Politics* 1 (2): 203–213.

Gourevitch, Peter A. and James Shinn. *Political Power & Corporate Control: The New Global Politics of Corporate Governance.* Princeton: Princeton University Press, 2005.

Goyer, Michel. "Institutional Complementarity and Change: Assessing the Impact of the Transformation of Corporate Governance in France and Germany." Paper presented to a Workshop on Institutional Change in Contemporary Capitalism, London School of Economics, June 2005.

———. "The Transformation of Corporate Governance in France." In Pepper Culpepper, Peter A. Hall, and Bruno Palier, eds., *Changing France: The Politics that Markets Make.* London: Palgrave Macmillan, 2006.

Greif, Avner and David D. Laitin. 2004. "A Theory of Endogenous Institutional Change." *American Political Science Review* 98 (4) (November): 633–652.

Guillén, Mauro. 2000. "Corporate Governance and Globalization: Is There Convergence across Countries?" *Advances in International Comparative Management* 13: 175–204.

———. *The Limits of Convergence.* New York: Cambridge University Press, 2003.

———. *The Rise of Spanish Multinationals: European Business in the Global Economy.* New York: Cambridge University Press, 2005.

Gunther, Richard, José Ramón Montero, and Joan Botella. *Democracy in Modern Spain.* New Haven: Yale University Press, 2004.

Hacker, Jacob and Paul Pierson. 2002. "Business Power and Social Policy." *Politics & Society* 30 (2): 277–325.

Haggard, Stephen. *Pathways from the Periphery.* Ithaca: Cornell University Press, 1990.

Haggard, Stephen and Mathew McCubbins. "Political Institutions and the Determinants of Public Policy: an Introductions." http://polisciexplab.ucsd.edu/mccubbin/mchag/chap1.htm.

Haggard, Stephan and Robert Kaufman. *The Political Economy of Democratic Transitions.* Princeton: Princeton University Press, 1995.

Hall, Peter A. 1994. "Central Bank Independence and Coordinated Wage Bargaining: Their Interaction in Germany and Europe." *German Politics and Society* (Winter): 1–23.

———. "Institutions and Economic Performance: The Evolution of the Field from the Perspective of Political Science." Lecture to the GAAC Workshop on Institutions and Economic Performance in Advanced Economies since 1945, Wissenschaftszentrum, Berlin, July 1998.

———. "The Political Economy of Europe in an Era of Interdependence." In Herbert Kitschelt, Peter Lange, Gary Marks, and John D. Stephens, eds., *Change and Continuity in Contemporary Capitalism.* New York: Cambridge University Press, 1999, pp. 1–70.

———. "Organized Market Economies and Unemployment in Europe: Is It Finally Time to Accept Liberal Orthodoxy." In Nancy Bermeo, ed., *Context and Consequence: The Effects of Unemployment in the New Europe.* New York: Cambridge University Press, 2000.

———. "Preference Formation as a Political Process: The Case of Monetary Union in Europe." In Ira Katznelson and Barry Weingast, eds., *Preferences over Time.* New York: Russell Sage Foundation, 2005.

———. "The Evolution of Varieties of Capitalism in Europe." In B. Hancké, M. Rhodes, and M. Thatcher, eds., *Beyond Varieties of Capitalism: Contradictions, Complementarities, and Change.* Oxford: Oxford University Press, 2007.

Hall, Peter and Daniel Gingerich. "Varieties of Capitalism and Institutional Complementarities in the Macroeconomy: An Empirical Analysis." *MPIfG Discussion Paper 04/5.* Cologne: Max Plank Institute for the Study of Societies, September 2004.

Hall, Peter A. and David Soskice, Eds. *Varieties of Capitalism: The Institutional Foundations of Comparative Advantage.* Oxford: Oxford University Press, 2001.

Hall, Peter A. and Kathleen Thelen. "Institutional Change in Varieties of Capitalism." Paper presented at the Annual Meeting of the American Political Science Association, Washington DC, September 1, 2005.

Hall, Peter A. and Robert Franzese, Jr. 1998. "Mixed Signals: Central Bank Independence, Coordinated Wage Bargaining, and European Monetary Union." *International Organisation* (Summer): 502–536.

Hamel, Gary and C. K. Prahalad. *Competing for the Future.* Cambridge: Harvard Business School Press, 1996.

Hancké, Bob. "Revisiting the French Model: Coordination and Restructuring in French Industry." In Peter Hall and David Soskice, eds., *Varieties of Capitalism: The Institutional Foundations of Comparative Advantage.* Oxford: Oxford University Press, 2001.

———. *Large Firms and Institutional Change: Industrial Renewal and Economic Restructuring in France.* Oxford: Oxford University Press. 2002.

Hancké, Bob, Martin Rhodes, and Mark Thatcher. *Beyond Varieties of Capitalism: Conflict, Contradictions, and Complementarities in the European Economy.* New York: Oxford University Press, 2007.

———. "Introduction." In Bob Hancké, Martin Rhodes, and Mark Thatcher., eds., *Beyond Varieties of Capitalism: Conflict, Contradictions, and Complementarities in the European Economy.* New York: Oxford University Press, 2007a.

Hancké, Bob and Andrea Monika Herrman. "Wage Bargaining and Comparative Advantage in EMU." In B. Hancké, M. Rhodes, and M. Thatcher, eds., *Beyond Varieties of Capitalism: Contradictions, Complementarities, and Change.* Oxford: Oxford University Press, 2007b.

Hassel, Anke. "What Does Business Want? Labor Market Reforms in CMEs and Its Problems." In B. Hancké, M. Rhodes, and M. Thatcher, eds., *Beyond Varieties of Capitalism: Contradictions, Complementarities, and Change.* Oxford: Oxford University Press, 2007.

Hassel, Anke and Bernhard Ebbinghaus. "From Means to Ends. Linking Wage Moderation and Social Policy Reform." In Giuseppe Fajertag and Philippe Pochet, eds., *Social Pacts in Europe. New Dynamics.* Brussels: European Trade Unions Institute, 2000.

Hassel, Anke and Hugh Williamson. "The Evolution of the German Model: How to Judge the Reforms in Europe's Largest Economy." Paper prepared for the Anglo-German Foundation for the Study of Industrial Society, 2004.

Hellman, Joel. 1998. "Winners Take All: The Politics of Partial Reform in Postcommunist Transitions." *World Politics* 5 (2) (January): 203–234.

Hine, Robert C. 1989. "Customs Union Enlargement and Adjustment: Spain's Accession to the European Community." *Journal of Common Market Studies* XXVIII (1) (September): 1–27.

Hirshman, Albert. *Exit, Voice and Loyalty.* Cambridge: Harvard University Press, 1970.

Hoepner, Martin. "Corporate Governance in Transition: Ten Empirical Findings on Shareholder Value and Industrial Relations in Germany." Max Planck Institute for the Study of Societies, Discussion Paper, No. 5, 2002.

———. "The German Party Paradox." Max Planck Institute for the Study of Societies, Discussion Paper, 2003.

Hoepner, Martin and Gregory Jackson. "An Emerging Market of Corporate Control? The Case of Mannesmann and German Corporate Governance." Max Planck Discussion Paper. Max Planck Institüt für Gesellschaftsforschung, Cologne, 2001.

Howell, Chris. 2003. "Varieties of Capitalism: And Then There Was One?" *Comparative Politics* (October): 102–124.

Huber, Evelyne. *Models of Capitalism: Lessons for Latin America.* University Park, PA: The Pennsylvania State University Press, 2002.

Huber, Evelyne and John D. Stephens. *Development and Crisis of the Welfare States: Parties and Politics in Global Markets.* Chicago: University of Chicago Press, 2001.

Hundt, Reed. *In China's Shadow.* New Haven: Yale University Press, 2006.

ILO, 1997. *World Employment Report 1996–1997.* Geneva, ILO.

Iversen, Torben. 1998. "Wage Bargaining, Central Bank Independence, and the Real Effects of Money." *International Organization* 52(3): 469–504.

———. *Contested Economic Institutions. The Politics of Macroeconomic and Wage-Bargaining in Organized Capitalism.* New York: Cambridge University Press, 1999.

———. *Capitalism, Democracy and Welfare.* New York: Cambridge University Press, 2005.

———. "Economic Shocks and Varieties of Government Responses." In B. Hancké, M. Rhodes, and M. Thatcher, eds., *Beyond Varieties of Capitalism: Contradictions, Complementarities, and Change.* Oxford: Oxford University Press, 2007.

Iversen, Torben and Anne Wren. 1998. "Equality, Employment and Budgetary Restraint." *World Politics* 50 (July); 507–546.

Iversen, Torben and David Soskice. "An Asset Theory of Social Policy Preference." Paper presented at the Workshop on Social Equality, Harvard University, 2000.

Iversen, Torben and Thomas Cusak. 2000. "The Causes of Welfare State Expansion: Deindustrialization or Globalization." *World Politics* 52: 313–349.

Jackson, Gregory. "Contested Boundaries: Ambiguity and Creativity in the Evolution of German Co-Determination." In Wolfgang Streeck and Kathleen Thelen, eds., *Beyond Continuity: Institutional Change in Advanced Political Economies.* Oxford: Oxford University Press, 2004, pp. 229–254.

Jacoby, Sanford M. *The Embedded Corporation: Corporate Governance and Employment Relations in Japan and the United States.* Princeton: Princeton University Press, 2005.

Jiménez Aguilar, J. "EL Nuevo Dialogo Social Desde la Perspectiva de las Organizaciones Empresarialies." Paper presented during the *Jornadas sobre el Dialogo Social.* Cursos de Verano de la Universidad Complutense, El Escorial, July 9, 1997.

Jimeno, Juan Francisco. 1997. "La Negociació Collectiva. Aspectes Institucionals i les Seves Conseqències Econòmiques." *Revista Econòmica de Catalunya* (32) (July): 78–86.

Jimeno, Juan Francisco and Luís Toharia. 1993. "The Effects of Fixed Term Employment on Wage. Theory and Evidence from Spain." *Investigaciones Económicas* XVII (3): 475–494.

John Stephens and Evelyn Huber Stephens. *Development and Crisis of the Welfare States: Parties and Policies in Global Markets.* Chicago: Chicago University Press, 2001.

Johnson, Chalmers A. *MITI and the Japanese Miracle the Growth of Industrial Policy, 1925–1975.* Stanford, CA: Stanford University Press, 1982.

Johnson, Juliet. 1997. "Russia's Emerging Financial-Industrial Groups." *Post-Soviet Affairs* 13 (4): 333–365.

Jordana, Jacint. 1996. "Reconsidering Union Membership in Spain, 1977–1994. Halting Decline in a Context of Democratic Consolidation." *Industrial Relations Journal* 27 (3): 51–69.

Katzenstein, Peter. *Small States in World Markets.* Ithaca: Cornell University Press, 1985.

Kaufman, Robert, Carlos Bazdresch, and Blanca Heredia. *Mexico: Radical Reform in a Dominant Party System.* In Stephan Haggard and Steven Webb, eds., *Voting for Reform.* New York: Oxford University Press, 1994.

Kenyon, Tom and Graeme Robertson. "Heinz Capitalism: How Many Varieties Are There?" Paper Presented at the APSA Annual Meeting, Chicago, September 2–5, 2004.

Kesselman, Mark. *The Politics of Globalization.* Boston: Houghton Mifflin Co., 2007.

Kim, Eui-Young. 1993. "The Developmental State and the Politics of Business Interest Associations." *Pacific Focus* VIII (2) (Fall): 31–60.

Kitchelt, Herbert, Peter Lange, Gary Marks, and John Stephens, Eds. *Change and Continuity in Contemporary Capitalism.* New York. Cambridge University Press, 1999.

Knetter, Michael M. 1989. "Price Discrimination by U.S. and German Exporters." *American Economic Review* 79 (1): 198–210.

Knight, Jack. *Institutions and Social Conflict.* New York: Cambridge University Press, 1992.

———. "Models, Interpretation and Theories: Constructing Explanations of Institutional Emergence and Change." In Jack Knight and Iai Sened, eds., *Explaining Social Institutions.* Ann Arbor: University of Michigan Press, 1995, pp. 95–120.

Kotler, Philip, Somkid Jatusripitak, Suvit Maesincee, and Somkid Jatusri, Eds. *The Marketing of Nations: A Strategic Approach to Building National Wealth.* New York: Free Press, 1997.

Kreile, Michael. "West Germany: Dynamics of Change." In Peter Katzenstein, ed., *Between Power and Plenty.* Madison: University of Wisconsin Press, 1978, pp. 191–224.

Krueger, Anne. 1974. "The Political Economy of the Rent-Seeking Society." *American Economic Review* 64 (3) (June): 291–303.

Lake, David A. and Robert Powell. *Strategic Choice and International Relations.* Princeton, NJ: Princeton University Press. 1999.

Larkings, Christopher. 1998. "The Judiciary and Delegative Democracy in Argentina." *Comparative Politics* 30 (4) (July): 423–443.

Lehmbruch, Gerhard and Phillippe Schmitter, Eds. *Patterns of Corporatist Policy-Making.* London: Sage. 1982.

Levy, Brian and Pablo Spiller, Eds. *Regulations, Institutions, and Commitment, Comparative Study of Telecommunications.* Cambridge: Cambridge University Press, 1996.

Levy, Jonah D. *Tocqueville's Revenge State, Society, and Economy in Contemporary France.* Cambridge: Harvard University Press, 1999.

Lichbach, Mark. *The Cooperator's Dilemma.* Ann Arbor: University of Michigan Press, 1996.

Lijphart, Arend. *Patterns of Democracy Government Forms and Performance in Thirty-Six Countries.* New Haven: Yale University Press, 1999.

Locke, Richard M. *Remaking the Italian Economy.* Ithaca: Cornell University Press, 1995.

Magone, Jose. *European Portugal.* New York: St. Martin's Press, 1997.

———. "Attitudes of Southern European Citizens Towards European Integration." In António Costa Pinto and Nuno Severiano Teixeira, eds., *Southern Europe and the Making of the European Union.* New York: Columbia University Press, 2002.

Malo, Miguel Angel. 2001. "Elecciones Sindicales y Comportamiento de los Sindicatos Españoles. Una Propuesta." *Estudios Sobre la Economía Española # 93.* Madrid: FEDEA.

Malloy, James, Ed. *Authoritarianism and Corporatism in Latin America*. Pittsburgh: University of Pittsburgh Press, 1977.

Manow, Philip and Eric Seils. "Adjusting Badly: The German Welfare State, Structural Change and the Open Economy." In Fritz Scharpf and Vivien Schmidt, eds., *Welfare and Work in the Open Economy*. Oxford: Oxford University Press, 2000, pp. 264–307.

Manzano, Daniel. *Sistema Financiero Español*. Madrid: Ediciones Empresa Global, 2005.

March, James G. and Johan P. Olsen. *Rediscovering Institutions: The Organizational Basis of Politics*. New York: Free Press, 1989.

Mares, Isabela. "Firms and the Welfare State: When and How does Social Policy Matter to Employers." In Peter Hall and David Soskice, eds., *Varieties of Capitalism: The Institutional Foundations of Comparative Advantage*. Oxford: Oxford University Press, 2001.

———. *Taxation, Wage Bargaining, and Unemployment*. New York: Cambridge University Press, 2006.

Martin, Cathie Jo. 1997. "Mandating Social Change: The Business Struggle over National Health Reform." *Governance* 10 (4) (October): 397–428.

———. *Stuck in Neutral: Business and the Politics of Human Capital Investment Policy*. Princeton, NJ: Princeton University Press, 2000.

Martin, Cathie Jo and Duane Swank. 2004. "Does the Organization of Capital Matters? Employers and Active Labor Market Policy at the National and Firm Levels." *American Political Science Review* 98 (4) (November): 593–612.

Martin, Cathie Jo and Kathleen Thelen. "Varieties of Coordination and Trajectories of Change: Social Policy and Economic Adjustment in Coordinated Market Economies." Paper presented at the 2007 Annual Meeting of the American Political Science Association, Chicago, August 30–September 2, 2007.

McDermott, Gerald. "The Politics of Institutional Renovation and Competitive Upgrading: Lessons from the Transformation of the Argentine Wine Industry." Paper presented at the Annual Meeting of the American Political Science Association, Washington DC, September 1–4, 2005.

Menz, Georg. *Varieties of Capitalism and Europeanization: National Response Strategies to the Single European Market*. New York: Oxford University Press, 2005.

Miguélez, Faustino and Carlos Prieto, Eds. *Las Relaciones de Empleo en España*. Madrid: Siglo XXI, 1999.

Milanovic, Branko. 2003. "The Two Faces of Globalization: Against Globalization as We Know It." *World Development Journal* 31 (4): 667–683.

Milgron, Paul and John Roberts. *Economics, Organization and Management*. New Jersey: Prentice Hall, 1992.

Millen, Joyce V. and Timothy Holtz. "Dying for Growth, Part I: Transnational Corporations and the Health of the Poor." In Jim Yong Kim et al., eds., *Dying for Growth: Global Inequality and the Health of the Poor*. Monroe, ME: Common Courage Press, 2000.

Miller, Gary. 1997. "The Impact of Economics on Contemporary Political Science." *Journal of Economic Literature* 35 (September): 1173–1204.

Moe, Terry. 2005. "Power and Political Institutions." *Perspectives on Politics* 3 (2) (June): 215–234.

Molina, Oscar and Martin Rhodes. 2005. "Conflict, Complementarities and Institutional Change: Reforming Production & Protection Systems in Mixed

Market Economies." Paper Presented at the 2005 Annual Meeting of the American Political Science Association, Washington DC, September 1–4.

———. "Conflict, Complementarities and Institutional Change in Mixed Market Economies." In B. Hancké, M. Rhodes, and M. Thatcher, eds., *Beyond Varieties of Capitalism: Contradictions, Complementarities, and Change.* Oxford: Oxford University Press, 2007.

Moral, Simón Sánchez Moral. *Natalidad industrial y redes de empresas en España.* Madrid: Ediciones Empresa Global, 2005.

Morgan, Glen, Richard Whitley, and Eli Moen, Eds. *Changing Capitalism.* New York: Oxford University Press, 2005.

Morlino, Leonardo. "The Europeanisation of Southern Europe." In António Costa Pinto and Nuno Severiano Teixeira, Eds., *Southern Europe and the Making of the European Union.* New York: Columbia University Press, 2002.

Moscoso, Leopolodo. "Social Democracy and Industrial Conflict. The Breakdown of Concertation in Spain, 1982–1994." Paper presented at the Iberian Study Group, CES-Harvard University, September, 1995.

Murillo, María Victoria. "Union Politics, Market-Oriented Reforms and the Reshaping of Argentine Corporatism." In Douglas Chalmers, Carlos M. Vilas, Katherine Hite, Scott B. Martin, Kerianne Piester, and Monique Segarra, eds., *The New Politics of Inequality in Latin America: Rethinking Participation and Representation.* New York: Oxford University Press, 1997.

Nelson, Joan. "Poverty, Equity and the Politics of Adjustment." In Haggard, Stephan and Robert Kaufman, eds., *The Politics of Economic Adjustment.* Princeton, NJ: Princeton University Press, 1992.

Newton, Michael T. (with Peter J. Donaghy). *Institutions of Modern Spain: A Political and Economic Guide.* New York: Cambridge University Press, 1997.

Nickell, Stephen. "Labour Market Institutions and Unemployment in OECD Countries." CESifo DICE Report No.2: 1326, 2003.

Nordhaus, W. 1989. "Alternative Approaches to the Political Business Cycle." *Brooking Papers of Economic Activity* 2: 1–49.

North, Douglass C. *Institutions, Institutional Change and Economic Performance.* New York: Cambridge University Press, 1990.

OECD. *Annual Employment Outlook.* Paris: OECD, 2007.

———. The *Globalization of Labor, World Economic Outlook.* Washington DC, 2007a.

———. *Education at a Glance.* Paris: OECD, 2007b.

Offe, Claus and Helmut Wiesenthal. 1980. "Two Logics of Collective Action." *Political Power and Social Theory* 1: 67–115.

———. "Two Logics of Collective Action: Theoretical Notes on Social Class and Political Form." In Claus Offe, ed., *Disorganized Capitalism.* Cambridge: MIT Press, 1986.

Olson, Mancur. *The Logic of Collective Action Public Goods and the Theory of Groups.* Cambridge, MA: Harvard University Press, 1965.

———. *The Rise and Decline of Nations.* New Haven: Yale University Press, 1982.

———. 1986. "A Theory of the Incentives Facing Political Organizations." *International Political Science Review* 7 (2) (April 1986): 165–189.

Ortega y Gassett, José. *Invertebrate Spain.* New York: Howard Fertig, 1974.

Ostrom, Elinor. *Governing the Commons.* New York: Cambridge University Press, 1990.

O'Sullivan, Mary. "Studying Firms to Understand Institutions: Globalisation, the 'French Touch' and the French Financial System." Mimeo, 2005.

Pack, Sasha D. *Tourism and Dictatorship: Europe's Peaceful Invasion of Franco's Spain*. New York: Palgrave, 2006.

Pagano, Marco and Paolo Volpin. "The Political Economy of Corporate Governance." Centro Stude in Econia e Finanza, Departimento di Scienze Economiche, Universitya degli Studi di Salerno, Working Paper No. 29, 2002.

Palier, Bruno. "Ambiguous Agreement, Cumulative Change: French Social Policy in the 1990s." In Wolfgang Streeck and Kathleen Thelen, eds., *Beyond Continuity: Institutional Change in Advanced Political Economies*. Oxford: Oxford University Press, 2005, pp. 127–144.

Pardo Avellaneda, Rafael and Joaquín Fernández Castro. "Las Organizaciones Empresariales y la Configuración del Sistema de Relaciones Industriales." In Miguélez, Faustino and Carlos Prieto, eds., *Las Relaciones Laborales en España*. Madrid: Siglo XXI, 1995.

Pelzman, Samuel. 1976. "Toward a More General Theory of Regulation." *The Journal of Law and Economics* XIX (August): 211–240.

Pérez, Sofía. *Banking in Privilege*. Ithaca: Cornell University Press, 1997.

———. "Yet the Century? The Return to National Social Bargaining in Italy and Spain, and Some Possible Implications." Paper prepared for delivery at the 1998 Annual Meeting of the American Political Science Association, Boston, August, 1998.

———. 2000. "From Decentralization to Reorganization. The Resurgence of National-Level Social Bargaining in Italy and Spain." *Comparative Politics* 32 (4) (July): 437–458.

Pérez-Díaz, Victor. "Políticas Económicas y Pautas Sociales en la España de la Transición. La Doble Cara del Neocorporatismo." In J. Linz, ed., *España. Un Presente Para el Futuro*. Madrid: Instituto de Estudios Económicos, 1984.

———. 1985. "Los Empresarios y la Clase Política." *Papeles de Economía Española* 22.

———. "From Civil War to Civil Society: Social Capital in Spain from the 1930s to the 1990s." In Robert D. Putnam, ed., *Democracies in Flux: The Evolution of Social Capital in Contemporary Society*. New York: Oxford University Press, 2002.

Perraton, Jonathan and Ben Clift, Eds. *Where Are National Capitalisms Now?* New York: Palgrave, 2004.

Petrazzini, Ben. "Telephone Privatization in a Hurry: Argentina." In Ravi Ramamurti, ed., *Privatizing Monopolies*. Baltimore and London: Johns Hopkins University Press, 1996.

Pierson, Paul. *Politics in Time: History, Institutions, and Social Analysis*. Princeton: Princeton University Press, 2004.

Pontusson, Jonas. *Inequality and Prosperity*. Ithaca: Cornell University Press, 2005.

Porter, Michael. *Competitive Advantage Creating and Sustaining Superior Performance*. New York and London: Free Press, Collier Macmillan, 1985.

———. *The Competitive Advantage of Nations*. New York: The Free Press, 1990.

———. *The Basque Country: Strategy for Economic Development*. Cambridge: Case Study. Harvard Business School, March 11, 2005.

Powell, Walter and Paul DiMaggio. *The New Institutionalism in Organizational Analysis*. Chicago: University of Chicago Press, 1991.

Pridham, Geoffrey. "The Politics of the European Community: Transnational Networks, and Democratic Transitions in Southern Europe." In G. Pridham, ed., *Encouraging Democracy: The Institutional Context of Regime Transition in Southern Europe*. Leicester: Leicester University Press, 1991.

Pridham, Geoffrey. "European Integration and Democratic Consolidation in Southern Europe." In António Costa Pinto and Nuno Severiano Teixeira, eds., *Southern Europe and the Making of the European Union*. New York: Columbia University Press, 2002.

Przeworski, Adam and Michael Wallerstein. 1988. "Structural Dependence of the State in Capital." *American Political Science Review* 82: 11–30.

Regini, Marino. 1997. "Still Engaging in Corporatism? Recent Italian Experience in Comparative Perspective." *European Journal of Industrial Relations* 3 (3): 259–278.

———. "Social Institutions and Production Structure. The Italian Variety of Capitalism in the 1980s." In Colin Crouch and Wolfgang Streeck, eds., *Political Economy of Modern Capitalism*. London: Sage Publications, 1997a.

———. "Between De-Regulation and Social Pacts. The Responses of European Economies to Globalization." CEACS, Working Paper 1999/133. Madrid: Centro de Estudios Avanzados en Ciencias Sociales, 1999.

———. 2000. "Between Deregulation and Social Pacts. The Responses of European Economies to Globalization." *Politics & Society* 28 (1) (March): 5–33.

———. 2003. "Tripartite Concertation and Varieties of Capitalism." *European Journal of Industrial Relations* 8 (3): 251–263.

Regini, Marino and Ida Regalia. 1997. "Employers, Unions, and the State: The Resurgence of Concertation in Italy?" *West European Politics* 25 (1): 210–230.

Rhodes, Martin. "Globalization, Labour Markets and Welfare States. A Future of Competitive Corporatism?" In Martin Rhodes and Yves Meny, eds., *The Future of European Welfare*. New York: St. Martin's Press, 1998, pp. 178–203.

Richards, Andrew and Javier García Polavieja. "Trade Unions, Unemployment and Working Class Fragmentation in Spain." Working Paper # 112. Madrid: Centro de Estudios Avanzados en Ciencias Sociales, 1997.

Rieger, Elmar and Stephan Leibfried. *Limits to Globalization*. Oxford: Polity, 2003.

Rippon, Hon Geoffrey. "Costs and Benefits of the Enlargement." In Various Authors, *España y el Mercado Común: Políticas y Alternativas*. Madrid: Instituto Nacional de Industria, 1980.

Roca, Jordi. *Pactos Sociales y Políticas de Rentas*. Madrid: Ministerio de Trabajo y Seguridad Social, 1993.

Rodrik, Dani. 1996. "Understanding Economic Reform." *Journal of Economic Literature* 36: 9–41.

———. *Has Globalization Gone Too Far?* Washington, DC: Institute for International Economics, 1997.

Roe, Mark. *Strong Mangers, Weak Owners: The Political Roots of American Corporate Finance*. Princeton, NJ: Princeton University Press, 1994.

———. *Political Determinants of Corporate Governance*. Oxford: Oxford University Press, 2003.

Rogowski, Ronald. *Commerce and Coalitions: How Trade Affects Domestic Political Alignments*. Princeton, NJ: Princeton University Press, 1989.

Rothstein, Bo. *Social Traps and the Problem of Trust*. Cambridge: Cambridge University Press, 2005.

Royo, Sebastián. *From Social Democracy to Neoliberalism: The Consequences of Party Hegemony in Spain 1983–1996*. New York: St. Martin's Press, 2000.

———. 2001. "The Collapse of Social Concertation and the Failure of Socialist Economic Policies in Spain." *South European Society & Politics* 6/1 (Summer): 27–50.

————. *A New Century of Corporatism? Corporatism in Southern Europe*. Westport: Praeger, 2002.

————. 2002a. "A New Century of Corporatism? Spain and Portugal in Comparative Perspective." *West European Politics* 52 (3) (July): 77–104.

————. 2003. "The 2004 Enlargement: Iberian Lessons for Post-Communist Europe." *South European Society & Politics* 8 (1–2.): 287–313.

————, Ed. *Portugal, Espanha e a Integração Europeia: Um Balanço*. Lisbon: Instituto de Ciencias Sociais da Universidade de Lisboa, June 2005.

————. "Spain and Portugal in the European Union: Mission Accomplished?" In Eleanor E. Zeff and Ellen B. Pirro, eds., *The European Union and the Member States: Cooperation, Coordination, and Compromise*. New York: Lynne Rienner Publishers, 2006.

————. "The Challenges of EU Integration: Iberian Lessons for Eastern Europe." In Joaquín Roy and Roberto Domínguez, eds., *Towards the Completion of Europe: Analysis and Perspectives of the New European Union Enlargement*. Miami: Jean Monnet EU Chair, University of Miami, 2006a.

————. 2006b. "Beyond Confrontation: The Resurgence of Social Bargaining in Spain in the 1990s." *Comparative Political Studies* (November): 969–995.

————. 2007. "Varieties of Capitalism in Spain: Business and the Politics of Cooperation." *European Journal of Industrial Relations* 13 (1) (Spring): 47–65.

————. "Regional Integration and Economic Development in the Iberian Peninsula and Mexico." In Various Authors, *Economic Integration—Global Experiences*. Pune, India: Icfai University Press, 2007a.

————. "The Europeanization of Portuguese Interest Groups? Trade Unions and Employers' Associations." In Antonio Costa-Pinto and Nuno Severiano Texeira, eds., *The Europeanization of Portuguese Democracy*. Lisbon: PJSS, 2007b.

————. 2007c. "Lessons from the Integration of Spain and Portugal to the European Union." *PS: Political Science and Politics*. American Political Science Association. XL (3) (October): 689–693.

————. "The Euro and Economic Reforms: The Case of Spain." In Joaquín Roy and Pedro Gomis-Porqueras, eds., *The Euro and the Dollar*. Aldershot, UK: Ashgate Publishing, 2007d.

Royo, Sebastián and Paul C. Manuel, Eds. *Spain and Portugal in the European Union: The First Fifteen Years*. London: Frank Cass, 2003.

————. 2003. "Some Lessons from the Fifteenth Anniversary of the Accession of Portugal and Spain to the European Union." In *South European Society & Politics* 8 (1–2) (Summer/Autumn): 1–30.

Sabel, Charles. *Work and Politics*. New York: Cambridge University Press, 1982.

————. "Learning by Monitoring." In Neil Smelser and Richard Swedberg, eds., *The Handbook of Economic Sociology*. Princeton: Princeton University Press, 1994.

Salvati, M. 1995. "The Crisis of Government in Italy." *New Left Review* (213): 76–95.

Sánchez Albornoz, Claudio. *España. Un Enigma Histórico*. Mexico DF: Hispano Americana, 1977.

Schaede, Ulrike. *German Financial System*. Cambridge: Harvard Business School, 1999.

Schamis, Hector. 1999. "Distributional Coalitions and the Politics of Economic Reform in Latin America." *World Politics* (January): 236–268.

Scharpf, Fritz W. "The Political Calculus of Inflation and Unemployment in Western Europe." CES Working Chapter Series #6, Cambridge MA: CES-Harvard University, 1987.

Scharpf, Fritz W. *Crisis and Choice in European Social Democracy.* Ithaca, NY: Cornell University Press, 1991.

———. *Games Real Actors Play. Actor-Centered Institutionalism in Policy Research.* Boulder, CO: Westview Press, 1997.

Scharpf, Fritz and Vivien Schmidt. *Welfare and Work in the Open Economy: From Vulnerability to Competitiveness.* Oxford: Oxford University Press, 2000.

Schenone, Osvaldo H. "Public Sector Behavior in Argentina." In Felipe Larraín and Marcelo Selowsky, eds., *The Public Sector and the Latin American Crisis.* International Center for Economic Growth, San Francisco, 1991.

Scheve, Kenneth F. and Matthew J. Slaughter. 2007. "New Deal for Globalization." *Foreign Affairs* 86 (4) (July/August): 34–47.

Schmidt, Vivien. *The Futures of European Capitalism.* New York: Oxford University Press, 2002.

———. Bringing the State Back into the Varieties of Capitalism and Discourse Back into the Explanation of Change. Paper presented at the Annual Meeting of the American Political Science Association, Philadelphia, PA, August 31–September 3, 2006.

Schmitter, Philippe. *Interest Conflict and Political Change in Brazil.* Stanford: Stanford University Press, 1971.

———. 1974. "Still the Century of Corporatism?" *Review of Politics* 36 (1) (January): 85–121.

———. "Interest Intermediation and Regime Governability in Western Europe and North America." In S. Berger, ed., *Organizing Interests in Western Europe.* New York: Cambridge University Press, 1981.

———. "Neo-Corporatism and the State." In Wyn Grant, ed., *The Political Economy of Corporatism.* New York: St. Martin's Press, 1985.

Schmitter, Philippe and Wolfgang Streeck. *The Organization of Business Interests.* MPIfG Discussion Paper 99/1, 1999 [1981].

Schneider, Ben Ross. Why Is Mexican Business So Organized? Paper presented at the meetings of the American Political Science Association in Atlanta, September 1999.

———. *Business Politics and the State in Twentieth-Century Latin America.* New York: Cambridge University Press, 2004.

Sebastián, Miguel. "Spain in the EU: Fifteen Years May Not Be Enough." Paper presented at the conference *From Isolation to Europe: 15 Years of Spanish and Portuguese Membership in the European Union,* Minda de Gunzburg Center for European Studies, Harvard University, November 2–3, 2001.

Sen, Amartya. 2002. "How to Judge Globalism." *The American Prospect* 13 (1).

Shafer, D. Michael. *Winners and Losers.* Ithaca: Cornell University Press, 1994.

Shafer, Robert. *Mexican Business Organizations.* Syracuse: Syracuse University Press, 1973.

Shapiro, Ian, Stephen Skowronek, and Daniel Galvin, Eds. *Rethinking Political Institutions: The Art of the State.* New York: NYU Press, 2007.

Shepsle, Kenneth. "Institutional Equilibrium and Equilibrium Institutions." In Herbert Weisberg, ed., *Political Science: The Science of Politics.* New York: Agathon, 1986, pp. 51–81.

Shiva, Vandana. *Stolen Harvest: The Hijacking of the Global Food Supply.* Cambridge: South End Press, 2000.

Shonfield, Andrew. *Modern Capitalism.* New York: Pickering & Chatto Ltd; New edition, 1994.

Siaroff, Alan. 1999. "Corporatism in 24 Industrial Democracies: Meaning and Measurement." *European Journal of Political Research* 36 (2) (October): 175–205.

Sikkink, Kathryn. *Ideas and Institutions.* Ithaca: Cornell University Press, 1991.

Skocpol, Theda. "Bringing the State Back In." In Peter Evans, Dietrich Rueschemeyer; and Theda Skocpol, eds., *Bringing the State Back In.* New York: Cambridge University Press, 1985.

Snyder, Richard. *Politics after Neoliberalism: Reregulation in Mexico.* New York: Cambridge University Press, 2001.

Solé, C. "Neocorporatisme i pluralism en les societats democràtiques; un debat obert." In *Chapters. Revista de Sociologia*, No. 245, Universitat Autonoma de Barcelona, 1985, pp. 13–23.

Soskice, David. 1990. "Wage Determination: The Changing Role of Institutions in Advanced Industrialized Countries." *Oxford Review of Economic Policy* 6 (4): 36–61.

———. "Divergent Production Regimes. Coordinated and Uncoordinated Market Economies in the 1980s and 1990s." In H. Kitschelt, Peter Lange, Gary Marks, and John D. Stephens, eds., *Continuity and Change in Contemporary Capitalism.* New York: Cambridge University Press, 1999, pp. 101–134.

———. "Macroeconomics and Varieties of Capitalism." In B. Hancké, M. Rhodes, and M. Thatcher, eds., *Beyond Varieties of Capitalism: Contradictions, Complementarities, and Change.* Oxford: Oxford University Press, 2007.

Steinmo, Sven, Kathleen Thelen, and Frank Longstreth, Eds. *Structuring Politics. Historical Institutionalism in Comparative Analysis.* New York: Cambridge University Press, 1992.

Stephens, John and Evelyn Huber Stephens. *Development and Crisis of the Welfare States: Parties and Policies in Global Markets:* Chicago: Chicago University Press, 2001.

Stigler, George. 1971. "The Theory of Economic Regulation." *Bell Journal of Economics and Management Science* 2 (1) (Spring): 3–21.

Stiglitz, Joseph. *Globalization and Its Discontents.* New York: W.W. Norton and Company, 2002.

———. 2002a. "Globalism's Discontents." *The American Prospect* 13 (1) (January): 16–21.

Stoleroff, Alan D. 1992. "Between Corporatism and Class Struggle. The Portuguese Labour Movement and the Cavaco Silva Governments." *West European Politics* 15 (4): 118–150.

Streeck, Wolfgang. "On the Institutional Conditions for Diversified Quality Production." In Egon Matzner and Wolfgang Streeck, eds., *Beyond Keynesianism.* Aldershot: Elgar, 1991, pp. 21–61.

———. *Social Institutions and Economic Performance.* Beverly Hills: Sage, 1992.

———. "Pay Restraint without Incomes Policy: Institutionalized Monetarism and Industrial Unionism in Germany." In Ronald Dore, Robert Boyer, and Zoe Mars, eds., *The Return of Incomes Policy.* London: Pinter, 1994, pp. 118–130.

———. "The German Economic Model: Does It Exist? Can It Survive?" In Crouch and Streeck, eds., *The Political Economy of Modern Capitalism.* London: Sage, 1997.

———. "Taking Uncertainty Seriously: Complementarity as a Moving Target." Workshop Proceedings of the Osterreichische Nationalbank, 1, 2004, pp. 101–115.

Streeck, Wolfgang and Kathleen Thelen, Eds. *Beyond Continuity: Institutional Change in Advanced Political Economies.* New York: Oxford University Press, 2005.

Swank, Duane. *Global Capital, Political Institutions, and Policy Change in Developed Welfare States.* New York: Cambridge University Press, 2002.

Swenson, Peter. 1991. "Bringing Capital Back In, or Social Democracy Reconsidered: Employer Power, Cross-Class Alliances and Centralization of Industrial Relations in Denmark and Sweden." *World Politics* 43 (4): 513–544.

———. *Capitalists against Markets.* New York: Oxford University Press, 2001.

Tarrow, Sidney. *Power in Movement.* New York: Cambridge University Press, 1998.

Terry Moe. "The Politics of Structural Choice." In Oliver E. Williamson, ed., *Organization Theory: From Chester Barnard to the Present and Beyond.* Oxford: Oxford University Press, 1990.

Thacker, Strom. 1999. "NAFTA Coalitions and the Political Viability of Neoliberalism in Mexico." *Journal of Interamerican Studies and World Affairs* 41 (2) (Summer): 57–90.

Thelen, Kathleen. *Union of Parts: Labor Politics in Postwar Germany.* Ithaca: Cornell University Press, 1991.

———. "Why Germany Employers Cannot Bring Themselves to Dismantle the German Model." In Torben Iversen, Jonas Pontusson, and David Soskice, eds., *Unions, Employers and Central Banks.* New York: Cambridge University Press, 2000, pp. 138–169.

———. "Varieties of Labor Politics in the Developed Democracies." In Peter Hall and David Soskice, eds., *Varieties of Capitalism. The Institutional Foundations of Comparative Advantage.* New York: Oxford University Press, 2001, pp. 77–103.

———. *How Institutions Evolve: The Political Economy Skills in Germany, Britain, the United States and Japan.* New York: Cambridge University Press, 2004.

Thelen, Kathleen and Ikuo Kume. 1999. "The Effects of Globalization on Labor Revisited: Lessons from Germany and Japan." *Politics and Society* 27 (December): 477–505.

Thorp, Rosemary and Francisco Durand. "A Historical View of Business-State Relations: Colombia, Peru, and Venezuela Compared." In Sylvia Maxfield and Ben Ross Schneider, eds., *Business and the State in Developing Countries.* Ithaca: Cornell University Press, 1997.

Thorsten Beck, George Clarke, Alberto Groff, Philip Keefer, and Patrick Walsh. *New Tools and New Tests in Comparative Political Economy: The Database of Political Institutions.* World Bank, July 1999.

Tiberghien, Yves. *Political Mediation of Global Market Forces.* Ph.D. Dissertation, Stanford University, 2002.

Tilly, Charles. 1995. "Globalization Threatens Labor's Rights." *International Labor and Working-Class History* 47 (Spring): 1–2.

Toral, Pablo. *The Reconquest of the New World: Multinational Enterprises and Spain's Direct Investment in Latin America.* Ashgate: Great Britain, 2001.

Torre, Juan Carlos. *El proceso político de las reformas económicas en América Latina.* Buenos Aires: Paidos, 1998.

Tovias, Alfred. "The Southern European Economies and European Integration." In António Costa Pinto and Nuno Severiano Teixeira, eds., *Southern Europe and the Making of the European Union.* New York: Columbia University Press, 2002.

Treisman, Daniel S. 1998. "Fighting Inflation in a Transitional Regime: Russia's Anomalous Stabilization." *World Politics* 50 (2) (January): 235–265.

Tsebelis, George. *Nested Games: Rational Choice in Comparative Perspective.* Berkeley: University of California Press, 1990.

Van der Meer, Marc. "Spain." In Bernard Ebbinghaus and Jelle Visser, eds., *The Societies of Europe. Trade Unions in Western Europe since 1945.* New York: Grove's Dictionaries, Inc., 2000.

Vaitsos, Constantino. "Economic Effects of the Second Enlargement." In Dudley Seer and Constantine Vaitsos, eds., *The Second Enlargement of the EEC.* New York: St Martin Press, 1982.

Vickers, John and George Yarrow. *Privatization: An Economic Analysis.* Cambridge: MIT University Press, 1995.

Vogel, Steven K. *Freer Markets, More Rules.* Ithaca: Cornell University Press, 1996.

———. "Routine Adjustment and Bounded Innovation: The Changing Political Economy of Japan." In Wolfgang Streeck and Kathleen Thelen, eds., *Beyond Continuity: Institutional Change in Advanced Political Economies.* Oxford: Oxford University Press, 2004, pp. 145–168.

Von Prodzynski, Ferdinand. "Ireland: Corporatism Revived." In Anthony Ferner and Richard Hyman, eds., *Changing Industrial Relations in Europe.* Oxford: Blackwell, 1999.

Wade, Robert Hunter. "The Disturbing Rise of Poverty and Inequality: Is It a "Big Lie?" In David Held and Mathias Koening-Archibugi, eds., *Taming Globalization: Frontiers of Governance.* Cambridge: Polity, 2003.

Watson, Michael. 2003. "Ricardian Political Economy and the Varieties of Capitalism Approach: Specialisation, Trade and Comparative Institutional Advantage." *Comparative European Politics* 1 (2): 227–240.

Weinstein, Barbara. *For Social Peace in Brazil.* Chapel Hill: University of North Carolina Press, 1996.

Whitley, Richard. *Divergent Capitalisms: The Social Structuring and Change of Business Systems.* Oxford: Oxford University Press, 1999.

Williamson, John, Ed. *The Political Economy of Policy Reform.* Washington, DC: Institute for International Economics, 1994.

Wolf, Martin. *Why Globalization Works.* New Haven: Yale University Press, 2004.

Wood, Stewart. *Capitalist Constitutions: Supply Side Reform in Britain and West Germany* 1960–1990. Ph.D. Dissertation, Harvard University, 1997.

———. "Employer Preferences, State Power and Labor Market Policy and Germany and Britain." In Peter Hall and David Soskice, eds., *Varieties of Capitalism.* New York: Oxford University Press, 2001.

World Bank. *From Plan to Market: World Development Report 1996.* Washington, DC: The World Bank, 1996.

———. *World Development Report.* New York: Oxford University Press, 1997.

Zuckerman, Leo. "Inflation Stabilization in Mexico: The Economic Solidarity Pact." M.Sc. Thesis, Oxford University, 1990.

Zysman, John. *Governments, Markets, and Growth: Financial Systems and Politics Industrial Change.* Ithaca, NY: Cornell University Press, 1984.

Index